Die Mauer

Monument des Jahrhunderts / Monument of the Century

Wolfgang Georg Fischer
Fritz von der Schulenburg

mit einer Chronologie von / with a chronology by
Hans-Jürgen Dyck

Ernst & Sohn

© 1990
Ernst & Sohn
Verlag für Architektur und technische Wissenschaften
Berlin
ISBN 3-433-02327-1

Alle Rechte vorbehalten, insbesondere die der Übersetzung
in fremde Sprachen.
All rights reserved, especially those of translation
into other languages.

Reproduktionen/Reproductions:
Reprogesellschaft L. Wahl mbH, Berlin

Satz und Druck/Type-setting and printing:
Druckerei Ludwig Vogt, Berlin

Bindearbeiten/Binding:
Buchbinderei Bruno Helm, Berlin

Übersetzungen/Translations:
Martin Crellin, William C. Flowe, Philip N. Hewitt und Michael Robinson.

Herstellerische Betreuung/Production coordination:
Fred Willer

Gewidmet
den Opfern einer anderen Diktatur, Dr. jur. Günther Fischer (1907 in Wien geboren, 1943 in Auschwitz ermordet) und Fritz-Dietlof Graf von der Schulenburg (1902 in London geboren, 1944 in Plötzensee/Berlin ermordet) sowie den Opfern der unlängst zu Ende gegangenen Diktatur, vor allem jenen, die ihr Leben an der Mauer in Berlin und an der innerdeutschen Grenze lassen mußten.

Dedicated
to the victims of a different dictatorship, Dr. jur. Günther Fischer (born in Vienna in 1907, murdered in Auschwitz in 1943) and Fritz-Dietlof Graf von der Schulenburg (born in London in 1902, murdered in Plötzensee/Berlin in 1944), and to the victims of the dictatorship which has just fallen, particularly to those who died at the Wall and on the inner-German border.

Ein persönliches Anliegen

Berlin ist für die Autoren dieses Mauerbuchs keine Stadt unter vielen. Es ist die Geburtsstadt des Photographen und die Stadt, in der sein Vater als Beteiligter am Attentat des 20. Juli 1944 von den Nazis hingerichtet wurde. Berlin ist für den Verfasser der Texte der letzte nachweisbare Ort, von dem aus der Bruder seines Vaters 1943 den Weg nach Auschwitz und in den Tod antreten mußte.

Bewußtes Zeugnis vom sichtbaren Ende einer Diktatur abzulegen, war ihnen daher ein Herzensbedürfnis, denn beim Untergang des Tausendjährigen Reiches sind sie noch Kinder gewesen. Sie haben das euphorische Glücksgefühl am 9. November 1989 mit vielen geteilt und wollten es sichtbar machen. Sie glauben, daß die Aktendeckel zu den Protokollen der Untaten der beiden größten politischen Verbrecher des 20. Jahrhunderts, Hitler und Stalin, erst jetzt zugeschlagen werden können, und sie wollen zur Wahrheitsfindung im Sinne der Menschenrechte ihren Beitrag leisten.

Mit dem Ruf »Wir sind das Volk!« hat ein neues Kapitel der deutschen und europäischen Geschichte begonnen. Dieses Buch ist Glückwunschschreiben und Mahnmal zugleich.

Wir danken jenen, die am Zustandekommen maßgeblich beteiligt waren, vor allem Hans-Jürgen Dyck, Museum Haus am Checkpoint Charlie, und dem enthusiastischen Team des Verlags Ernst & Sohn. Wir freuen uns, daß wir sie in den Chor jener einbeziehen konnten, die glauben, daß der Ruf *in tyrannos* am Ende nicht überhört werden kann!

Wolfgang Georg Fischer
Fritz von der Schulenburg
London
Sommer 1990

A personal matter

For the authors of this book on the Wall Berlin is not merely a city amongst the many in this world. It is the birthplace of the photographer and the city where his father was executed by the Nazis for his part in the July 20 rebellion against Hitler. For the author of the texts, it is the place from which news was last received from his father's brother before he was sent to his death in Auschwitz.

It was therefore a calling from the heart that caused them to travel to Berlin to bear witness to the end of a dictatorship. Upon the fall of the last dictatorship to reign in Germany, the Thousand Year Reich, they had still been children. The euphoria that filled them as the Wall fell on November 9, 1989, was an emotion they shared with many others and a feeling they wished to make visible. They believe that, finally, it has become possible to close the files on the atrocities perpetrated by the two biggest criminals of the 20th century, Hitler and Stalin, and the authors hope to make their contribution to the search for truth.

The demonstrators' chant of »We are the people« has opened a new chapter in German and European history. This book is meant both as a message of congratulations and as a reminder, and warning, of the past.

We wish to thank all those who helped in making this book, in particular Hans-Jürgen Dyck of the Checkpoint Charlie Archives and the enthusiastic team at the publishers Ernst & Sohn. We are pleased to add our voices to the choir of people who believe that the cry of *in tyrannos* cannot be overheard!

Wolfgang Georg Fischer
Fritz von der Schulenburg
London
Summer 1990

»Ich bin ein Berliner!« Präsident John F. Kennedy mit dem Regierenden Bürgermeister Willy Brandt und Bundeskanzler Konrad Adenauer an der Mauer, 1963.

"I am a Berliner!" President John F. Kennedy with the Governing Mayor Willy Brandt and the West German Chancellor Konrad Adenauer at the wall, 1963.

**Zehn Fragen zur »Mauer«
an den Zeitzeugen Willy Brandt**
Ein Gespräch in Bonn, Bundeshaus, 13. März 1990,
mit Wolfgang Georg Fischer

Wolfgang Georg Fischer:
Darf ich Sie bitten, Herr Brandt, den 13. August 1961 in Ihr Gedächtnis zurückzuholen, nicht im Sinne der hohen Politik, sondern auch als einen Tag im Leben der Familie Brandt, ganz persönlich. Wo hat Sie die Nachricht von der Grenzsperrung ereilt, was war Ihre unmittelbare Reaktion, was sagten Sie zu Ihrem engsten Kreis und zu Ihrer Familie, was hatten Sie an diesem Tage gegessen und wo, wie waren Sie gekleidet?

Willy Brandt:
Ich war in der Nacht vom 12. auf den 13. August 1961 mit dem Zug, in einem Sonderwagen, von Nürnberg nach Kiel auf dem Wege. Ich hätte damals den Wahlkampf in Kiel für die Bundestagswahlen im September eröffnen sollen. Am frühen Morgen, ich weiß nicht, so um vier, wurde ich geweckt, in Berlin wäre Dramatisches im Gange. Bin in Hannover aus dem Zug, mit dem ersten Flugzeug von Hannover nach Berlin! Ich wußte, daß die Lage kritisch war, denn die Zahl der Flüchtlinge in Berlin war gewachsen, von Tag zu Tag. Man mußte damit rechnen, daß dagegen Vorkehrungen getroffen würden, wenn ich auch nicht damit gerechnet habe, daß die Sperren diese Form annehmen und sich gerade an diesem Tag ereignen würden.
Meine Familie, nach der Sie fragen, habe ich überhaupt erst am späten Abend gesehen, denn ich bin, als ich angekommen war, an den Potsdamer Platz gefahren, dann zum Brandenburger Tor, dann in mein Büro, dann zu den alliierten Kommandanten und habe gespürt, welche große Beunruhigung bei den Westberlinern eintrat, die befürchteten, daß dies auch eine direkte Bedrohung für West-Berlin darstellen könnte — was es ja nicht war! Es war, nebenbei gesagt, an diesem Tag auch noch nicht die eigentliche Mauer da. Die Mauer wurde erst einige Tage später errichtet. Es waren Stacheldrahtverhaue, Sperren unterschiedlicher Art, aber natürlich schon die Abriegelung, der dann der Mauerbau folgte. Hinterher kann man jetzt sagen, man hätte nicht so überrascht sein dürfen ...
Da habe ich meinen Mitarbeitern gesagt, jetzt kommt es darauf an, eine schädliche Reaktion in West-Berlin zu vermeiden und die Alliierten dazu zu bewegen, sich der sowjetischen Seite gegenüber zu äußern. Das war sehr mühsam! Es dauerte ja einige Tage, bis auch nur ein Protest eingelegt wurde.
Im Grunde hing das alles mit dem Berlinstatus zusammen. Wir auf deutscher, in diesem Falle auf Westberliner Seite gingen

**Ten Questions Concerning the »Wall«,
put to the Eyewitness Willy Brandt**
An interview in Bonn, Bundeshaus, 13 March 1990,
with Wolfgang Georg Fischer

Wolfgang Georg Fischer:
Herr Brandt, may I ask you to think back to 13 August 1961, not at the level of high politics, but as a day in the life of the Brandt family, a personal memory. Where were you when you heard the news about the closing of the border, what was your immediate reaction, what did you say to your most intimate associates and family, what did you eat on that day and where, what clothes were you wearing?

Willy Brandt:
On the night of the 12—13 August 1961 I was on a train, in a special carriage, on the way from Nuremberg to Kiel: it was around the time of the September 1961 general election, and I was supposed to open the campaign in Kiel. I was woken up, I don't know at four or thereabouts, and told that something dramatic was happening in Berlin, I got off the train in Hanover, and took the first plane to Berlin. I knew the situation was critical, because the number of refugees in Berlin was increasing rapidly from day to day, we inevitably sensed something would be done about it, even though I hadn't reckoned on closure of the border taking the form it did, or that it would happen on the day it did.
My family, you asked after them, I didn't see them at all until late evening, because as soon as I got to Berlin I went to Potsdamer Platz and the Brandenburg Gate, then to my office, then to see the Allied commanders. I realized how worried the West Berliners were, they were afraid it could be a direct threat to West Berlin as well, which of course it wasn't. And by the way, the Wall itself didn't appear that day. The actual Wall wasn't built until a few days later. There were barbed wire entanglements, barriers of various different kinds, the city was sealed off like that, and then the Wall was built. With hindsight it is possible to say that we shouldn't have been so surprised ...
Then I said to my colleagues, what we have to do now is avoid harmful reactions in West Berlin and get the Allies to say something to the Soviet side. That was very hard work. It was a few days later they even made a single protest.
Basically it was all connected. We on the German, in this case the West Berlin, side worked on the basis that, in terms of overall responsibility for the city, the four powers were involved, all involved together. Then it quickly became clear that the guarantee for West Berlin was absolutely sound nothing could shake that, but the basis they were actually working on was that any

davon aus, daß die Gesamtverantwortung für die Stadt alle vier Mächte gemeinsam zu tragen hätten. Es stellte sich dann aber rasch heraus, die Garantie für West-Berlin, die war deutlich, daran wurde nicht gerüttelt, aber eigentlich ging man davon aus, jeder kann mit seinem Teil machen, was er will. Es dauerte ein wenig, die eigenen Mitbürger hiermit vertraut zu machen.

Wolfgang Georg Fischer:
Und Ihr ganz persönliches Leben im Strudel der Ereignisse, Herr Brandt?

Willy Brandt:
Was man vor so vielen Jahren gegessen hat, das weiß ich wirklich nicht mehr. Ich glaube, ich habe an dem Morgen Kaffee getrunken und habe eine Suppe in mein Amtszimmer kommen lassen. Mir war nicht nach viel Essen zumute an dem Tag, aber ich habe spät abends zu Hause noch etwas gegessen. Wie ich gekleidet war, weiß ich nicht. Aber es gibt Photos, auf denen man das erkennen könnte.

Wolfgang Georg Fischer:
Haben Sie in den fast dreißig Jahren Mauergeschichte je Angst, ganz elementare Angst empfunden: Jetzt könnte einer auf den Raketen- oder Atombombenknopf drücken ...?

Willy Brandt:
Ja, aber nicht so, als ob jemand etwas in Bewegung setzte, was Berlin betreffen würde, wohl aber, daß die Krise um Berlin zu einem Konflikt führen könnte. Das sind ja zwei verschiedene Dinge. Nicht Angst, aber die Sorge mußte da sein, wird ja mittlerweile auch durch Quellen belegt. Da war zunächst die Kuba-Krise von 1962, ein Zusammenhang ist sicher festzustellen. Keiner weiß ja auch, was geschehen wäre, wäre die Kuba-Krise nicht so beigelegt worden, wie sie zwischen Kennedy und Chruschtschow beigelegt worden ist. Es hat auch in der Zeit zwischen dem Mauerbau vom August 61 und der Kuba-Krise im Oktober 62 Situationen gegeben, in denen aliierte Freunde, mit denen ich zu tun hatte, damit rechneten, daß ein Handstreich stattfinden könnte, ein sowjetischer Handstreich, und der hätte ja, wenn er stattgefunden hätte, Reaktionen nach sich ziehen können, die — nicht notwendigerweise, wie gesagt — einen atomaren Anschlag in Berlin oder auf Berlin bezogen, ausgelöst hätten. Damit habe ich eigentlich nie gerechnet, sondern eher damit, daß von der Berlin-Krise die eine oder die andere Weltkrise hätte ausgelöst werden können.

one of the powers could do what they liked with their part. And it took some time to make this clear to our fellow citizens.

Wolfgang Georg Fischer:
And your personal life, that is to say ...

Willy Brandt:
As far as what I ate all those years ago is concerned, I can't really remember. I think I had some coffee that morning, and had some soup sent up to my office. I didn't really feel much like eating that day, I propably had something else to eat at home late in the evening. I don't know how I was dressed either. But there are photographs, you could find out from there.

Wolfgang Georg Fischer:
In almost thirty years of the Wall were you ever afraid, really deeply afraid, did you think someone might press the button and launch rockets, or even the atomic bomb ...?

Willy Brandt:
Yes, but not in the sense that someone might set something off that could affect Berlin, but that the Berlin crisis could lead to conflict. Those are two quite different things. Not fear, but there was definitely that anxiety, as has since been proved by various sources. The Cuba crisis of 1962 certainly has to be seen in this context. And of course nobody knows what would have happened if the Cuba crisis had not been settled in the way it was settled between Kennedy and Khrushchev. And in that period between the building of the Wall in August 1961 and the Cuba crisis in October 62 there were a number of situations in which Allied friends I was dealing with thought that something might happen, that the Russians might do something, and if that had happened it could have caused reactions, but that wouldn't necessarily have unleashed an atomic attack in or on Berlin. I actually never thought that would happen, but I did think that something or other could have been triggered by the Berlin crisis.

Wolfgang Georg Fischer:
Hand on your heart, Herr Brandt, if on New Year's Eve 1988/89 someone had wanted to bet you that the Wall fall within the year, which side would you have been on?

Willy Brandt:
I wouldn't have bet that it would happen, I'd have said it would certainly take a bit longer.

Wolfgang Georg Fischer:
Hand aufs Herz, Herr Brandt, hätte jemand mit Ihnen in der Neujahrsnacht 1988/89 auf den Fall der Mauer innerhalb Jahresfrist wetten wollen, hätten Sie dafür oder dagegen gewettet?

Willy Brandt:
Ich hätte sicher nicht dafür gewettet, sondern hätte gesagt, das wird sicher noch etwas länger dauern ...

Wolfgang Georg Fischer:
Sie sagen in Ihrer Autobiographie: »Die Geschichte kennt kein letztes Wort.« Können Sie sich vorstellen, daß der funkelnagelneue Freiheitsteppich, der nun von der ehemaligen »Zonengrenze« bzw. DDR-Grenze, also von der Mauer bis zur russischen Westgrenze (und vielleicht auch schon weiter) reicht, jemals zurückgerollt wird?

Willy Brandt:
Ich sehe das nicht, jedenfalls nicht für die jetzt voraussehbare Zeit, ein Zurückrollen durch erneutes Ausdehnen der sowjetischen und der russischen Macht, nein, wohl aber halte ich die Demokratie für die Länder zwischen Rußland und Deutschland für keineswegs gesichert, denn die Ablösung des Stalinismus und des Post-Stalinismus, die stellt sich ja nicht nur in der Form von alten Überlegungen dar, sondern mancherorts auch in Gestalt von nationalistischen Verirrungen unterschiedlicher Art. Insofern mache ich einen Unterschied zwischen den beiden möglichen Vorgängen und sage nein zu der Frage, ob für die Zeit, die man jetzt überblicken kann, ein militärisches, machtpolitisches Auffüllen des Raums in Betracht kommt. Ich sage ja zu der Gefahr, daß die junge Demokratie, die ja erst noch keine Demokratie im erprobten Sinne sein kann, noch erheblichen Herausforderungen ausgesetzt sein wird.

Wolfgang Georg Fischer:
Mit der Mauer als schrecklicher Realität jahrelang zu leben und dennoch als politischer Humanist für die betroffenen Menschen Hilfe, Beistand und Erleichterung zu erkämpfen, ohne je zu erlahmen, das war eines Ihrer vielen Verdienste. Worauf sind Sie in diesem Zusammenhang, mit gutem Recht, besonders stolz?

Willy Brandt:
Also ich weiß nicht, ob stolz die richtige Bezeichnung ist. Das überlasse ich lieber anderen ... Nein, ich glaube eher, ich habe etwas dazu beitragen können in Berlin und danach in Bonn, daß etwas abgewischt werden konnte vom deutschen Schild, wenn Sie so wollen, und daß die beiden Begriffe Deutschland und Frie-

Wolfgang Georg Fischer:
You say in your autobiography: "In history there are no last words." Can you imagine that the brand new carpet of freedom that now stretches from the former "Zone frontier" which became identical with the GDR border and the Wall to the Western borders of Russia (and perhaps even further) will ever be rolled back again?

Willy Brandt:
I can't see, at least not for the foreseeable future, that it could be rolled back by a new demonstration of Soviet or Russian power, but I don't consider that democracy is definitely secure in the countries between Russia and Germany: Stalinism and post-Stalinism aren't necessarily smoothly replaced by old and familiar approaches, in some places thera are nationlistic aberrations of various kinds. I would make that distinction between the two possible ways of proceeding, and I say no to the question of whether, within the immediately foreseeable future, the area will be taken over in a way that could be called military, or by the use of power politics. I say yes to the danger that democracy, and it isn't really democracy yet, will have to face up to considerable challenges and provocation.

Wolfgang Georg Fischer:
One of your many achievements was to live with the Wall as a terrible reality for years, and yet to fight tirelessly for help, support and relief for the people affected. In this context, what are you particularly proud of and quite rightly?

Willy Brandt:
Well, I don't really know that proud is the right word. I'd rather leave that for other people to say ... No, myself I'd actually say that I think first of all I helped, in Berlin and after that in Bonn, to make it possible for something to be wiped of the German record, as it were, to help to make it possible to mention the concepts of Germany and peace in the same breath again. I changed the notion of Germany a little, after the Berlin period as well, and then as Foreign Minister and Chancellor in Bonn I managed to do a bit of preparatory work on making it possible not just to talk about peace in Europe but actually to take some action about it, and seen together that really is quite a lot ...

Wolfgang Georg Fischer:
The Wall in its physical form is already history. But the great difference in awareness and prosperity between East and West will create an invisible wall for a long time. However, the two parts of Germany will grow together more quickly than other parts of

den wieder im guten Zusammenhang genannt werden konnten. Ich habe in meiner Berliner Zeit, und dann später als Außenminister und Regierungschef in Bonn, ein Stück Vorbereitung dafür leisten können, daß über europäische Friedensordnung jetzt nicht mehr nur geredet, sondern hiervon gehandelt wird, und das ist ja insgesamt eine ganze Menge ...

Wolfgang Georg Fischer:
Die Mauer in ihrer physischen Form ist bereits Geschichte! Das Bewußtseins- und Wohlstandsgefälle zwischen Ost und West wird dennoch für lange Zeit eine unsichtbare Mauer bilden. Die beiden Teile Deutschlands aber werden auf Grund ihrer gemeinsamen Geschichte und Sprache schneller zusammenwachsen als andere Teile Europas. Wie lange wird es dauern, nach Ihrer Meinung, bis der Ausgleich hergestellt ist, und worin sehen Sie die größten Schwierigkeiten?

Willy Brandt:
Ich glaube, man muß mit einem halben Jahrzehnt rechnen, bis in allem Wesentlichen der ökonomische Ausgleich da ist. Der wird ja dadurch sehr erschwert, daß die Produktivität in der bisherigen DDR unvergleichlich viel niedriger liegt als in der Bundesrepublik. Auf der anderen Seite ist der jetzt dazukommende Teil der Bevölkerung sehr viel kleiner. Also zu den 60 oder 62 Millionen kommen im besten Fall etwa 16 oder 17 Millionen dazu. Das ist für einen relativ wohlhabenden Staat wie die Bundesrepublik zu verkraften, und es wird dann von einem bestimmten Punkt während dieser fünf Jahre sogar ein Sprung stattfinden, denn die wirtschaftliche Aufforstung der bisherigen DDR wird ja mit einer Technologie erfolgen, die der durchschnittlichen technischen Ausrüstung in der Bundesrepublik voraus ist. Man wird nicht dort hingehen mit alten Maschinen, sondern man wird herangehen an die Firmen, ihre Partnerschaft machen, dann aber hineingehen mit Anlagen, die dem modernsten Stand der Technik entsprechen.

Wolfgang Georg Fischer:
Ein Vergleich drängt sich auf, England und Deutschland nach 1945! Das war eine ähnliche Situation. Die alten Maschinen in Deutschland waren zum Großteil zerstört, da bot sich die Chance, vom Gestern direkt auf das Morgen des Wirtschaftswunders umzuschalten ...

Willy Brandt:
Es ist noch etwas zugespitzter hier! Aber trotzdem, ich glaube mit allem Drum und Dran, in einem halben Jahrzehnt wird das Wesentliche einfacher sein.

Europe because of their common history and language. How long will it take in your opinion for a balance to be established, and what do you see as the greatest difficulties?

Willy Brandt:
I think it'll take a good five years for the fundamental economic position to even out. It's made more difficult by the fact that productivity in the GDR so far is incomparably much lower than in the Federal Republic. On the other hand the additional population is very much smaller than West Germany's. So there'll be 16 or 17 million at the most, to add to 60 or 62 million. A relatively prosperous state like the Federal Republic can cope with that and at a certain point during these five years there'll even be a leap forward, because economic restocking of the former GDR will ensue, with technology that will be ahead of the average technical standard in the Federal Republic. We won't be taking old machines over there, we'll go into their firms, set up partnerships and then put in equipment with absolutely up-to-date technology.

Wolfgang Georg Fischer:
Just like England and Germany in 1945, really. That was a similar situation. The old machines in Germany were mostly destroyed, so it was possible to switch from the past directly to the future of the economic miracle.

Willy Brandt:
The situation here is rather more acute. But nevertheless, I think that despite all the fuss and bother it'll all be a lot simpler in five years time.

Wolfgang Georg Fischer:
And do you think the greatest difficulties will arise from economic or political awareness?

Willy Brandt:
I think they are economic, and by that I mean economic not just in the narrowest sense, but economic including social matters, that is building a social safeguard into the unification process for pensioners and savers, and also for employees who won't have a job temporarily or even for a longer period, because this kind of process necessarily involves shedding workers. This I think is the main problem. And there's definitely something else, connnected with this: we mustn't give people in the present GDR the impression that they are simply being taking over ...

Wolfgang Georg Fischer:
... swallowed up.

Wolfgang Georg Fischer:
Werden sich die größten Schwierigkeiten nach Ihrer Meinung aus der Umschaltung des ökonomischen oder des politischen Bewußtseins ergeben?

Willy Brandt:
Ich glaube, das ökonomische; d.h. ökonomisch nicht eng gesehen, sondern ökonomisch mit Einschluß des Sozialen, also, die soziale Absicherung des Einigungsvorgangs, z.B. auf Rentner und Sparer bezogen, auch auf Arbeitnehmer, die vorübergehend oder längere Zeit keinen Arbeitsplatz haben werden, weil der Angleichungsprozeß notwendigerweise mit der Freisetzung von Arbeitnehmern verbunden sein wird — dies ist, glaube ich, das Hauptproblem! Und da kommt dazu, sicherlich, oder verbunden hiermit, der Umstand, daß die Menschen in der heutigen DDR nicht den Eindruck haben möchten, als würden sie einfach vereinnahmt, als würden sie ...

Wolfgang Georg Fischer:
... geschluckt.

Willy Brandt:
Dabei meinen sie fälschlicherweise, sie könnten wirtschaftlich ausgeschlachtet werden. Das ist ja ein Irrtum! Also betrifft es mehr das Selbstgefühl von Menschen, die unter schwierigeren Bedingungen als denjenigen in Westdeutschland gelebt haben. Sie möchten, daß ihre Art von Erfahrung und Empfindung nicht mit Gewalt im Wiedervereinigungstaumel aufgelöst wird.

Wolfgang Georg Fischer:
Ein sehr menschliches, aber subjektives Problem ...

Willy Brandt:
Sicher. Auch ein Lebensgefühl. Die Familie hat eine größere Rolle gespielt in diesen Jahren, weil man sich aus dem öffentlichen Leben sehr stark zurückgezogen hat in den Kreis der Familie und in seine Freundschaftskreise. Man hat dort noch mehr Zeit gehabt, zu lesen und miteinander zu sprechen. Ein weniger freies, aber auch weniger hektisches Leben. Das sind psychologische Faktoren, die jetzt mit hineinspielen.

Wolfgang Georg Fischer:
Plötzlicher Verlust einer »Biedermeierkultur« ...?
Bei der Bitte um Nennung von drei bestimmenden Figuren der Mauergeschichte — aus der westlichen Welt, aus der östlichen und eines der Opfer —, welche Namen kommen Ihnen spontan in den Sinn und in welchem Zusammenhang?

Willy Brandt:
But they do mistakenly think they could be exploited economically. They really are wrong about it. It's more the self-esteem of people who have lived under more difficult conditions than people in West Germany and don't want their way of experiencing and sensing things to be forced out in the reunification process.

Wolfgang Georg Fischer:
All right, a humanitarian problem, a very personal one ...

Willy Brandt:
Definitely. It's also part of the way they see life. The family has played a greater role in these years because people have shown a very strong tendency to withdraw from public life into their families and circles of friends. They've had more time to read and talk to each other. A less free life, but a less hectic one. These are psychological factors that have to be taken into consideration.

Wolfgang Georg Fischer:
A "Biedermeier culture", abruptly lost? ...
If you were asked to name three decisive figures in the history of the Wall — one from the West, one from the East, and one of the victims — which names come spontaneously into your mind, and in what context?

Willy Brandt:
From the West I would choose John F. Kennedy, not because he was at the heigth of his wits at the time the incident occured, but more because he did a great deal to help absorb the shock the incident caused, and then his visit to Berlin in June 1963 was a very significant event, not just because it was a source of strength and courage for West Berliners, but because at that time he anticipated many things we have actually experienced in the last few years. He talked about "winds of change" that would blow in the East as well, he made the realities of our coming together clear. But he was also of course simply the President who was there when the Wall was built.
In the East I would say Ulbricht, he was the top man at the time in the Communist government in East Berlin. Of course one could say Khrushchev rather than him. I deliberately put Ulbricht first, because he had difficulty in getting Khrushchev go give him the green light for the Wall. The then boss of the Soviet Union hesitated for a long time before he agreed to it.
Victim of the wall, there the first one I think of, without neglecting any of the others, is young Peter Fechter, a twenty-year-old building worker who tried to get across in August 62 — some did

Willy Brandt:
Auf den Westen bezogen, John F. Kennedy, nicht weil er besonders auf der Höhe war, als der Vorgang selbst sich abspielte, wohl aber weil er sehr viel dafür getan hat, die Erschütterung auffangen zu helfen, die der Vorgang auslöste. Sein Besuch dann im Juni 63 bleibt ein Vorgang von ganz großer Bedeutung, nicht nur weil er den Westberlinern Mut gemacht hat, sondern weil er dort einiges vorweggenommen hat, was wir später dann, in den letzten Jahren, erlebt haben. Er hat von den »Winden der Veränderung« gesprochen, die am Osten nicht vorbeiziehen werden, er hat den steigenden Druck des Zusammenwachsens deutlich gemacht. Aber er war eben auch der Präsident, der da war, als die Mauer errichtet wurde.
Im Osten, würde ich sagen, Ulbricht, damals erster Mann der kommunistischen Herrschaft in Ost-Berlin. Man könnte natürlich statt dessen auch Chruschtschow sagen. Ich sage bewußt Ulbricht an erster Stelle, weil er Mühe hatte, Chruschtschow dazu zu bekommen, ihm grünes Licht für die Mauer zu geben. Der damalige erste Mann der Sowjetunion hat lange gezögert, bevor er seine Zustimmung gegeben hat.
Opfer der Mauer, da denke ich, ohne andere zurückzusetzen, an diesen jungen zwanzigjährigen Bauarbeiter Peter Fechter im August 62, der herüber wollte — einige haben das ja immer wieder versucht — und auf den dann geschossen wurde, und der schrie und dem niemand helfen konnte. Auch die amerikanischen Soldaten, die in unmittelbarer Nähe waren, fühlten sich nicht befugt, ihn dort herauszuholen.

Wolfgang Georg Fischer:
»Wir sind jetzt das glücklichste Volk auf der Welt!«
Diesen schönen, überschwenglichen Satz hat der Regierende Bürgermeister von Berlin, Walter Momper, nach dem Fall der Mauer ausgesprochen.
Würden Sie dem noch zustimmen können oder überwiegt jetzt schon die Sorge?

Willy Brandt:
Mein Freund Momper hat ja damals im November in Berlin nicht gesagt, wir werden immer das glücklichste Volk der Welt sein, sondern er hat gesagt, wir sind es, an diesem Tag!
Die Leute sind sich um den Hals gefallen, und viele haben geweint, vor allem die Familien, die lange getrennt waren. Aber sonst ist es ja natürlich richtig, daß die Freude immer noch groß ist. Man spürt das, wenn man mit den Menschen spricht, wenn sie in großer Zahl versammelt sind, ob in Rostock oder Magdeburg oder Chemnitz oder Frankfurt an der Oder oder Potsdam, das weiß ich. Ich nenne nur einige Städte, in denen ich in der

keep on trying. He got shot, and screamed, and nobody could help him. Even the American soldiers who were immediately to hand didn't feel authorized to bring him out.

Wolfgang Georg Fischer:
"Now we are the happiest people in the world!"
This beautiful, bubbly sentence was spoken by Walter Momper, the governing mayor of Berlin, afther the Wall came down. Do you find you agree, or is anxiety now the predominant factor?

Willy Brandt:
My friend Momper didn't actually say on that day in November in Berlin that we'd always be the happiest people in the world, but he said we are — today that is. People fell into each others' arms and a lot of them wept, especially families who had been separated for a long time. But otherwise of course it's right that people are still very very happy. You sense that when you're talking to people who have come together in large numbers, whether they're in Rostock or Magdeburg or Chemnitz or Frankfurt an der Oder or Potsdam, I know that. I've only mentioned a few of the towns I've been to recently. But joy that the division of the country, something people felt was unnatural, is a thing of the past, is mixed with uncertainty. They're uncertain whether, as the wonderful process of reunification moves forward, step by step, but steadily, whether as it's happening the interests, the legitimate interests, of ordinary people will be taken sufficiently into account. The export of somewhat rougher election practices from the Federal Republic into the other part of Germany displeased people in quite a lot of places: they're not used to that sort of thing. In reality they haven't had elections for decades and they didn't think it was possible that political forces fighting to make themselves felt can sometimes be a bad thing, as well a very good one. So the original feeling is still there, and other feelings have now come along as well.

Wolfgang Georg Fischer:
And those other feelings are probably somewhat stronger now!?
A vision of the future in 1995, reunified Germany in a united Europa five years today, a futurist ideas-game. What would that look like, and how would it work?

Willy Brandt:
It works quite simply if you're clear about what united Europe means, because the present GDR will become part of the European Community. That doesn't even need a new agreement within the European Community. Of course it does need consultation with the present members of the Community, but Brussels

letzten Zeit gewesen bin. Aber die Freude, daß die Teilung, als widernatürlich empfunden, zu Ende geht, mischt sich mit Unsicherheit. Unsicherheit, ob nun die göttliche Vereinigung schrittweise, aber deutlich vor sich gehen wird, ob dabei die Interessen, die legitimen Interessen der einfachen Menschen hinreichend Berücksichtigung finden werden. Auch der Export etwas ruppiger Wahlkampfformen aus der Bundesrepublik in den anderen Teil hat mancherorts eher befremdet; die sind das nicht gewohnt. Die haben ja in Wirklichkeit seit Jahrzehnten keine Wahlen gehabt und haben sich nicht gedacht, daß das nicht nur ein schöner, sondern manchmal auch ein unschöner Vorgang ist, wenn politische Kräfte um ihren Einfluß ringen. Also, es ist das eine noch da, und es ist jetzt das andere hinzugekommen.

Wolfgang Georg Fischer:
Das andere ist wahrscheinlich etwas stärker, jetzt ...?
Zukunftsvision 1995, das vereinigte Deutschland im geeinten Europa, heute in fünf Jahren, als futuristisches Gedankenspiel! Wie sähe das aus, wie könnte das funktionieren?

Willy Brandt:
Das funktioniert ganz einfach, wenn man sich klar darüber ist, was das heißt, »Geeintes Europa«, denn die heutige DDR wird Teil der Europäischen Gemeinschaft sein. Dazu bedarf es nicht einmal eines neuen Vertrages über die Europäische Gemeinschaft. Es bedarf freilich der Konsultation mit den jeweiligen Mitgliedern der Gemeinschaft, aber Brüssel sitzt ja schon dran an allen Details, was Wirtschaft und Währungseinheit angeht. Und die meisten von uns hier in Bonn, wie aber auch diejenigen auf der anderen Seite, sind dafür, daß der deutsche Vorgang die weitere Entwicklung der Europäischen Gemeinschaft in keiner Weise behindern darf, sondern, daß der dort festgelegte Fahrplan für den Ausbau der Gemeinschaft für die Währungsunion, auch für die Stärkung der politischen Komponenten der Europäischen Gemeinschaft, daß an diesem Fahrplan nichts geändert wird. Nun gibt es gleichwohl Sorgen, zumal bei den neuen südeuropäischen Partnern der Europäischen Gemeinschaft, daß der deutsche Vorgang sie etwas in den Hintergrund schieben könnte, da zumal die ökonomischen Potentiale sich stärker nicht auf den hinzukommenden Teil Deutschlands konzentrieren, sondern auch auf das sonstige Mittel- und Osteuropa ausweiten werden. Ich glaube, das wird sich relativ rasch einpendeln. Schwieriger ist die Frage — aber nicht nur für die Deutschen —, wenn man mit dem geeinten Europa nicht allein die Europäische Gemeinschaft meint, sondern wenn man damit auch das neue Verhältnis zwischen der leicht erweiterten Europäischen Gemeinschaft und den anderen europäischen Staaten meint, mittel- und osteuropäischen Staaten, etwas, das

is already working on all the details affecting the economic situation and currency union. And most of us here in Bonn, like people over there as well, are keen that what happens in Germany should not in any way hamper further development of the European Community. A timetable has been set for extending the Community and for currency union, and also for strengthening political components within the Europan Community, and they don't want anything in this timetable to be changed. Now there is also anxiety, especially among the new Southern European partners in the European Community, that events in Germany could push them somewhat into the background, especially as economic potential will be concentrated not just on the part of Germany that is joining, but also on the rest of Central and Eastern Europe. I think that will settle down relatively quickly. A more difficult question, and not only for the Germans, is if by a united Europe you don't only mean the European Community alone, but the new relationship between the slightly extended European Community and other European states, Central and Eastern European states, in other words something that will emerge from association between what used to be Comecon, and the Community, something that could go in the direction of a confederation, a possibility for the beginning of the next century suggested by President Mitterrand. I cannot see what difficulties could be caused by joining the two parts of Germany together as far as this course of events is concerned, a course of events with large implications well beyond the EC. The opposite is more likely to be the case: the former Eastern part of Germany, the part that was in the Warsaw Pact, will bring with it experience that could help us to settle questions that are still open, especially questions of economic co-operation with the Poles, the Czechs, the Hungarians etc.

Wolfgang Georg Fischer:
There is a fear in certain circles, especially in England, that now, in the context of renewed Germany unity, the energy used to suppress the evil deeds in German history could result in nationalistic extremes again, a fear from the past, something indeterminable smouldering in the back of the minds of people who still remember World War II ...

Willy Brandt:
This is part of the burden that we will carry with us for quite a while. That is not always easy to explain to young people in Germany, who often feel that they are called to answer to a large extent for the sins of their grandfathers; it's not even their fathers any more. But I believe that extension and enlargement of Germany is quantitatively not insignificant, but that qualitatively nothing will change.

sich ergeben wird aus den Verbindungen zwischen dem bisherigen Comecon, den anderen Staaten und der Gemeinschaft, etwas, was in die Richtung einer Konföderation gehen könnte, wie es Präsident Mitterrand kürzlich als eine Möglichkeit für den Beginn des nächsten Jahrzehnts angedeutet hat. Für diesen Vorgang, diesen größeren, über die EG hinausgehenden Vorgang sehe ich nicht, wie sich Schwierigkeiten ergeben könnten aus dem Zusammenfügen der Teile Deutschlands. Eher im Gegenteil, der bisherige östliche Teil Deutschlands, der im Warschauer Pakt war, bringt ein Stück Erfahrung ein, das uns helfen kann bei der Regelung der offenen Fragen, zumal auch der ökonomischen Fragen der Zusammenarbeit mit den Polen, den Tschechoslowaken, den Ungarn etc.

Wolfgang Georg Fischer:
Die Angst gewisser Kreise, vor allem auch in England, daß die Verdrängungsenergie zur Unterdrückung der Untaten innerhalb der deutschen Geschichte nun im Rahmen der neuen deutschen Einheit nationalistisch ausgewertet werden und das Faß wieder zum Überlaufen bringen könnte, eine von der Vergangenheit her gespeiste Angst, das ist natürlich etwas, was eher unbestimmbar ist, aber im Hintergrund des Bewußtseins von Menschen schwelt, die noch wache Erinnerungen an den Zweiten Weltkrieg haben ...

Willy Brandt:
Das ist ein Stück der Last, die wir noch eine ganze Weile mit uns tragen werden. Das ist den jungen Leuten in Deutschland nicht immer leicht zu erklären, die sich häufig stark in Anspruch genommen fühlen für die Sünden ihrer Großväter; es sind mittlerweile nicht mehr die Väter! Aber ich glaube, daß die Erweiterung und Vergrößerung Deutschlands zwar quantitativ nicht unerheblich ist, aber daß sich qualitativ nichts ändert.
Sehen Sie, die ökonomische Potenz, die die DDR einbringt, ist zu vergleichen mit der des Bundeslands Hessen. Das ist nicht alle Welt. Die Sorgen wegen ökonomischer Dominanz werden doch reduziert, wenn nicht sogar überflüssig, durch Deutschlands festes Eingefügtsein in die Europäische Gemeinschaft. Eine ökonomische Dominanz wird gezügelt bzw. verhindert, indem sich Deutschland eben nicht als Nationalstaat, sondern als Teil der Europäischen Gemeinschaft entwickelt. Dies wird noch mehr auf militärischem Gebiet der Fall sein. In bezug auf die künftige militärpolitische Struktur Deutschlands wird erst recht die Einfügung in einen größeren Zusammenhang wichtig sein. Keiner weiß heute schon genau, wie das aussehen wird, denn das wird ein Ergebnis der Verhandlungen mit den vier Mächten und mit den anderen europäischen Staaten. Aber auf beiden Gebieten, dem ökonomischen und dem militärpolitischen, werden Deutschland Zügel angelegt,

You see, the economic potential that the GDR will bring with it is comparable with that of the West German Land of Hessen. That is not a great deal. The worries people have about economic dominance are reduced, if not made completely superfluous, by the fact that Germany is firmly embedded in the European Community. Economic dominance is curbed or prevented by the fact that Germany is developing not as a national state, but as part of the European Community. This will be all the more the case in the military field. As far as Germany's future military structure is concerned this is to an even greater extent a matter of incorporation into a larger context — no-one today knows precisely what it will turn out like, as it will be based on negotiations with the four powers and with the other European powers. But in both fields, that of the economy and that of military and political status, Germany is being reined in, if I may put it like that. But that can be done in a form that the Germans accept, a form they agree with and do not see as an insult. And so I believe that here one need not anticipate any real relapses in matters that remind us of the past.

Wolfgang Georg Fischer:
Finally — three wishes! One each for the two parts of Germany, the Federal Republic and the GDR, and one for the united Germany of the near future. What would these three wishes be?

Willy Brandt:
For West Germany, that it should not treat the smaller section that is now joining it arrogantly, and behave like a rich uncle. For East Germany, that people there do not lose their self-esteem and self-confidence, and do not let other people make them lose it, and thirdly for the whole of Germany that it should take a very positive attitude to two fundamental European matters that lie before us to be a loyal member of the European Community and to make urgent efforts towards pan-European co-operation. In Germany we have never allowed awareness to flag, even in the younger generation, that Prague and Budapest and Warsaw are European cities too. And then I would also wish that the pan-German state, united Germany, might help to create an awareness of global questions in Europe, questions that go beyound our continent. By this I mean of course concern about many people in other parts of the world whou are hungry and for whom we could do rather more than we do now, now that armaments don't have to be stockpiled to the extent hitherto necessary, to say nothing about environmental matters impinging upon us from the outside, in the face which people are only just beginning to understand the concept of interdependence.

wenn man so will. Das kann man aber in einer Form tun, die die Deutschen akzeptieren, die sie einsehen und nicht als Kränkung empfinden. Also ich glaube, daß man hier keine wirklichen Rückfälle in Dinge erwarten darf, die uns an die Vergangenheit erinnern.

Wolfgang Georg Fischer:
Zum Abschluß — drei freie Wünsche! Je einen für die beiden Teile Deutschlands, BRD und DDR, und einen für das geeinte Deutschland der nahen Zukunft. Wie würden Sie diese drei Wünsche formulieren?

Willy Brandt:
Auf Westdeutschland bezogen, daß es dem kleineren Teil, der jetzt dazukommt, nicht überheblich und in der Attitüde des reichen Onkels begegnen möchte. Auf Ostdeutschland bezogen, daß die Menschen dort ihr Selbstgefühl, ihr Selbstbewußtsein nicht reduzieren und nicht durch andere reduzieren lassen, und drittens auf Gesamtdeutschland bezogen, daß es sich sehr bewußt hineinstellen möge in beide europäische Grundsätze, die vor uns liegen, loyal als Mitglied der Europäischen Gemeinschaft und drängend in bezug auf die gesamteuropäische Zusammenarbeit, weil man eben doch in Deutschland, gerade auch im anderen Teil, nie das Bewußtsein, auch in der jungen Generation nicht, hat untergehen lassen, daß Prag und Budapest und Warschau europäische Städte sind. Und dann füge ich noch hinzu, ich wünsche mir, daß der gesamtdeutsche Staat, das vereinigte Deutschland, mithelfen möchte, in Europa den Sinn für die globalen Fragen zu schaffen, die über unseren Kontinent hinausgehen. Damit meine ich natürlich die Sorge um die Vielen in anderen Teilen der Welt, die Hunger leiden und für die man etwas mehr als jetzt tun kann, wenn Rüstungsmittel nicht mehr im bisher erforderlichen Maße aufgestockt werden müssen, ganz zu schweigen von den von außen her auf uns zukommenden Umweltfragen, die ja manche erst jetzt das Wort von der Interdependenz richtig verstehen lassen.

Wolfgang Georg Fischer:
Ich danke Ihnen für dieses Gespräch, Herr Brandt, und freue mich, daß Sie als Zeitzeuge Nummer eins der Berliner Mauer auch deren Fall miterleben und mitfeiern konnten! Prosit!

Wolfgang Georg Fischer:
Thank you very much for this interview, Herr Brandt. I am happy that you as the witness Number One as it were to the History of the Berlin Wall, were also able to see it coming down and rejoice with us in the celebrations! Cheers!

Wolfgang Georg Fischer

2 x Wall
Anno Domini 1964 x Anno Domini 1989 = zero hour

I. The Berlin Wall Symphony, 1964
in Words and Four Movements
Extracts from the diary

Berlin, Friday, February 28, 1964

Having never been to Berlin before 2.30 p.m. February 28, 1964, my images of Berlin are initially literary ones. A celluloid Berlin composed of newsreel pictures.
The roaring Twenties: Hanussen the hypnotist performing at a Ball/*cut*/The Belgian beauty queen Mademoiselle Cameron/*cut*/ Robert Musil next to Herwarth Walden in the Romanisches Café/*cut*/Walden and Flechtheim fighting for a picture painted by Chagall/*cut*/Somebody introduces himself at Café Grössenwahn: "My name is Billy Wilder, well, actually Samuel Wilder. I'm from Vienna, well, actually from Krakau"/*cut*/"Please, take a seat." says the man of street-literature facing him, who adds, "What can I do for you?"/*cut*/"If you could perhaps buy me a cup of coffee ..."/*cut*/

"Two dark eyes,
two eggs in a glass,
a drop of lifeblood
with rum ..."

But this luggage of literary snippets is too light-weight for a heavy trip to Berlin. Even if I were to add Peter Panther or Gottfried Benn or *All Quiet on the Western Front.* There is a small collection of books from the Weimar Republic in my mind/*cut*/
The strongest images remain my own quasi-political memories of Berlin: the harsh, shouting voices of Hitler and Goebbels, transmitted throughout the world from Berlin; voices which I remember hearing on a crackly "Volksempfänger" radio as an evacuee in Gurten, a town halfway between Ried and Braunau[1] in the Inn region of Austria. The never-to-be-forgotten moment shortly after 5 o'clock on the afternoon of July 20, 1944, when the first sentence spoken by the newscaster, "This morning, an attempt was made to assassinate the Führer," sent our hopes soaring, only to be dashed again within almost the same breath by the second: "The Führer is alive."
It was in the short space of time between these two sentences that my first political image of "Berlin" crystallized.

und dem zweiten Satz: »Der Führer lebt«, als eben diese Hoffnungen ebenso maßlos in Sekunden abzusinken begannen. Zwischen diesen beiden Sätzen hat sich mein erstes politisches Vorstellungskristall »Berlin« gebildet. Im Kindheitstagebuch des damals Elfjährigen steht: »Wien, Donnerstag, 20. Juli 1944. — Heute wurde ein Attentat auf Adolf Hitler verübt.«
Rote Hinweispfeile und Unterstreichungen als versteckte Zeichen für die Bedeutung des Tages. Eingeklebte Zeitungsblätter der Sonderausgabe des *Völkischen Beobachters*, Berlin, 21. Juli 1944: »Wie das Deutsche Nachrichtenbüro erfährt, ist das Komplott der verbrecherischen Offiziersclique völlig zusammengebrochen.«

Erster Satz: Ankunft in Berlin

Und nun das Reale, Flug mit Pan American von Stuttgart nach Berlin-Tempelhof, Ankunft um 14.30 Uhr. In den hohen, flugzeugüberdeckenden Hallen die stehengebliebene Architektur des Tausendjährigen Reichsstils ... Das gewohnte Mercedestier bringt uns ins Hotel Kempinski, Ecke Kurfürstendamm. Die übliche Luxushotelhallenfauna und -flora, Liftboys, vom Leben enttäuschte Zigaretten- und Postkartenverkäuferinnen, »Menschen im Hotel«, würde Vicki Baum sagen, Pelzdamen, denen unten Seidenstrumpfbeinchen hübsch heraustehen, Herrenflauschmäntel, die aufgeregt wie der »Richtige Fischer«[2] hin- und hergehen. Flugkarten bestellen, Blumensträuße kaufen, Telegramme wegschicken, der lächelnde Portier mit den gekreuzten Schlüsseln am »Offizierskragen«. Also ehrlich gesagt, unter uns, ganz im Vertrauen, auf diese Weise kann ich meine Berlin-Vorstellungen nicht überprüfen. Hier kommt kein Blauer Engel mehr, auch wenn ich nach ihm rufe. Die Bekanntschaft eines Reichspropagandaministers kann ich auch nicht mehr machen, selbst wenn ich mich bis zum Tiergartenbunker durchfrage. Der alte Curtius[3] ist tot. Seine Söhne leben in Krefeld und Bonn. Den Bildgießer Noack, der jetzt alle Henry-Moore-Plastiken gießt, und Will Grohmann, das lebendige Dresdner Kunstgreislein, Herrn Professor Reidemeister, Generaldirektor der Berliner Museen, und die Familie Lemmer in Zehlendorf werde ich im Verlaufe der Begebenheiten sehen.

Zweiter Satz: Die Mauer auf dem Stadtplan

Einstweilen bleibt nichts anderes zu tun, als im Zimmer des Hotels Kempinski wie jeder andere Dutzendreisende in der Stadt des politischen Tourismus den Stadtplan auszubreiten und staunend den Verlauf der visuell eindrucksvollsten Trennungslinie zwischen Ost und West festzustellen — immer an der Wand lang: Die stachelige Schnörkellinie auf dem Stadtplan beginnt bei der

In the diary of the eleven-year-old child I was at the time this event is described simply: "Vienna, Thursday, July 20, 1944. Today, an attempt was made on Adolf Hitler's life."
A splattering of red arrows and lines serve as a coded message to the observer of the day. Newspaper cuttings have been pasted in from July 21, 1944, from the special edition of the *Völkischer Beobachter*, Berlin:
"The German News Office has now received confirmation that the plot organized by the criminal clique of army officers has completely collapsed."

First Movement: Arrival in Berlin

And now back to reality, to a Pan Am flight from Stuttgart to Berlin-Tempelhof, scheduled to land at 2.30 p.m. The huge aircraft hangars look like huge fossils of the monumental architectural style of the Thousand Year Reich ... the ever-present Merc whisks us off to the Kempinski Hotel on the corner of Kurfürstendamm. The standard luxury hotel fauna and flora, lift attendants, disillusioned women selling postcards and cigarettes, "People in Hotels" as Vicki Baum would say, ladies clad in fur coats from which pretty, silk-stockinged legs protrude, gentleman's velveteen overcoats strutting back and forth like the "Real Fischer"[2].
Booking aeroplane tickets, buying bunches of flowers, sending telegrammes, the smiling doorman sporting crossed-keys insignia on his "officer's collar". To be honest, just between the two of us, in confidence, I can't check the validity of my Berlin images in this style. There is no Blue Angel to be found here, even if I call for one. This is no place to meet the Reich's propaganda minister, even if I manage to ask my way to the bunker at Tiergarten. Old Curtius[3] is dead. His sons now live in Krefeld and Bonn. Later on during this trip, I will be meeting up with Noack, who runs a sculpture-casting foundry and who now casts all Henry Moore's statues and Willi Grohmann, Dresden's living éminence grise of art, Professor Reidemeister, General Director of the Berlin Museums, and the Lemmer family in Zehlendorf.

Second Movement: The Wall on the Map

For the time being, there is nothing else to do but to spread out the map of the city in my room in the Kempinksi Hotel, as would any other run-of-the-mill traveller to the city of political tourism, and to gaze astounded at the world's most striking demarcation line between East and West — "immer an der Wand lang" as the old song goes.
A snaking line of barbed-wire begins at Waltersdorfer Chaussee turns to cross the Havel river and the Jungfernsee to travel

Waltersdorfer Chaussee mit den eingezeichneten Spanischen Reitern, dreht sich über die Havel und den Jungfernsee nach Norden, schlängelt sich an Spandau vorbei — sitzt dort nicht noch der Reichsjugendführer und Gauleiter von Wien, Baldur von Schirach? — und knickt östlich der Oranienburger Chaussee wieder nach Süden, bis der gezeichnete Stacheldraht wieder an die rot und in Vogelperspektive eingezeichnete Mauer, die Berliner Mauer, stößt, die von Nord nach Süd mit zahlreichen Knickungen, einer Knickungsbucht beim Brandenburger Tor und neun Maueröffnungen die Stadt durchzieht. Eine Schandmauer, wenn man den Begriff von der westlichen Vorstellung ableitet, eine Friedensmauer, wenn man den Namen gemäß der östlichen Sprachverordnungen in den Mund nehmen will. Eine chinesische Mauer, die irrtümlich von Russen in deutscher Erscheinungsform aufgestellt wurde, wenn man die Sache *sub specie aeternitatis* sieht. Man sollte daher nicht von London und Köln oder Stuttgart, nicht von Moskau und Warschau oder Leipzig anreisen, um die Mauer zu sehen. Man sollte von Peking kommen, um nicht erstaunt zu sein! Während ich die neun Maueröffnungen auf der Karte betrachte und die Kartenlegende — von Pankow zur Zeit genehmigte Grenzübergänge, seit 23. August 1961 — studiere, beginnen plötzlich eine Baßbariton- und eine Sopranstimme im Nebenzimmer Tonleitern auf und ab zu singen. »Walter Berry und Christa Ludwig«, sagt das Zimmermädchen flüsternd, »von der Wiener Staatsoper!«

Dritter Satz: Überschreiten der Mauer

Berlin, Montag, 2. März 1964

Ich habe mir einen Wagen zur Fahrt nach Ost-Berlin bestellt. Das muß man anmelden. Ein Chauffeur mit Sonderpaß muß beigestellt werden. Eine Reiseführerin des anderen Deutschlands muß einen auf der anderen Seite der Mauer erwarten und die Rundfahrt mitmachen.
Abfahrt um 10 Uhr vom Hotel Kempinski. An der Westfront der Mauer zunächst vorbei am Brandenburger Tor: die vom Bildgießer Noack (wir werden ihn heute nachmittag sehen) wiederhergestellte Quadriga fährt in östlicher Richtung davon. In der Bernauer Straße hat man die Häuser evakuiert und aus ihren Vorderfronten einen »Mauerteil« gemacht, bis zum zweiten Stock die Fenster zugemauert, Schießscharten ausgespart.
Man konnte die Leute nicht in Ostberliner Häusern lassen, wo die Haustore nach Westen gehen, welche Gefahren! Straße überqueren: Nescafé, *Frankfurter Allgemeine*, am Ende gar die *New York Times* oder die *Herald Tribune* kaufen; im weiteren Verlauf der Begebenheiten — nach Westen aus den oberen Stockwerken

North, twisting past Spandau — isn't that where the Reich's youth leader and Gauleiter of Vienna, Baldur von Schirach is now incarcerated? — before taking a sharp turn just East of Oranienburger Chaussee towards the South again, where the drawing of barbed wire joins up again with the red-coloured, bird's eye view of the Wall, the Berlin Wall, which follows a jagged path from North to South, making a short, arching diversion around the Brandenburg Gate and interrupted by nine holes, representing crossing-points. The Wall of Shame, to take the western view, or the Wall of Peace, to take the official term prescribed by the East. A Chinese Wall mistakenly cast by Russians in a German mould, *sub specie aeternitatis*. People shouldn't come to see it from London or Cologne, or from Stuttgart, or from Moscow, Warsaw or Leipzig. People should come from Peking — at least they wouldn't be overwhelmed!
I sit looking at the nine openings in the Wall shown on the map and at the map's key — crossing-points approved by Soviet command in Pankow since August 23, 1961 — when suddenly a bass baritone and a soprano begin to practice their scales in the next room. "Walter Berry and Christa Ludwig," whispers the maid, "from the Viennese State Opera!"

Third Movement: Crossing the Wall

Berlin, Monday, March 2, 1964

I have asked for a car to take me over to East Berlin. You have to apply for it specially. They have to get hold of a chauffeur with a special pass. A guide from the other Germany must be waiting for you on the far side of the Wall and must accompany you on the tour.
We set off at around 10 a.m. from the Kempinski Hotel. We pass the western side of the Wall at the Brandenburg Gate: the Quadriga, the chariot rider atop the Gate (restored by the sculpture-caster Noack whom we will visit this afternoon) gallops towards the East. In Bernauer Strasse the houses have been evacuated and their fronts now form part of the Wall, the windows of the first and second floors have been bricked up except for slits left for the guards' guns.
It was impossible to leave people living in houses facing the West — think of the danger! They might cross the street: take a Nescafé, buy the *Frankfurter Allgemeine*, maybe even the *New York Times* or the *Herald Tribune*; as things developed, they might even jump out of the upper windows, they might even miss the blanket stretched out to break their fall: pools of blood and an announcement of their death in western newspapers …!

springen, das Sprungtuch verfehlen: Blutflecken und eine Todesnachricht in westlichen Zeitungen hinterlassen ...!
Von den Häusern der Bernauer Straße fallen Verputz, Ziegelsteine, Gesimsteile auf den westlichen Gehsteig. Es ist nicht nur politisch gefährlich, hier auf und ab zu gehen! Vorbei an den moosgrünen Schupos am Checkpoint Charlie, einige Autolängen durch Niemandsland. Ich kenne dieses kribbelige Gefühl noch von der Ennsbrückenüberquerung her.[4] Eine Schrankenaufwärtsbewegung jetzt, und ein freundlich grinsender »Russe« mit nach oben zusammengebundener Mütze sagt hier sächselnd, wir sollten die Papiere bereithalten. Er ist ja auch Sachse und nicht Russe, und für die russengraugrüne Uniform kann er nichts. Eine dicke Frau unbestimmten Alters steigt zu, blond, eher bieder, so zwischen Lehrersfrau und Krankenkassenbeamtin. »Ich begrüße Sie zu einer Stadtrundfahrt. Mein Name ist Nowak.« Meine Neugierde, wie sich die anbefohlene Propaganda um meine Ohren legen wird, ersticke ich zunächst in dem Satz: »Mein Name ist Fischer!«

Vierter Satz: Rundfahrt in Ost-Berlin

Vorbei an dunklen Halbruinen, darauf mit Weißletternschrift auf rotem Grund: »Der Sozialismus hat schon begonnen.«
Vor dem brettervernagelten Berliner Dom meine Frage:
»Werden hier noch Gottesdienste gehalten?«
»Nein«, sagt Frau Nowak, »nur ab und zu.«
»Was ist dann drin?«
»Das Gebäude«, sagt Frau Nowak, »beherbergt die Theologische Fakultät!«
Vor dem gespenstischen Rathaus, niemand geht ein und aus, spricht Frau Nowak von Bürgermeister Ebert, dem Sohn des republikanischen Ebert seligen Weimarer Andenkens. Ob ich Sonderwünsche hätte? Ja, ich möchte zur Museumsinsel und in eine Buchhandlung. Gut, der westliche Chauffeur und Frau Nowak bringen mich hin und stellen mich unter einer Brücke ab.
Ich gehe an einer Volkspolizeiunterkunft vorbei, wo wieder ein sächsischer »Russe« Wache steht, vermerke neben ihm eine blumengeschmückte Gedenktafel — oder ein Grab?
»Im Andenken an den 24jährigen Volkspolizisten — gemeißelter Name —, der im Kampf gegen Westberliner Polizei etc ... fiel.«
Ich überquere die bröckelige Brücke über die Spree und stehe vor Museumstoren und weiß nicht, was mich dahinter erwartet. Über die Eingangstreppen hat man einen behelfsmäßigen Brettersteg gelegt. Wird hier noch Mörtel geführt? Was wird über diesen Brettersteg in das große, pompöse Haus gebracht? Ich sehe keine Arbeiter. Ich sehe nur wenige Besucher. An der Kleidung erkennt man sie als West-Touristen, Westdeutsche. Ich »Falscher Fischer«,[5]

The houses in Bernauer Strasse shed plaster, roof tiles and chunks of window ledge onto the footpath on the western side. It is not just politically dangerous to walk around here!
Past the moss-green-clad West Berlin police, the "Schupos," at Checkpoint Charlie. I recognize the butterflies in my stomach from the time we crossed the bridge over the river Enns[4]. The upward swing of a barrier and the friendly smile of a "Rusky," sporting a Russian-style hat with tied-up earflaps. Our "Rusky" says, with a Saxon accent, we should get our papers ready. The accent shouldn't come as such a surprise really, after all he is from Saxony and not from Russia, and it is scarcely his fault that he has to wear the Russian-grey uniform. A fat woman of undefinable age clambers into the car with us, mousy blond, rather tame, something of a cross between school teacher's wife and health insurance clerk. "Welcome to the tour of the city. My name is Nowak." I am eager to know what form the state propaganda will take, but I manage to suppress my inquisitiveness and simply reply: "My name is Fischer."

Fourth Movement: Tour of East Berlin

We pass dark, delapidated buildings which act as hoardings for white lettering on a red background proclaiming: "Socialism has already begun."
In front of the boarded-up Cathedral of Berlin I ask a question: "Is mass still held there?"
"No," replies Frau Nowak, "only now and again."
"What's in there?"
"The building," says Frau Nowak, "houses the Theology Faculty."
In front of the ghostly Town Hall, which no one enters and no one leaves, Frau Nowak talks of Mayor Ebert, the son of Friedrich Ebert, the socialist Chancellor during the Weimar Republic. She asks if I have any particular wishes? I reply that I would like to see the Museum Island and a bookshop. Fine. The western chauffeur and Frau Nowak take me there and drop me off under a bridge. I pass by a Volkspolizist barracks where another Saxon "Rusky" stands guard and I spot, next to him, a memorial plaque decorated with flowers, or is it perhaps a grave? "To the memory of the 24-year-old Volkspolizist — his name engraved in the stone — who fell in the battle ... etc. against the West Berlin police." I cross the crumbling bridge over the river Spree and stand in front of the gates to the museum, not knowing what awaits me beyond. A makeshift footbridge of planks has been placed across the steps leading to the entrance. Are they still repairing it? Just what are they carrying across these planks into the pompous building beyond? I can't see any workers, only a few visitors to the museum. Their clothes give them away as tourists from the West, West

ein Wiener aus London, stelle mich dazu. Das erzene Reiterstandbild des Großen Kurfürsten wächst neben dem Brettersteg staubig aus dem Boden, besser — versinkt ... Wird es der märkische Sand bald ganz zudecken?

Aus dem Dunkel der schlecht beleuchteten Vorhalle, Hin- und Hergehen der Museumsdiener in abgeschabten Anzügen und krawattenlosen Hemden. Ein Rollkragenpullover oder ähnliches ersetzt das Buntfleckchen des bourgeoisen Krawattenknopfes.

Ein Diener schlurft mit mir gleichzeitig auf die Toilette. Beim seifenlosen Händewaschen merke ich, wie er eine Pappdose aus der Rocktasche zieht und grauen Scheuersand über seine Hände streut. Sollte ich ihn um Sand bitten, wie man jenseits der Mauer um Feuer bittet? In der vorgeschichtlichen Sammlung biete ich einem Diener ein Zigarillo an. Er ergreift es gierig, sagt, so etwas bekommt man bei uns nicht mehr, will meinen Namen und meine Adresse wissen, zeigt mir ein Notizbuch, vollgeschrieben mit Namen und Adressen westlicher Besucher. Ist das sein armseliges Gebetbuch der Freiheit — Namen, die jenseits der Mauer ihre Träger haben — oder will er nur Bettelbriefe schreiben? Träumt er von Flucht und bedeuten diese Namen utopische Fluchtziele? Ist er am Ende nichts als ein Spitzel? Er bedankt sich für die Zigarillogeste.

Ich gehe weiter, vermerke neben dem Pergamonaltar die zweit- und drittklassigen Ausstellungsobjekte. Die erstklassigen stehen in Berlin-Dahlem, Arnimallee. Kaufe mir einen Katalog. Die graue Katalogfrau schreibt umständlich eine Quittung für die Pfennigrechnung. Der sächsische »Russe« am Mauerloch muß ja bei der Rückfahrt über meine Ausgaben in Ost-Berlin Bescheid wissen.

Ich lasse die Ausstellungsräume mit den belehrenden Tafeln, z.B. »Rokoko = der letzte Glanz der dekadenten Herrscherklasse vor der Bewußtwerdung der Arbeiterklasse«, hinter mir, steige die schwach beleuchtete Prunktreppe hinab, lasse das staubige Reiterstandbild des Großen Kurfürsten links liegen, überquere den seltsamen Brettersteg, vorbei an dem Wächter, der Scheuersand in der Tasche trägt, hinaus auf die steinerne Balustrade über der Spree, über die Brücke, vorbei an der Wache mit Russenmütze, vorbei am blumengeschmückten Grab, zurück zu Frau Nowak.

Über die Karl-Marx-, ehemals Stalinallee, zur Karl-Marx-Buchhandlung. Auf der Fahrt erzählt Frau Nowak vom ostzonalen Rationierungssystem. Jeder Fleischerladen hätte seine gesetzliche Kundenkarte. Nur ein registrierter Kunde bekäme Fleisch in seinem gesetzlich vorgeschriebenen Fleischerladen ...

Buchladen. Die große Karl-Marx-Buchhandlung. Am Treppenaufgang haben sich die zwei Erzväter in billigem Warenhaus-Dutzenderz lebensgroß als Begrüßer aufgestellt, Marx- und Engelsbüsten ringsum, verkäufliche Devotionalien. Die roten Buchrücken der endlos langen Karl-Marx-Gesamtausgabe. Ich

Germans. I join them, a "False Fischer"[5], a Viennese from London. The iron statue of the Kurfürst, the Great Elector, on horseback, covered in dust, rises up next to the planks — or perhaps more appropriately sinks — soon to be covered completely by the sand of the Mark Brandenburg.

The museum attendants float in and out of the gloom of the poorly-lit entrance hall in thread-bear suits and open-collared shirts. A polo-neck jumper or something similar replaces the splash of colour provided in the West by the bourgeois tie.

One of the attendants scuffs along beside me towards the toilets. While washing my hands, I notice him extract a paper cup full of grey-coloured dish-washing grit from his jacket pocket and spread it over his hands. Should I ask him for some in the same way as you'd ask for a light on the other side of the Wall? In the Prehistoric Collection I offer a cigarillo to one of the attendants. He grabs it greedily, asks for my name and address, shows me a notebook crammed with names and addresses of other visitors from the West. It is a rather pathetic prayer book of freedom — names whose bearers live beyond the Wall, or does he want to write begging letters? Does he dream of escape and these names represent his utopian destinations? Is he, in reality, nothing more than an informer? He thanks me for the cigarillo.

I go on, and take note of the second-rate and third-rate exhibits. Only the Pergamon Alter stands out. The better exhibits are in Berlin-Dahlem, Arnimallee, in the West. I buy a catalogue. The grey catalogue-lady laboriously writes out a receipt for an amount which can be counted in Pfennigs. The Saxon "Rusky" at the hole in the Wall will need evidence of my purchases when I go back.

I leave behind me the exhibition halls and their didactic descriptions, including, for example, "Rococo = the last flourish of the decadent ruling class before the rise in working class consciousness." I descend the weakly-illuminated but magnificent stairway, pass the dusty statue of the Kurfürst, I cross the strange plank footbridge, pass the attendant who carries grit in a paper cup in his pocket, out onto the stone balustrade across the Spree, across the bridge, past the guard with his Russian hat, past the grave with flowers, back to Frau Nowak.

Across Karl-Marx-Allee, which used to be called Stalin-Allee, to the Karl-Marx bookshop. On the way, Frau Nowak explains about the system of food rationing in the East. Every butcher's shop has its own official rationing cards. Only a customer with an official ration card can get meat and only in the butcher's shop to which he is assigned.

The bookshop. The big Karl-Marx book shop. On the steps to the entrance the shopper is greeted by the two founding fathers of communism, dozens of cheap-looking, life-size, department-store-style busts of Marx and Engels — devotionals for sale. I notice the

bitte, mir die Abteilung »Geistes- und Literaturgeschichte« zu zeigen. Frau Nowak ist eher betreten, bringt mich in den Oberstock. Ich greife mir Prospekte und Zeitschriften heraus:
Weimarer Beiträge, Zeitschrift für deutsche Literaturgeschichte, 1963/III, S. 576:
»Gedanken zur bevorstehenden Ehrung Jacob Grimms 1963«, »Molevolistische Strömungen im klassischen Weimar«, »Das Renaissancebild Johannes R. Bechers — Ausdruck einer sozialistischen, nationalen Literaturkonzeption«, »Operativität, Volkstümlichkeit und nationale Bedeutung von J.R. Bechers Ballade *Kinderschuhe aus Lublin*«, »Bemerkungen über Sprachporträts in Bernhard Seegers Roman *Herbstrauch*«, dann »Über die deutsche Sprache und die beiden Deutschland«, daraus ein Zitat:
»Die unter der Arbeiter- und Bauernmacht in der Deutschen Demokratischen Republik fortschreitende politische, ökonomische und kulturelle Umwälzung und die ebenfalls alle Lebensformen ergreifende Abspaltung Westdeutschlands vom deutschen Nationalverband unter dem Diktat der Monopolbourgeoisie sind auch an der deutschen Sprache nicht vorübergegangen ...«
Die gekauften Heftchen und Zeitschriften werden wieder mit Quittungen versehen.
Kehrtwendung des Wagens auf der Karl-Marx-Allee. Ich entdecke, daß Frau Nowak in der Karl-Marx-Buchhandlung ein englisches Buch gekauft hat, irgendeinen nichtssagenden Roman. Aber wie leuchten ihre Augen nach dem einmaligen Fang!
»Ein englisches Buch bekommt man hier fast nie zu kaufen«, sagt Frau Nowak. Der Inhalt ist ihr gleichgültig. Etwas in der Sprache des offiziellen Feindes zu lesen, das ist ihr wichtig! Ein Protestfunke, wenn auch vielleicht unbewußt. Wie leicht hätte ich ihr ein paar englische Zeitschriften und Bücher mitbringen können, aber so bleibt nur die Bedrückung — das ewige Nichtwissen um die wahren Bedürfnisse des Nächsten —, ein kurzer Absatz im langen Kapitel über die Erbsünde ...
In dem graugrünen Heftchen, von der grauen Frau im Museum gekauft (Horst Redecker, *Das Dilemma der Dekadenz*, Berlin 1958), finde ich allerdings Stellen, die meinem persönlichen Bedrückungsdilemma mit falschem Optimismusfanfarenklang kurzfristig Auflösung durch befreiendes Lachen bringen:
»... daß die Arbeiterklasse der legitime Erbe aller großen kulturellen Leistungen der Menschheit ist, der Hüter und Mehrer der Kultur in der Epoche des zu Ende gehenden Kapitalismus. Das ist auch ein Beweis dafür, daß die Sowjetunion, schon seit dem ersten Jahre ihres Bestehens, allen bürgerlichen Verleumdungen zum Trotz, das höchste kulturelle Niveau der Menschheit repräsentierte.«
Zurück zum Mauerloch Friedrichstraße, Halt am Straßenrand, um die Einkaufsquittungen vorzuzeigen und von der eingetauschten

red spines of the endless volumes that make up the complete set of works of Karl Marx. I ask to be shown the section on "History of Literature and Humanities". Frau Nowak seems a little put out at this suggestion but leads me to the top floor. I sample a few brochures and magazines:
A Weimar journal for essays on literary history, 1963/III, page 576:
"Thoughts on the coming celebration of Jacob Grimm, 1963", "Molevolist thought in classical Weimar", "The renaissance image of Johannes R. Bechers — the expression of a socialist, nationalist concept of literature", "Operativity, popular tradition and national significance of ballad *Kinderschuhe aus Lublin* by J.R. Bechers", "Comments on the linguistic character portrayals in the novel *Herbstrauch* by Bernhard Seegers", then "On the German language in the two Germanys", including the following quotation:
"The progressive political, economic and cultural revolution under workers' power in the German Democratic Republic and the similarly all-embracing decision of West Germany to form a separate state under the dictatorship of the bourgeoisie has naturally left its mark on the German language ..."
Once again, receipts are provided for the books and magazines. We make a U-turn on Karl-Marx-Allee. I discover that Frau Nowak has bought a book published in English. It is only a bland novel of some kind but her eyes display a glint of joy at making this unique catch. "It is almost impossible to get a book in English." explains Frau Nowak. The contents would seem to be irrelevant, what is important is the chance to read something in the language of the enemy. So a spark of rebellion after all, even if perhaps an unconscious one. It would have been so easy for me to have brought over a few English magazines and books, but as it is I am left feeling slightly sad — this eternal ignorance of the real needs of your neighbour, another short paragraph in the long chapter on original sin ...
The grey-green pamphlet which I had bought from the woman in the museum (Horst Redecker, *The Dilema of Decadence*, Berlin, 1958) manages to wrench me away from my depressing thoughts by presenting a false fanfare of socialist optimism which triggers liberating laughter:
"... the working class is the legitimate heir to all great cultural achievements of humanity, the guardian and disseminator of culture in the epoch of dying capitalism. This is also proof that the Soviet Union, notwithstanding the slander of the bourgeoisie, has, since the very first year of its existence, represented the highest level of human culture."
Back to the hole in the Wall in Friedrichstrasse, where we stop at the edge of the road to have our receipts stamped and the amount compared with the amount of Ostmark we now wish to exchange back. Frau Nowak says good-bye and gets out of the

Ostmarksumme abzuziehen. Frau Nowak verabschiedet sich und steigt mit dem englischen Buch unterm Arm aus dem Mercedestier und verschwindet, am sächsischen »Russen« vorbei, der freundlich lächelt, die Quittungen übernimmt und den Schlagbaum hochzieht. Das Mercedestier rollt im Schrittempo durch.

Nachspiel: Ein Siegesdenkmal nach dem anderen ...

Gießerei Hermann Noack[6], Fehlerstraße, Berlin

Noack junior (der Vater starb vor zwei Jahren), ein stämmiger kleiner Mann mit Bäuchlein und beginnender Glatze, berlinert wie nur einer, läuft wie ein Wiesel durch die Werkstatthallen, läßt den neuen Kran knarren, zeigt stolz auf den erhöhten Dachstuhl des Ateliers, führt die runden Mörtelformen vor, in welche die Güsse noch »eingepackt« sind. Da stehen mit schwarzer Kreide dick die Namen »Heiliger« und »Moore« auf dem Mörtel. Noack erwähnt, kurz und ohne Pathos, obwohl er auf seine handwerklichen Fähigkeiten mit Recht stolz sein könnte, das zerbrochene Gipsmodell der Moore-Plastik für das Lincoln Center, New York, das er wieder zusammengeflickt hat.
Auf die Frage des »Falschen Fischer«, wie es der Firma zwischen 1945 und 1950 gegangen sei, sagt er fröhlich:
»Ach, sehr gut. Wir gossen ein Siegesdenkmal nach dem anderen für die Russen, eine Gedenkplatte nach der anderen. Wir konnten mit der Arbeit gar nicht nachkommen in dieser Zeit. Die Russen zahlten mit Naturalien: Butter, Kartoffeln, Eier, halbe und ganze Schweine. Das war was wert damals! Wir waren die erste Berliner Fabrik im April 1945, in der wieder Rauch aus dem Schornstein gestiegen ist. Dann hämmerten wir die Quadriga am Brandenburger Tor zurecht, und jetzt können wir uns auch nicht beklagen. Ich mußte wegen Henry Moore den Betrieb vergrößern und anbauen lassen!«
Diese Bronzepferde da, Reichssportfeldrenaissance, und diese Bronzetafeln dort im Garten, will der »Falsche Fischer« wissen, werden die jetzt eingeschmolzen?
»Das Bronzepferd da vielleicht«, sagt Noack, »aber die Ehrentafel, die da am Zaun lehnt, die Ehrentafel der Berliner Universität für Professor Hahn, was damit geschieht, wissen wir auch nicht. Hahn will keine Ehrentafel, und die Universität kann ja das schwere Ding auch nicht heimlich aufstellen ...«

Merc with the English book tucked under her arm and disappears past the Saxon "Rusky", who offers a friendly smile, takes our receipts and lifts the barrier to let us pass. The Mercedes crawls slowly across.

The encore: One memorial to victory after another ...

The Hermann Noack[6] foundry, Fehlerstrasse, Berlin

Noack junior (the father had died two years previously) is a stout man with a bit of a belly and a bald patch. He has a thick Berlin accent and runs like a weasel through the workshops, putting the new crane through its paces for our benefit and proudly showing off the studio's raised roof truss and the round brick moulds into which the casts are packed. The names "Heiliger" and "Moore" have been written onto the bricks in thick lines of black chalk. Although he can justifiably be proud of his skills as a craftsman, Noack mentions briefly, and in a matter-of-fact way, that he has just patched up the broken plaster model for the Moore sculpture for the Lincoln Center in New York.
When asked by the "False Fischer" how business was between 1945 and 1950, he replies cheerfully: "Very good. We cast one memorial to victory after another for the Russians, one memorial plaque after another. We couldn't keep up with the orders. The Russians paid in kind: with potatoes, eggs, half a pig, sometimes a whole one. And that was worth something in those days! We were the first Berlin factory to have smoke coming out of the stack after April 1945. Then we went to work on the Quadriga above the Brandenburg Gate and got it into shape. And we can't complain now, either. Thanks to Henry Moore, I have had to expand the business and to add an extension."
The "False Fischer" enquires whether the bronze horse over there, a Third Reich stadium renaissance piece, and the bronze plaques in the garden are to be melted down.
"The bronze stallion perhaps," replies Nowak, "but we don't know what's to be done with the plaque of honour leaning against the fence over there, the Berlin University plaque for Professor Hahn. Hahn doesn't want it and the university can hardly put up that great heavy thing inconspicuously ..."

II. Bericht von der gefallenen Mauer, 1989

Die letzte Pirsch am antifaschistischen Schutzwall mit Schutzengel Uwe, Oberstleutnant der DDR-Grenztruppen, promovierter Fachlehrer für Marxismus-Leninismus.

Widmung
Für Heinrich, Karl und Kurt, die Altmeister ironischer Polittexte; für Heinrich Heine, Karl Kraus und Kurt Tucholsky.

Moritat vom Ende:

1. Die letzte Phase — 1989
»Mich hat interessiert die Tragödie dieses Sozialismus. Jetzt sieht es aus wie eine Farce. Das ist die letzte Phase. Aber es war eine Tragödie!« (Dramatiker Heiner Müller, in: *Der Spiegel*, 31/1990, 30. Juli 1990, S. 140)

2. Eislers Blick auf West-Berlin — 1961
»Siehst du, das ist unser Berlin! Überall, wo jetzt ein Licht angeht, sitzt einer und träumt davon, uns die Gurgel durchzuschneiden!« (Gerhart Eisler, der spätere Vorsitzende des staatlichen Rundfunkkomitees von Pankow nach West-Berlin blickend, zu seinem Neffen Georg Eisler, Sohn des Komponisten der DDR-Hymne, Hanns Eisler, 1961. Zitiert nach: *Der Spiegel*, 31/1990, 30. Juli 1990, S. 140)

3. Die Stimmen auf den Plätzen — 1989/1990
»Wir sind das Volk!«
»Auch wir sind das Volk!« (Ruf von 3000 demonstrierenden Volkspolizisten in Leipzig, 25. Januar 1990)

Am 6. Dezember 1989, einem Mittwoch, sind sie zur Stelle, pünktlich um 9 Uhr, am Checkpoint Charlie: Fritz Graf von der Schulenburg, das Chronisten-Auge, und Wolfgang Georg Fischer, die federführende Chronisten-Hand. Die natürlichen Werkzeuge im Anschlag und nichts wie hinüber!
Chronisten der bröckelnden Mauer sind sie schon Anfang November gewesen, westliche Schauseite, jetzt ist die östliche dran. Sie wollen aber deswegen nicht zu dieser späten Stunde der fast dreißigjährigen Mauerexistenz noch fünf nach zwölf von einer irrtümlich abgefeuerten Grenzerkugel ins rote Jenseits befördert werden, obwohl der hier so lange als volkseigen apostrophierte Zeitgeist schon seit Wochen nur mehr röchelnd durch den Medienäther gegeistert war.
Am 9. November ist er dann mit Knall aus der vom Chefpropagandisten Karl-Eduard von Schnitzler so lange verwalteten Äther-

II. Report on the Fallen Wall, 1989

A last opportunity to go hunting along the Anti-fascist Wall of Protection in the company of a guardian angle, in the guise of Uwe Karsch, Lieutenant Colonel of the GDR Border Guards and holder of a Masters Degree in Marxist-Leninist Education

Dedication
to Heinrich, Karl and Kurt, the grand old masters of ironic political comment.
To Heinrich Heine, Karl Kraus and Kurt Tucholsky

The "end is nigh" ballad:

1. The final phase — 1989
"It was the tragedy of socialism that interested me. Now it looks like a farce. This is the final phase. But it really was a tragedy!" (The playwright Heinrich Müller in *Der Spiegel*, 31, 1990, July 30th, 1990, page 140).

2. Eisler's view of West Berlin — 1961
"You see, that's Berlin for you! Behind every one of those lights out there is someone who dreams of slitting our throats!" (Gerhart Eisler, the later Chairman of the State Broadcasting Committee, looking from Pankow in East Berlin across to West Berlin, talking to his nephew Georg Eisler, son of the composer of the national anthem of the GDR, Hans Eisler, 1961, quoted from *Der Spiegel*, 31, 1990, July 30th, 1990, page 140).

3. Voices from the streets — 1989/1990
"We are the people!"
"We are the people, too!"
(The chant of 3,000 Volkspolizist demonstrators in Leipzig, January 25, 1990).

On December 6, 1989, a Wednesday, they are assembled on the dot of 9 a.m. at Checkpoint Charlie: Fritz von der Schulenburg, the camera-equipped Chronicler's Eye, and Wolfgang Georg Fischer, the pen-yielding Chronicler's Hand. Their tools are at the ready and there is no time to be lost — off, across the Wall!
As chroniclers of the crumbling Wall they were present from the very beginning of November — on the Western side. Now it is time for the Eastern side. Nevertheless, our chroniclers have no desire, at this late hour in the almost thirty-year history of the Wall, to be propelled into the next, socialist-red world by the accidental firing of a border guard's gun. They remained wary, despite the fact that the Party's artificial version of the "People's

flasche entwichen und hat endlich die sehnlich erhofften Löcher in die Mauer gerissen. »Sudel-Ede« — besser noch »Sudel-Edel« selbst, wie der mit Adelsprädikat beschwerte Genosse genannt wird, hatte sich allerdings schon am 30. Oktober im Äther aufgelöst, nicht ohne letzte Worte von der Hygiene des Äthers zu hinterlassen. Am Bildschirm jedenfalls ward er seither — außer in heiteren Talkshows — nicht mehr gesehen!

Chronisten sind aber habituell vorsichtig veranlagte Gesellen, darum hat »Die Hand« schon vor der Reise bei der DDR-Botschaft in London vorsorglich »Polizeischutz« angefordert und auch zugesagt bekommen. »Das Auge« hat, ebenso vorsorglich, empfohlen, beim Übergang Checkpoint Charlie nur die britischen Pässe vorzuzeigen, obwohl sie ja beide keine Engländer sind, sie leben nur seit 25 Jahren auf der Insel, der in Berlin geborene Fritz und der in Wien geborene Wolfgang.

Vor dem Checkpoint steht schon das Empfangskomitee — zivil ausgedrückt — bereit, Polizeischutz könnte man es auch nennen, wollte man eher militärisch formulieren, bestehend aus einer strammen Person in blitzblanken Stiefeln, russische Pelzmütze auf dem Kopf, freundlich lächelnd, jedoch kerzengerade, grüne Mappe unter dem Arm, tadellos adjustiert, das muß man ihr lassen.

Die Person stellt sich als Oberstleutnant der DDR-Grenztruppen vor, für uns abkommandiert vom Ministerium für Verteidigung, NVA, Nationale Volksarmee, Pressestelle.

Sie stehe voll und ganz zu unserer Verfügung, ein Dienstwagen mit Fahrer warte auf der anderen Seite, die Formalitäten beim Überqueren des Wildwechsels von West nach Ost, einfach läppisch, das sei im Handumdrehen erledigt.

Auf geht's zur letzten Pirsch am antifaschistischen Schutzwall zu dritt, zwei Westler in Zivil, ein Ostler in Uniform, laßt die Räuber durchmarschieren!

Wie hat man doch diese Menschenschleuse für Diplomaten und Westler aus dem nichtdeutschen Ausland seit 1964, als ich mich hier zum ersten Mal durchzwängen mußte, verschönt: Topfpflanzen in Kugelhumus, weiße Häkelvorhänge, gutgehaltene Toiletten mit funktionierenden Seifenspendern, Zollbeamtinnen, die dick und freundlich wirken wie Toilettenfrauen im Wiener Volkstheater bei einer Nachmittagsvorstellung für die reifere Jugend. Richtig heimelig könnte man sich da fühlen, wie in einem Jungpionierlager der FDJ für Auserwählte, aber unter ständiger Volkskontrolle, wenn nicht der Wagenspiegel auf Rädern noch da wäre, mit dem die Grenzsoldaten die Unterseite der Autos auszuspiegeln hatten, um verdächtige Luftlöcher im doppelten Kofferraum mit verbrecherischen Republikflüchtlingen strafaktenkundig zu machen. Der Geisterflug von einer Welt in die andere dauert keine fünf Minuten, immer in fürsorglicher Begleitung unseres

Spirit", which it had nurtured with such tender, loving care for so long, has, for several weeks now, been dying a slow death. Suddenly, on November 9, the genuine People's Spirit burst out of the corked-up bottle held by propaganda chief (and bête noire of East German television viewers) Eduard von Schnitzler, ripping long yearned-for holes in the Wall. Comrade von Schnitzler, "Sudel-Edel" the mud-slinging aristocrat himself, the red-blooded stalinist with a blue-blooded name, disappeared in a puff of smoke before that, on October 25, but not without a few last comments about maintaining the hygiene of the GDR ether. But there was nothing more to be seen of him on the country's television screens, except for the occasional appearance on non-political talk-shows.

But chroniclers are, by habit, cautious creatures and for this reason "the Hand" had already asked the GDR consulate in London for "police protection", which he was granted, before setting out for Berlin. "The Eye" had suggested that they use their British passports when crossing Checkpoint Charlie. Even though they are not English by birth, both Fritz, the native Berliner, and Wolfgang, the native Viennese, have been living in Britain for more than 25 years.

In front of the Checkpoint, the reception committee, to put it politely, is already waiting. Those with a military bent might just call it police protection: a committee consisting of one person in gleaming boots, a Russian hat, with a friendly smile and a green file tucked under his arm, but immaculately turned out. He introduces himself as a Lieutenant Colonel of the GDR border guards, seconded from the Ministry for Defence, by the National Army press department.

He is at our complete disposal, he assures us, a car with chauffeur is waiting on the other side, the formalities of crossing from West to East will be no problem, all over in a couple of minutes. So off we set, the three of us, on the last tour of the Anti-fascist Wall of Protection, two Westerners in civvies and an Easterner in uniform, let the hunt begin!

I notice the efforts that have been made since my first attempt to force entry in 1964 to embellish this air-lock for diplomats and non-Germans travelling between West and East: pot plants growing in spheres of humus, white net curtains, well-maintained toilets with soap dispensers that actually work, plump, friendly lady customs officials with something of the air of toilet attendants at the Vienna Volkstheater during a matinee for teenagers. It almost has a cosy feel to it, a bit like being in a "young pioneers'" camp for the elite, run by the East German youth organisation, the Freie Deutsche Jugend, under constant supervision of the People. Well, it would be cosy if it weren't for the castor-mounted mirrors on long handles for searching under cars for breathing holes

Ehrenkomitees, unseres Grenztruppenoffiziers, eines Schutzengels zur besonderen Verwendung sozusagen. Drüben wartet schon sein dunkelgrüner Dienstwagen Marke Wartburg, etwas verbeult zwar, aber durchaus funktionstüchtig. Ein muffiger Schlägertyp in Halbzivil, der keine Miene verzieht, läßt den Motor an — ihm möchte man in keinem System ohne schützende Polizeibegleitung begegnen, ihm möchte man sich nicht von der falschen Seite nähern müssen.

Erst im Wartburg gewinnt die militärische Person zivile Konturen, gibt Vor- und Familiennamen preis, Uwe und Karsch, läßt uns nochmals wissen, daß wir jetzt ganz freie Wahl hätten, auch die Ostseite der Mauer, das bisher unbemalte und sozusagen volkseigene Gesicht des antifaschistischen Schutzwalls, zu besichtigen. Chronisten, befehlt, ich folge euch: Todesstreifen, Wachtürme, Suchscheinwerfer, Panzersperren, Stacheldrahtverhaue, Gehege für scharfe Wolfshunde an Drahtläufen, damit die ausfallenden Biester sich nicht am Ende jetzt auch in die Waden der Grenztruppe verbeißen, bereits entfernte Stahlbetonplatten, Bereitstellungsflächen für in Reserve gehaltene Panzer, all die Herrlichkeiten legt uns der Schutzengel zu Füßen! Nimm, Kameraauge, was das menschliche Auge nicht fassen kann, ohne daß ihm die Welt in Tränen verschwimmt, nimm, Wort, was du nicht formulieren kannst, ohne daß es dir in der Kehle steckenbleibt!

»Mauern machen mich trübsinnig«, hat mir unlängst ein Teilnehmer des Zweiten Weltkriegs gesagt, »nicht nur die in Berlin, sondern überhaupt. Sie machen mir Komplexe. Das ist zwar eine jüdische Erfindung, aber es gibt sie. Wetten …?«

Und hier, jetzt, während wir auf eigenes Verlangen vom Schutzengel näher an die Mauer herangeführt werden — undeutsche Mauer von Jericho, wie du uns jetzt deine weiße Farbe der völligen Unbeflecktheit zuwendest, kilometerlanges Weiß vor dem Todesstreifen, du machst uns noch immer Angst … Gerade dieses Weiß soll jahrzehntelang das Morgenrot der sozialistischen Idee im Arbeiter- und Bauernparadies ersetzt haben? Ich dachte immer, in der Deutschen Demokratischen Republik hätte man eher alles grau in grau gehalten!

Wirft das Echo der Mauer noch Erichs Worte vom vergangenen Sommer zurück?

»Den Sozialismus in seinem Lauf«
So sagen wir immer
»Hält weder Ochs noch Esel auf!«

Die Antwort darauf ist dann wohl nicht mehr bis Wandlitz durchgedrungen:

»Die große Wende in ihrem Lauf
Hält weder Ochs noch Esel auf!«

and secret compartments for would-be escapees. Escapees who, not so long ago, would have been hauled off to court and denounced as criminals. The transfer from one world to another takes less than five minutes, accompanied throughout by our honorary reception committee, our border guard, our guardian angle with special duties. On the other side a dark-green, official car awaits us — an East German-made Wartburg, a little bit dented but in good working order. The driver, a bad-tempered thug half in uniform and half not, who doesn't so much as raise an eyebrow to greet us, starts the engine. He's a man you wouldn't want to meet anywhere, in any system, without high-ranking police protection, a man you wouldn't want to get on the wrong side of.

Once we are seated in the Wartburg, our military companion acquires a more civilian side, revealing his first and last names, Uwe and Karsch. He then informs us that we have a completely free hand to look at whatever part of the Eastern side of the People's Anti-fascist Wall of Protection we want — the side which has been guarded so courageously and ingeniously for such a long time. Chroniclers of the world, give your orders and I shall obey: the stretch of land they call the "death strip", the watch towers, the searchlights, the anti-tank devices, the barbed wire, the trained guard dogs in wire-mesh runs to prevent them from taking a lump out of the calves of a passing border guard, the L-shaped concrete slabs that have already been removed from the Wall, the parking areas for the tanks held for emergencies — our guardian angle lays all of these treasures before our eyes. Use a camera to record what the human eye cannot comprehend without the world dissolving into a haze of tears. Use a pen to describe the words which stick as a lump in the throat. "Walls make me sad," a veteran of the Second World War said to me recently, "not just the one in Berlin, but all walls. They make me neurotic. Neurotic complexes may be a Jewish invention, but they exist … I would bet on it …"

And now we are right up close to the Wall, at the behest of our guardian angel. A German Wall of Jericho, covered in the whiteness of immaculate purity. Here beyond the still-chilling Death Strip there is mile after mile of white. Of all colours, they chose this pure white as the substitute for the glowing red of the sun rising on the worker's paradise? I had always thought that the GDR liked to keep things a nice grey shade of grey?

Does the Wall still echo the words of Erich Honecker, the fool who uttered:

"Neither ox nor donkey
can halt the forward march of socialism."

Immerhin, ein Wendehals als Irrgast, um in der Sprache der politischen Ornithologie zu bleiben, hätte ja noch in letzter Minute mit dieser neuen Frohbotschaft im rosaroten Schnäbelchen in Wandlitz einfliegen können ...

Flieg, Vogerl, flieg ...

Aber es gibt jetzt auch schon Graffiti auf der Ostseite, allerdings erst nach dem 9. November, vor allem links und rechts der Maueröffnungen, die durch das Wegschaffen der L-förmigen Stahlbetonteile geschaffen wurden.
Da haben sich die malenden Ostler endlich auch mit Pinsel und Farbtopf hinwagen dürfen, um ihre eigenen Graffiti hinzusetzen: einen grinsenden Egon-Krenz-Kopf zum Beispiel, der jetzt wie ein böse auftauchender Hai aus dem Film »Jaws« (»Der weiße Hai«), über die Mauer geistert. Krenz als Kohlenklau daneben, starr durch ein gemaltes Mauerloch guckend, flankiert von einem gelbäugigen Mackie-Messer-Profil mit Sprechblase: »17 Millionen, Egon!«
Plötzlich entdeckt Fritz das rote Barett eines englischen Generals. Zunächst als einen roten Punkt, der sich vor dem Hintergrund der Mauerfläche hin- und herbewegt. Fritz setzt einen Augenblick seine Leica ab, kneift die Augen zum besseren Fixieren zusammen und sagt freudig erregt, jedoch leise wie der Jäger auf der Pirsch, dem endlich das Wild vor die Flinte gekommen ist:
»Mensch, ist doch nicht möglich, das ist der englische Stadtkommandant, General Corbett!«
»Kennst du ihn denn?« will ich, noch ungläubig, wissen.
»Nein, aber vom Fernsehen weiß ich, wie er aussieht!«
General Corbett mit der roten Pullmankappe der Fallschirmjäger stakt zwischen den beiden riesengroßen frischen Ost-Graffiti-Köpfen hin und her, zwischen dem Haifisch- und Kohlenklaukopf Krenz und der Märtyrerfigur eines Ostlers, dem auf dem Mauerfresko ein Reißverschluß längs durch den Leib gezogen wurde, als wär's ein einoperierter Körperteil. Was wird herauskommen, sobald sich dieser Reißverschluß öffnet und die nackte, tätowierte Ostlerhaut zum Vorschein kommt? Unbotmäßiges, nehme ich an, und auch die Wendehälse werden gackernd mit den Flügeln schlagen, wenn ihnen plötzlich die flotte Bezeichnung für die alte, jetzt notgetaufte SED entgegenleuchten wird:

S wie Sauwirtschaft
E wie Egoismus
D wie Diebstahl

Wenn dieser echt volkseigene Kosename für die Partei den Genossen Egon Krenz, Erich Honecker, Willi Stoph, Erich Mielke,

The reply from the demonstrators, which must have failed to get through to the compound for the privileged elite in Wandlitz, was equally simple:

"Neither ox nor donkey
can halt the overthrow of socialism"

Nevertheless a "Wendehals", a wryneck, an ornithological name which has been used in the GDR to describe the volte-face opportunists of political change, could have taken this happy message in its pink beak and flown across the no-longer guarded perimeter fence around the Wandlitz compound ...

"Fly away, Peter, fly away, Paul ..."

But the whiteness of the Eastern side of the Wall has now been marred by graffiti which did not appear until November 9. It is particularly prevalent on either side of the new holes that have been made by the removal of the L-shaped slabs of reinforced concrete that make up the Wall.
So finally the Easterners have dared to take up paint brush and spray and add their own graffiti: the grinning head of Egon Krenz, for instance, which now haunts the Wall like a shark from "Jaws". And next to that, Egon Krenz depicted as a "Kohlenklau", a sinister figure with a swag-bag familiar from the war, staring out of a painted hole in the Wall, flanked by a yellow-eyed "Mackie-Messer," a character from Brecht's Threepenny Opera, with a bubble coming out of his mouth with the words "17 million people gone, Egon!"
Suddenly Fritz spots the red beret of an English general. At first there is nothing to be seen but a red dot moving back and forth against the backdrop of the Wall. Fritz stops looking through the viewfinder of his Leica for a moment, screws up his eyes and says, with a gasp of happy excitement but as softly as a hunter who has finally got the prey he has been stalking in his sights:
"Hey, that's not possible, that's the British Commander of Berlin, General Corbett!"
"Do you know him?" I ask, still sceptical.
"No, but I know his face from the television."
General Corbett with the red beret of the parachute regiment strides between the two giant, freshly-painted heads, between the "Jaws" and the "Kohlenklau" versions of Egon Krenz and the picture of a martyred East German, a man with a zip fastener through his stomach, as if it had been implanted by surgery. What will come out when the zip is opened and the naked, tattooed skin of the East emerges? Something unpleasant, that's for sure. And the "political wrynecks" will flap their wings and squawk

Harry Tisch und Günter Mittag rechtzeitig, als die Zellenschlüssel der Stasi-Gefängnisse noch fest in ihren Händen waren, zu Ohren gekommen wäre, dann aber Gnade dir, frecher Ostler, der du deine Lippen zu dieser Gotteslästerung deiner alleinseligmachenden Staatspartei zu öffnen wagtest! Gnade dir, und ab mit dir in den Knast. Freundschaft, der Gruß, dann, Genosse, aber zum letzten Mal!

Halt einmal, sachte, übermorgen ist Mariä Empfängnis, und das Politbüro ist schon vor drei Tagen zurückgetreten. Egon hat das Handtuch geworfen, Erich H., Willi St. und Erich M. sind gleichzeitig aus der Partei ausgeschlossen worden, Harry T. und Günter M. unter dem Verdacht der Untreue bereits verhaftet. Am Ende wird's bald keine Partei mehr geben, doch wenn sie klebrig bleibt, dann aber, bitte, unter neuer Direktion:

S wie sauber
E wie Eintopf
D wie Durchhalten

bis das Allerärgste vorüber ist: Sauberste Eintopf-Partei Deutschlands, wie wär's? Da könnten doch nicht einmal die Pastoren mehr etwas dagegen sagen — da sei Gott vor! Besser noch, Hände falten und in ökumenischer Latinität *PDS* beten: Pater Dominus Sanctus, bitt' für uns, jetzt und in der Stunde des Absterbens unserer Partei! Amen!

Wir nähern uns General Corbett und beginnen mit ihm und seinen beiden Adjutanten ein ziviles Gespräch, auf englisch, small talk wie unter gentlemen zwischen dem ersten und zweiten Whisky im Club üblich, quite cold today, but sunny, fun to go out for a little stroll, isn't it? Schutzengel Uwe steht baff daneben, und Fritz will schon die Leica zum Erinnerungsphoto heben, General Corbett und Oberstleutnant Karsch für die Nachwelt, Offiziere aller Länder, vereinigt euch, aber Corbett lehnt lächelnd mit einer kleinen Handbewegung ab:

»Don't do that, please, it could make things difficult for me.«

Karschs berechtigte Frage bei der Weiterfahrt in der grünen Wartburg-Minna:

»Wer war denn das?«

»Das war der britische Stadtkommandant, General Corbett«, sagt Fritz.

»Na, hören Sie mal!« rügt Karsch, »und das haben Sie mir nicht gesagt! Da hätte ich doch ganz anders gegrüßt!«

Die beiden Chronisten blicken erstaunt auf ihn und seine russische Feldherrnmütze — ganz anders gegrüßt? Wie, was und womit?

Die Gnade der späten Geburt hat ihr Chronistenleben in Fragen des militärischen Protokolls auf dem Milchkindniveau gehalten; sie

when they spot what the graffiti artists have made of the old name for the GDR communist party, the SED:

S for Sauwirtschaft = a ruined economy
E for Egoismus = egoism
D for Diebstahl = theft

If these nicknames, the genuine People's Titles, for the Party and comrades Egon Krenz, Erich Honecker, Willi Stoph, Erich Mielke, Harry Tisch and Günther Mittag had been painted a little earlier, when the state security police, the "Stasi", still had the keys to the jails firmly in their hands, then the East German who was their author would have had to pray for mercy for this blasphemy against the almighty Party. God take mercy on your soul and off with you into prison.

But hold on, slow down, the day after tomorrow is the Festival of the Immaculate Conception and the Politburo resigned three days ago when Egon Krenz threw in the towel. Erich H., Willi St. and Erich M., have all been expelled from the Party, Harry T. and Günther M. have already been arrested on suspicion of treason. Soon there will be no Party left, or if it insists on hanging on, then we want a new look:

S for sauber = clean
E for Eintopf = hot pot
D for Durchhalten = grin and bear it

until the worst is over: Sauberste Eintopfspartei Deutschlands (the Cleanest Hot-Pot Party in Germany). How about that? Even the church wouldn't have anything to object to . Or even better, we take the new communist party with its new initials — PDS — Pater Dominus Sanctus. Father, pray for us as our party dies. Amen.

We approach General Corbett and strike up a conversation with him and his two adjutants, in English, small talk as practised between the second and third whiskey in the club. Quite cold today, but sunny, fun to go out for a little stroll, isn't it? Guardian angel Uwe looks on perplexed and Fritz is already preparing the Leica in order to record the event — General Corbett and Lieutenant Colonel Uwe Karsch captured for posterity, army officers of the world unite! But Corbett demurs with a raised hand and a smile: "Don't do that, please, it could make things difficult for me."

As we carry on our tour in the Wartburg, Uwe asks a fair question:

"Who was that?"

"That was the British Commander of Berlin, General Corbett" says Fritz.

waren weder HJ-Pimpfe noch FDJ-Pioniere und sind, ohne gedient zu haben, ins zivile Leben eingetreten. Wenn das Fritz-Dietlof Graf von der Schulenburg, der Vater des »Auges«, wüßte, als Sohn des Kaiserlich-Preußischen Militärattachés in London geboren, die Haare würden ihm zu Berge stehen! »Die Hand« bzw. dessen jüdische Vorfahren hätten da sicher viel weniger Skrupel, Offiziersrangklassen oder die Beförderungschancen im Generalstab konnten für sie von Haus aus keine steilen Lebensstufen gewesen sein, die es zu erklimmen galt.

Was konnte unser Schutzengel nur gemeint haben? Wäre er strammer gestanden, hätte er den Arm zackiger an die Russenmütze geworfen, hätte er die Stiefelabsätze lauter aneinandergeschlagen? Du wirst es nie erfahren, eiliger Photo-»Graf«, und du auch nicht, vom unruhigen Zeitgeist an die Mauer geschwemmter Talmudist ...

Jetzt aber geht's nicht mehr um Bananen, jetzt geht's um die Wurst! Die Wartburg-Minna nähert sich dem Brandenburger Tor, und ohne unseren Schutzengel kämen wir da nicht bis unter die Quadriga.

So aber verläuft alles ordnungsgemäß, ganz nach Generalstabsplan; dem Schlägertyp wird befohlen, die kleine Minna vor den Absperrzäunen hinter den bereitstehenden Grenzpanzern abzustellen, Karsch holt den Dienstausweis aus der Innentasche des langen Militärmantels, der diensthabende Offizier erstattet Meldung, mustert kurz den Dienstausweis, und schon öffnen zwei Grenzsoldaten die Gittertore der Absperrung.

So völlig einsam und ungestört wie im Blaubeerenwald werden wir wohl niemals wieder auf dem Platz hinter oder vor dem Brandenburger Tor ausschreiten können. Das ist noch nicht einmal dem amerikanischen Präsidenten gelungen, hier im Schlagschatten des Brandenburger Tors unbelästigt wie Alpenvereinswanderer auszuschreiten. Dem armen Kennedy damals, obwohl er nach eigenen Worten ein Berliner war, hat Luftschutzwart Ulbricht — diese Funktion hat er tatsächlich lange Jahre ausgeübt, und zwar im Moskauer Kominternhotel »Lux« während des Zweiten Weltkriegs — das Brandenburger Tor mit Vorhängen zugemacht, damit der amerikanische Präsident nur ja keinen Blick in das Arbeiter- und Mauernparadies werfen konnte. Im Moskauer »Lux« als Luftschutzwart Asche auf das Haupt jener Genossen zu streuen, die allnächtlich von Väterchen Stalin in die Lubjanka abkommandiert wurden und nie mehr wiederkommen durften, und dann dem frechen Millionärssohn aus Boston Vorhänge ins Brandenburger Tor zu hängen — das müssen Höhepunkte im politischen Leben einer sächsischen Lehrerseele gewesen sein, von denen sich Chronisten, wie wir es sind, nichts träumen lassen!

Fritz macht sich an die Leica-Arbeit, und ich stehe mit Karsch in der Säulenhalle, unschlüssig, was nun wirklich »vor« und was »hin-

"Hey," replies Uwe somewhat annoyed, "why didn't you tell me. I would have greeted him quite differently!"

The two chroniclers stare in amazement at him and the back of his Russian hat. He would have greeted him quite differently? How? What would he have said? The fortune to be have been born too late saved them from having to come to grasps with questions of military protocol. They were members neither of the Hitlerjugend of Nazi rule nor of the Freie Deutsche Jugend of Communist rule and they entered into civilian live without having to do military service. If only Fritz Dietlof Graf von der Schulenburg had known — the father of the "Eye" who was born in London, the son of the Prussian Kaiser's military attaché — he would turn in his grave! Mind you, "the Hand", or his Jewish forefathers, who have less cause for scruples about a lack of military knowledge, after all their background prevented any prospect of climbing the rungs of the military ladder from the very outset.

What on earth did our guardian angel mean? Did he mean he would have stood more smartly to attention, would he have brought up his hand to his Russian hat with greater alacrity, would he have knocked the heels of his boots together more sharply? They were never to find out, neither the photographer of noble military ancestry, nor the restless Talmudist ...

But now we are coming close to the climax of our tour. The Wartburg approaches Brandenburg Gate. Under normal circumstances we wouldn't get much closer, but our guardian angel makes it all possible. Everything goes smoothly, as if planned with military precision. The thug receives orders to park the car in front of the barriers behind the waiting tanks of the border guards. Karsch extracts his official ID card from the inside pocket of his long military overcoat, the duty officer salutes, glances briefly at the ID and within moments two regular border guards are opening the wire gate in the barrier fencing.

We will probably never again be able to walk across the square around the Brandenburg Gate in quite this fashion, totally undisturbed and completely alone, as if we were taking a stroll through Alice in Wonderland country. A feat that not even the President of the United States succeeded in accomplishing. Back then, when Kennedy, the man who was, in his own words, himself a Berliner, had wanted to take a walk-about around the Brandenburg Gate. But the leader of the GDR at that time, Walter Ulbricht, ordered curtains to be pulled across the Gate to prevent the President taking a peek at the walled-in worker's paradise. But that is not all he achieved in his life. Ulbricht was also an air warden. While exiled in the Soviet Union, Ulbricht volunteered to act as air warden at the "Lux" hotel in Moscow. It was a job which he performed for many years. To have acted as air warden to his comrades who were called away nightly to the Lubianka by Uncle Joe,

ter« dem Brandenburger Tor bedeutet. Die Quadriga auf dem Dach des Brandenburger Tors ist ja seit altersher in Marschrichtung Ost abkommandiert gewesen — nicht erst seit Bestehen der Deutschen Demokratischen Republik, um den Monopolkapitalisten und neugierigen Polittouristen auf der Besuchertribüne den grün patinierten Hintern zu zeigen.

Ob sie jetzt umgedreht wird, um endlich aus dem Kreisverkehr des politischen Ringelspiels gezogen zu werden? Man müßte diese Frage an die grün patinierten Wettkampfrösser stellen, deren Pferdeverstand sicher bei weitem jeden politischen Verstand rings um das Brandenburger Tor übersteigt. Lediglich das aus ihrem Siegeskranz gezwickte Eiserne Kreuz sollte man für immer weglassen, damit dessen innere Leere für alle Zeiten als Schlüsselloch in die Hohlheit festgefügter politischer Überzeugungen wirke, ein Siegeskranz als Wert ohne Muster und als Geschenk der Muse Klio an die wißbegierige Jugend des neuvereinten Berlins.

»Sehen Sie die Fahne da drüben?« sagt Oberstleutnant Karsch zu mir und deutet auf die bundesrepublikanische Fahne, die vom First des alten Reichstagsgebäudes unter der kalten Dezembersonne im Wind flattert, »die ist nämlich ungesetzlich!«

»Warum?« frage ich erstaunt.

»Berlin ist nicht Teil der Bundesrepublik!«

»Wirklich nicht? Ist mir neu!«

»Nein, ist nicht Teil der Bundesrepublik, Sie können mir glauben, steht im Abkommen!«

Ich hole Luft, trete aus dem Schatten des Brandenburger Tors, blicke nach oben und zeige auf die DDR-Flagge, Schwarz-Rot-Gold über dem Brandenburger Tor, aber mit Hammer und Zirkel.

»Und diese Flagge da oben, was ist mit der?«

»Das ist was anderes«, sagt der Schutzengel, »die ist ganz in Ordnung, denn Berlin ist Hauptstadt der Deutschen Demokratischen Republik, diese Stadt wurde uns von der Sowjetunion zum Geschenk gemacht!«

Richtig, wenn man mit Marx- und Engelszungen redet, aber der Pfeil seiner unentrinnbaren Dialektik geht haarscharf an der Mitte meines Herzens vorbei, denn ich erinnere mich auch gut an die Worte des Genossen Pieck, mit denen er sich für das »Geschenk« der weltberühmten Gemälde der Dresdner Galerie bei der sowjetischen Armee bedankte, als die geklauten Meisterwerke zum Anlaß der Staatsgründung von Moskau nach Dresden zurückgekarrt wurden. Diese Pieckschen Dankesworte im Vorwort zum ersten Nachkriegskatalog der Dresdner Gemäldegalerie haben schon in den ersten Semestern meines Kunstgeschichtestudiums für Augenblicke großer Heiterkeit gesorgt.

Jetzt ist aber auch die Zeit gekommen, beschließe ich, um den ersten Schuß aus meiner selbstgebastelten Nato-Konsum-Kanone abzufeuern. Sieht gar nicht wie Kanone und Munition aus, übri-

never to return, and to have drawn the curtains on the Brandenburg Gate in the face of the cheeky, millionaire's son from Boston — these must have been the high points in the political career of Ulbricht, the teacher from Saxony — high points which chroniclers of the likes of us can only dream about!

Fritz goes to work with his Leica and I remain together with Karsch in the hall of columns, uncertain what "in front of" and "behind" the Brandenburg Gate means any more. The Quadriga chariot on the top of the gate has long been turned towards the East, and not, as modern urban legend would have it, been placed in that direction by the German Democratic Republic in order to show green-tainted horses' backsides to the capitalists and political tourists standing on the wooden platforms in the West. The question of whether it will ever be turned back again and thus removed from the political circus would have to be directed to the four green-coloured thoroughbred stallions which pull the chariot. Their equine acumen is likely to exceed the political intelligence of those surrounding them. Only the Iron Cross, which has been stolen from the laurels of victory, should be permanently left out. The emptiness that would remain would serve for all time as a remainder of the vacuity of petrified political conviction, the laurels of victory as a meaningless symbol and as a gift from the Muse Clio to the knowledge-thirsty youth of a unified Berlin.

"Do you see the flag over there?" asks Lieutenant Colonel Karsch and points to the flag of the Federal Republic of Germany, which flutters in the wind from the roof of the old Reichstag beneath the cold December sun. "That's illegal!"

"Why?" I ask, baffled.

"Berlin is not part of the Federal Republic of Germany!"

"Really? That's news to me."

"No, really. It isn't, it's all written down in the Berlin treaty!"

I take a deep breath, step out from the shadow beneath the Brandenburg Gate and look up to where the flag of the GDR is hoisted on the top of the Gate, the same black, red and gold that make up the Federal German flag, but with the addition of a hammer and compass.

"What about that flag up there?"

"That's different," replies our guardian angel, "that's all right, Berlin is the capital of the GDR, it was given to us by the Soviet Union!"

Fine, if white man speaks with forked tongue of Marx and Engels, but the arrow fired from his inexhaustible sheath of dialectic misses my heart by a whisker. I recall the time Comrade Pieck thanked the Red Army for the return, upon the foundation of the GDR, of the world-famous paintings which adorn the Dresden Art Gallery — masterpieces which had been stolen and carted off to Moscow. Pieck's thanks were used as the foreword

gens, diese Reiseumhängetasche mit einer Flasche Scotch, Marke Black Label, noch im Kofferraum der Wartburg-Minna versteckt. Inzwischen hat auch mein Photograph schon mit seiner Leica-Kanone aus allen Rohren geschossen, seine Taschen wölben sich bereits unter der Last belichteter Kodak-Filme.

Wir verlassen den Ort der großen historischen Begebenheiten in zahlreichen deutschen Reichen und kehren zum Wartburg-Kofferraum zurück. Ich nehme die Whiskyflasche aus der Reisetasche und überreiche sie: »Für die vielen Mühen, die Sie mit uns gehabt haben heute morgen, Herr Oberstleutnant, eine kleine Aufmerksamkeit aus Great Britain!«

Ob er das nehmen wird? Diese Morgengabe meiner V.T.P., meiner Vereinigten-Trinker-Partei, das wird mir doch der Schutzengel nicht abschlagen, nicht nur Offiziere, auch Spirituosen aller Länder, vereinigt euch, Bruder Whisky und Genosse Wodka, macht doch aus euren Herzen keine Mördergrube, zwei Tage vor Mariä Empfängnis und knapp vier Wochen nach dem Fall des Mauerheiligtums.

Ohne Zögern greift Oberstleutnant Karsch wieder in die innere Militärmanteltasche, fischt sich aber diesmal nicht den Dienstausweis heraus, sondern eine säuberlich doppelt gefaltete Plastiktüte mit Henkel. Eins, zwei, drei, fertig ist die Zauberei, die Plastiktüte entfaltet, Abrakadabra, die Whiskyflasche verschwindet. Dann geht der Schutzengel mit der nun voll getarnten Whiskyflasche zur grünen Mini-Minna zurück und verstaut meine geheime Nato-Munition unter seinem Wagensitz. Die glasigen Stasi-Augen seines Fahrers können nichts mehr entdecken, geheime Kommandosache offenbar. So wird auch das dickste Packeis der eingefrorenen Fronten zum Schmelzen gebracht oder doch immerhin von Eisbrechern in Form von Whiskyflaschen wenigstens so weit aufgelockert, daß eine kleine Fahrtrinne zur Fahrt ins freie Meer entstehen könnte — von Sofia bis nach Hawaii visafrei!

Jetzt können wir ja zu reden beginnen.

»Ist Ihr Dienst an der Mauer ein schwerer Dienst gewesen, Herr Oberstleutnant?«

»Das kann man so nicht sagen, ich mache seit fünfundzwanzig Jahren Dienst an der Mauer, seit meinem achtzehnten Lebensjahr, zuletzt am britischen Abschnitt, da bin ich immer der Montgomery-Kaserne gegenübergelegen.«

»Ist das nicht auch langweilig, wenigstens ab und zu?«

»Das schon, gab mir aber auch Zeit und Gelegenheit zum Studium.«

»Was haben Sie studiert?«

»Marxismus-Leninismus.«

»Ein langwieriges Studium?«

»Kommt darauf an, bei mir hat es fünf Jahre gedauert, ich habe das als Fernstudium absolvieren können.«

to the first Dresden Art Gallery catalogue to appear after the war and were the cause of much merriment even then, during my early days of studying art history.

But now I think it is time to fire the first salvo from my home-made NATO consumer gun. But my tourist's shoulder bag, containing a bottle of Black Label scotch and still hidden in the boot of the Wartburg does not look much like a gun and ammunition. In the meantime, my Leica-armed photographer has been blasting away feverishly and his pockets are sagging under the weight of spent Kodak film cartridges. We leave this location of so many momentous events in so many German Reichs and return to the boot of the Wartburg. I remove the whiskey from the bag and present it to our guardian angel:

"With thanks for all that you have done for us this morning, Lieutenant Colonel, a little token of our esteem from Great Britain!"

Will he accept it? This promotional gift from my UDP, the United Drinkers' Party. Surely he won't turn it down? Not just army officers but spirits of the world unite! Brother Whiskey and Comrade Vodka, give yourselves a break, come on, it's now only two days before the Festival of the Immaculate Conception and four short weeks after the fall of the Sacred Wall.

Without hesitating, Lieutenant Colonel Karsch thrusts his hand into his coat pocket once more and produces, not an ID card, but a neatly folded plastic bag with a grip. Abracadabra and the plastic bag unfolds and the whiskey bottle disappears. Then the guardian angel returns to the car with the fully-camouflaged bottle and hides my secret NATO weapon beneath the seat. The driver's glassy, secret policeman's eyes will not find it, obviously this is a secret commando mission. And so the thickest pack ice of the frozen fronts begins to thaw, or at least loosen up sufficiently by an ice-breaker (in the form of a whiskey bottle) to leave a channel wide enough to allow us to make for the open sea — a no-visas-required trip from Sofia to Hawaii!

Now we can begin to talk.

"Has serving at the Wall been difficult, Lieutenant Colonel?"

"I wouldn't put it like that. I have been serving as a border guard at the Wall for over 25 years, since I was 18 years old. My last tour of duty was along the border to the British Sector, I was always at the point just opposite Montgomery Barracks."

"Hasn't it been boring, at least sometimes?"

"Sure, but it gave me time to study."

"What did you study?"

"Marxism-Leninism."

"A time-consuming subject?"

"Depends, I took five years; I graduated from a distant-learning course."

»Und was konnte man damit anfangen?«
»Zum Beispiel Fachlehrer sein, ich gebe jetzt Marxismus-Leninismus-Unterricht in der Truppe ...«
Pause, dann:
»... aber eines sage ich Ihnen, ich bin schwer enttäuscht worden ...«
Wieder Pause.
»... von denen da oben in den letzten sechs Wochen!«

Ach, Wandlitz,
Wo ist dein Antlitz,
Wenn der Kugelblitz
Durchs Schwimmbad
Der Genossen fährt?

Ich halte mich jedoch zurück, unser Schutzengel ist ja noch kein lockerer Begleiter für heitere Abende im Kabarettjargon à la Kurt Tucholsky, trotz Bruder Whisky und Genossen Wodka. »Stasi-Blick« kurvt uns weiter, immer an der Mauer lang, bis wir wieder zu einer Durchgangsstelle kommen, wo der neue, freie Wildwechsel zwischen westlichen Futterplätzen und Ostler-Paradiesen über vorsorglich auf dem ehemaligen Todesstreifen verlegte Bretterstege stattfindet. Behelfsmäßige Brücken von Mensch zu Mensch sozusagen, keine Luftbrücke wie 1948, sondern ein fester, erdgebundener Weg durch den Matsch, über den jetzt jeder gehen darf, nachdem der SED-Bezirkssekretär Günter Schabowski mit anfeuernden, revolutionären Worten der fiebernden Menge vor vier Wochen die Erlaubnis gegeben hat:
»... gilt diese Regelung unmittelbar.«
Rechts neben dem Durchgang wieder große Flächen frisch bemalter Mauer, diesmal abstrakt, durchsichtiges Rosé, schmutziges Weiß, hastig hingepinselt, könnte wie eine in die Vertikale gekippte Mark-Rothko-Freskierung aussehen, seltsam ...
»Ja, sehen Sie«, erklärt uns der Schutzengel, »da mußten wir dann den Soldaten Kommando geben drüberzumalen ...«
???
»Plötzlich hatten auch unsere Ostberliner Künstler begonnen, hier die Mauer zu bemalen, ohne vorher beim Grenzkommando um Genehmigung anzusuchen. Da mußten wir unseren Soldaten Pinsel und Farbtopf in die Hände drücken mit dem Kommando: Drübermalen! Hätten unsere Künstler vorher um Genehmigung angesucht, hätten sie diese heute auch ohne weiteres bekommen.
So ist uns ja nichts anderes übriggeblieben, als dieses Kommando zu geben. Sie werden das einsehen ...«
Ich aber frage mich: Brauchen die hier jetzt Kunstmaler oder Grenzsoldaten, Architekten oder Tapezierer, brauchen sie Artenschutz für Wendehälse, Zivildienstleistende oder Oberstleutnants, Blockflöten oder Knüppel?

"What can you do with a degree in Marxism-Leninism?"
"You can become a teacher. I now teach Marxism-Leninism to the other border guards ..."
A pregnant pause ...
"... but I'll tell you one thing, I've been really disappointed ..."
Another meaningful silence ...
"... by the party leadership in the last six weeks!"

"Oh, Wandlitz
Where is your face
When the ball lightning
rips through the comrades'
swimming pool?"

I remain cautious. Despite Brother Whiskey and Comrade Vodka, our guardian angle is no easy-going companion with a penchant for light-hearted evenings of Kurt Tucholsky-style satire. The chauffeur with the secret policeman's eyes drives us around some more, moving along the Wall until we come to another crossing point where the animals move between the Western feeding bowl and Eastern paradise on thoughtfully-placed planks across the former Death Strip. A very much down-to-earth path through the mud which anyone may now tread, ever since SED District Secretary Günter Schabowski gave the go-ahead for a free-for-all across the Wall in a delivery of fiery, revolutionary enthusiasm some four weeks ago:
"... this regulation becomes effective as of now — by order ..."
To the right of the hole there are once again huge areas of freshly-painted Wall, abstract images this time, a see-through pink, a dirty white, painted in haste, looking a bit like a Mark Rothlo fresco stood on edge, strange ..."
"You see," our guardian angel begins to explain, "we had to order the soldiers to paint over it ...!"
???
"Well, all of a sudden our artists from East Berlin began to paint the Wall at this point, without asking the border guards for permission. So we had to give the guards a pot of paint and a brush and order them to paint over it. If they had asked for permission, then they would have got it, straight-away, no problem. But as it was we really had no choice but to order the guards to paint over it. I'm sure you understand ...!"
I begin to ask myself: What do they need more — graffiti artists or border guards, architects or just people to wall-paper over the cracks, do they need to offer protection to endangered species such as "political wrynecks", do they need people doing alternative, non-military service or Lieutenant Colonels, the music of recorders or the sound of truncheons?

Die Marx- und Engelszungen jedenfalls haben vierzig Jahre lang das Alleinseligmachende und das Allmächtige verbreitet, und dieser atheistische Engelschor hat so lange seine roten Messen gesungen, bis die Gegenstimmen der Verzweifelten wieder einmal die Mauern von Jericho, diesmal vor Berlin, zu Fall gebracht haben. Aber dahinter wird zunächst vor allem Asche zum Vorschein kommen und nicht so schnell jener Vogel Phönix, der laut Überlieferung aus ihr aufzusteigen pflegt. Ruhet jetzt in Frieden, atheistische Engelschöre, oder singt euch selbst in den Kyffhäuserschlaf der Weltrevolution — aber das wäre eine zu einfache, gleichsam metaphysische Lösung ...!

>Vielleicht
>Fragt man uns
>Später
>Nach diesem Herbst
>Nach den gläsernen Tagen
>Und dem Morgen
>An dem die Melisse erfror
>Ach wir
>Die wir kaum noch Schatten warfen
>Und vor den Feuern in den Wipfeln
>Und der Fäulnis unter den Buchen
>Die Augen schlossen
>Waren in jenem Herbst
>Helden, Toren und Komödianten
>Nichts galt mehr ...
>Nicht unsere Lieben
>Nicht unsere Jahre
>Wir schliefen fast nie
>Ein jeder trug nun
>Am zweiten Gesicht
>Wir brauchten einander
>Genügten doch nicht
>Unsagbar schwer
>Pulsierte das Leben
>Von innen her
>Vielleicht
>Fragt man uns
>Später
>Nach diesem Herbst
>Als wir auf den Straßen
>Bevor der Winter nahte
>Die Zukunft gewannen
>Ach wir
>Die wir dann
>Im Gegenlicht die Augen schließen
>Wie werden wir müde sein
>(Helga Königsdorf, »Im Gegenlicht«)

The representatives of Marx and Engels have had forty years to spread the word of their Gospel, their Almighty. A choir of atheists had sung red songs of praise for as long as it took for their captive audience to strike up their own song and bring down the Walls of Jericho, this time in Berlin. But the first thing to emerge will be ash, and only later the Phoenix. Rest in peace, you choir of atheist angels or sing yourselves to sleep in the Kyfhäusser mountains of the world revolution — but that would be far too simple a metaphysical solution ...!

>"Perhaps
>People will ask us
>Later
>About this autumn
>About the glassy days
>And the morning
>Upon which the balm did freeze
>We
>We, who scarcely cast a shadow
>And who closed our eyes
>To the fire in the treetops
>And to the decay beneath the beeches
>We were heroes, fools, comedians
>That autumn
>Nothing mattered any longer
>Not our loves
>Not our age
>We rarely slept
>Each one of us
>Struggled with his other face
>We needed one another
>But were not enough
>Life pulsated
>From within
>Unbearably heavy
>Perhaps
>People will ask us
>Later
>About this autumn
>When we won our future
>On the streets
>As winter approached
>We
>We who
>Will close our eyes against the light
>How tired we will be
>(Helga Königsdorff, "Im Gegenlicht")

Wie wird's jetzt weitergehen, das Leben des Oberstleutnants der DDR-Grenztruppen, Uwe Karsch, geprüfter Fachlehrer für Marxismus-Leninismus, ein nebenberuflicher Zusatz seiner offenbar steilen Offizierslaufbahn, aus dem ihm jetzt leicht ein Strick gedreht werden könnte? Trotzdem ist er in diesen zwei Dezembermorgenstunden fast zum Freund geworden, ein wenig mit Hilfe von Bruder Whisky vielleicht, zum Menschen wie du und ich. Wollen wir hoffen, daß er keinem Republikflüchtling an der Mauer nachschießen mußte und daß er ihn auch nicht getroffen hätte, daß er den Schießbefehl an der Mauer nicht zu seinem pflichtgemäßen Kommando machen mußte ...
Die Gnade des Abkommandiertseins zum Marxismus-Leninismus-Unterricht vielleicht, wer weiß? Wer aber bin ich, um hier Richter zu spielen?
Wie ich höre, sind im Februar 1990 bereits eintausendfünfhundert ausgemusterte Stasis in den öffentlichen Schuldienst der DDR übernommen worden. Ich stelle mir eine rückgekoppelte Parallele vor: Im Jahre 1945 vier Monate nach dem Ende unseres Tausendjährigen Reichs wären eintausendfünfhundert Gestapo-Leute in den Schuldienst der vier Besatzungszonen in Deutschland und Österreich als Lehrer übernommen worden. Non scholae sed vitae discimus, nicht für die Schule, sondern für's Leben sollen wir lernen, wie der Lateiner sagt, aber für welch ein Leben, müßte man auf der Lehrerkonferenz der poststalinistischen Zyniker hinzufügen ...
»Und was wird jetzt mit der Mauer geschehen, nach Ihrer Meinung, Herr Oberstleutnant?«
Diese Gretchenfrage, besser Erichfrage der DDR hatte ich dem Schutzengel noch im Schatten des Brandenburger Tors gestellt.
»Die Mauer in der jetzigen Form, die wird fallen«, hatte er mir geantwortet, »aber die Grenze muß natürlich bleiben. Wir werden die Mauer voraussichtlich durch einen Zierzaun ersetzen!«

>»Die Lehre von Marx ist allmächtig ... Irren ist menschlich!«
>»Bleibe im Lande und wehre dich täglich!«
>»Es wird Zeit, daß der Stein zu blühen beginnt!«

Transparentlosungen bei den Demonstrationen vom Herbst 1989, die aber alle nicht die Durchschlagskraft jener vier großen Worte erreichen konnten:
»WIR SIND DAS VOLK«,
jene würdige Antwort, auch noch über dreihundert Jahre und viele Genossen hinweg, auf das absolutistische Glaubensbekenntnis des großen Ludwig:
»L'ETAT C'EST MOI!«
Kurz vor dem Heiligen Abend 1989 ist eine Weihnachtskarte aus Berlin in meinen Londoner Postkasten gefallen, von Oberstleutnant Karsch ...

How will things turn out — for Lieutenant Colonel Uwe Karsch of the GDR Border Guards, graduate teacher in Marxism-Leninism, an additional qualification for a man already with an apparently outstanding career behind him, a career for which many would like to have him strung up. And yet in these couple of hours on a December morning he has become something of a friend in the company of Brother Whisky, he has taken on human form, just like you or me. Let us hope that he never had to shoot at, and hit, someone trying to cross the Wall. If only it wasn't his duty to take aim and fire ...
Perhaps there is hope to be found in his assignment to other duties as a teacher of Marxism-leninism, who knows? After all, who am I to judge?
I heard that in February 1990, 1,500 former members of the "Stasi" state security police were sent out to continue their public service as teachers. I can't help but think, how would it have been in 1945 if, four months after the collapse of our Thousand Year Reich, 1,500 Gestapo officers had been taken on as teachers in the four zones of occupation in Germany and Austria. Non scholae sed vitae discimus, we shouldn't learn for school, but for life, as the latin scholars put it. But a teachers' conference composed of post-stalinist cynics would have to ask itself: "What kind of life?"
"And what do you think will become of the Wall now, Lieutenant Colonel?"
I posed our guardian angel this question in the shadow of the Brandenburg Gate.
"The Wall in its present form will fall," he replied, "but the border must remain, of course. We will probably replace the Wall with a fence."

>*"Marxist theory is almighty ... but we are only human!"*
>*"Stay in the GDR and fight!"*
>*"It is time for the stone to blossom!"*

Some of the slogans on the demonstrators' banners in the Autumn of last year, but which could never match the power of the four words that made up the favourite chant:
"WE ARE THE PEOPLE,"
a cry which transcends many Comrades and dictatorships, back over three hundred years, and which answers the favourite saying of Louis XIV:
"L'ETAT C'EST MOI!"
Shortly before Christmas 1989, I received a Christmas card at my London home, sent from Berlin, from Lieutenant Colonel Karsch.

[1] Geburtsort des GRÖFAZ (Größter Feldherr aller Zeiten, Spottname für Hitler).

[2] H.R. Fischer (geb. Wien 1903, gest. London 1977), vor der Emigration Verleger und Buchhändler in Wien, dann Kunsthändler, Vater des Tagebuchautors, wird in den Tagebüchern als der »Richtige Fischer« bezeichnet.

[3] Julius Curtius (geb. Duisburg 1877, gest. Heidelberg 1948), Reichsaußenminister 1929–31, Großvater meines Jugendfreunds Peter Curtius.

[4] Grenze zwischen Ober- und Niederösterreich und zwischen der amerikanischen und sowjetischen Besatzungszone in Österreich vor 1955.

[5] Im Gegensatz zu H.R. Fischer, meinem Vater, der als »Richtiger Fischer« bezeichnet wird.

[6] Die Verbindung zwischen Hermann Noack und Henry Moore wurde durch H.R. Fischer und seine in Berlin geborene Frau Elfriede geb. Lemmer hergestellt.

[1] The birthplace of the GROEFAZ (the popular nickname for Hitler during the Nazi period, composed by abbreviating the German for "the greatest field marshall of all times").

[2] H.R. Fischer (born in Vienna in 1903, died in London in 1977), a publisher and book dealer in Vienna before his emigration, then an art dealer, father of the diarist, is referred to in the diaries as the "Real Fischer".

[3] Julius Curtius (born in Duisburg 1877, died in Heidelberg 1948), Foreign Minister of the Third Reich, 1929–31, grandfather of my childhood friend, Peter Curtius.

[4] Border between Upper and Lower Austria and between the American and Soviet zones of occupation in Austria before 1955.

[5] As opposed to H.R. Fischer, my father, who is referred to as the "Real Fischer".

[6] Hermann Noack and Henry Moore were first introduced to one another by H.R. Fischer and his wife Elfriede, neé Lemmer, who herself was born in Berlin.

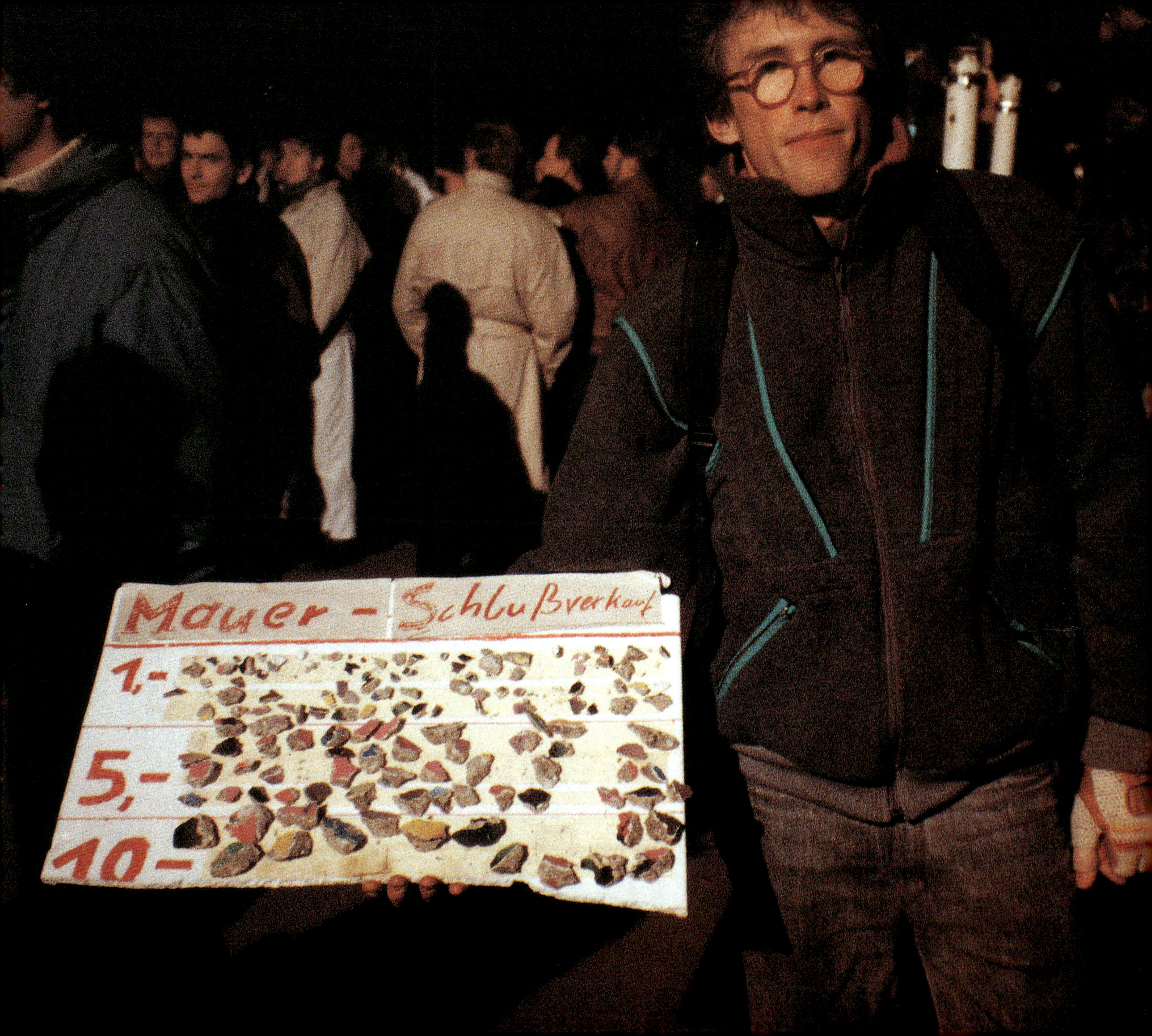
Mauer - Schlußverkauf
1,-
5,-
10-

»Vielleicht sollte ich springen ...?« Grenzsoldat auf dem Häuserfrontrest, der in der Bernauer Straße als »Mauer« fungiert, ein Abrißkommando bewachend. 1965.

"Maybe I should jump ...?" Border guard keeping watch over a demolition crew on top of what remains of a house that serves as the "wall" on Bernauer Straße. 1965.

»Mit Stein und Eisen gegen Beton.« Junge mit Brechstange.

"With stone and iron against concrete". A boy with a crowbar.

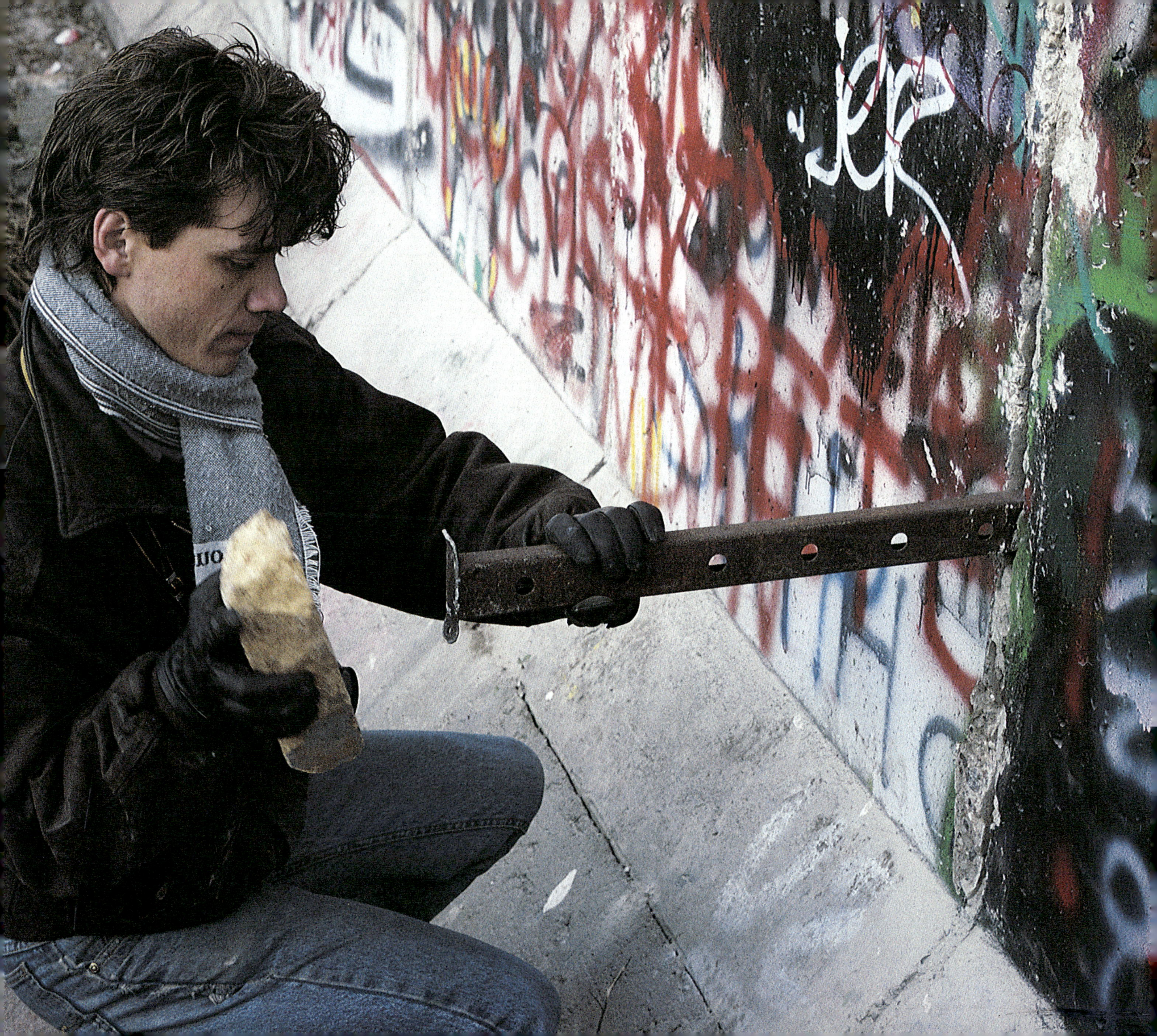

»Volkseigene Mauerinstand-
setzung.« Mauerreparatur
unter militärischer Aufsicht.
Elsenstraße, 1963.

"People's wall repair". Mend-
ing the wall under military
observation. Elsenstraße,
1963.

»Lange unerwiderte Liebes-
erklärung.« Graffito »Ich liebe
Dich«.

"Declaration of love long
unanswered". Graffiti:
"I love you".

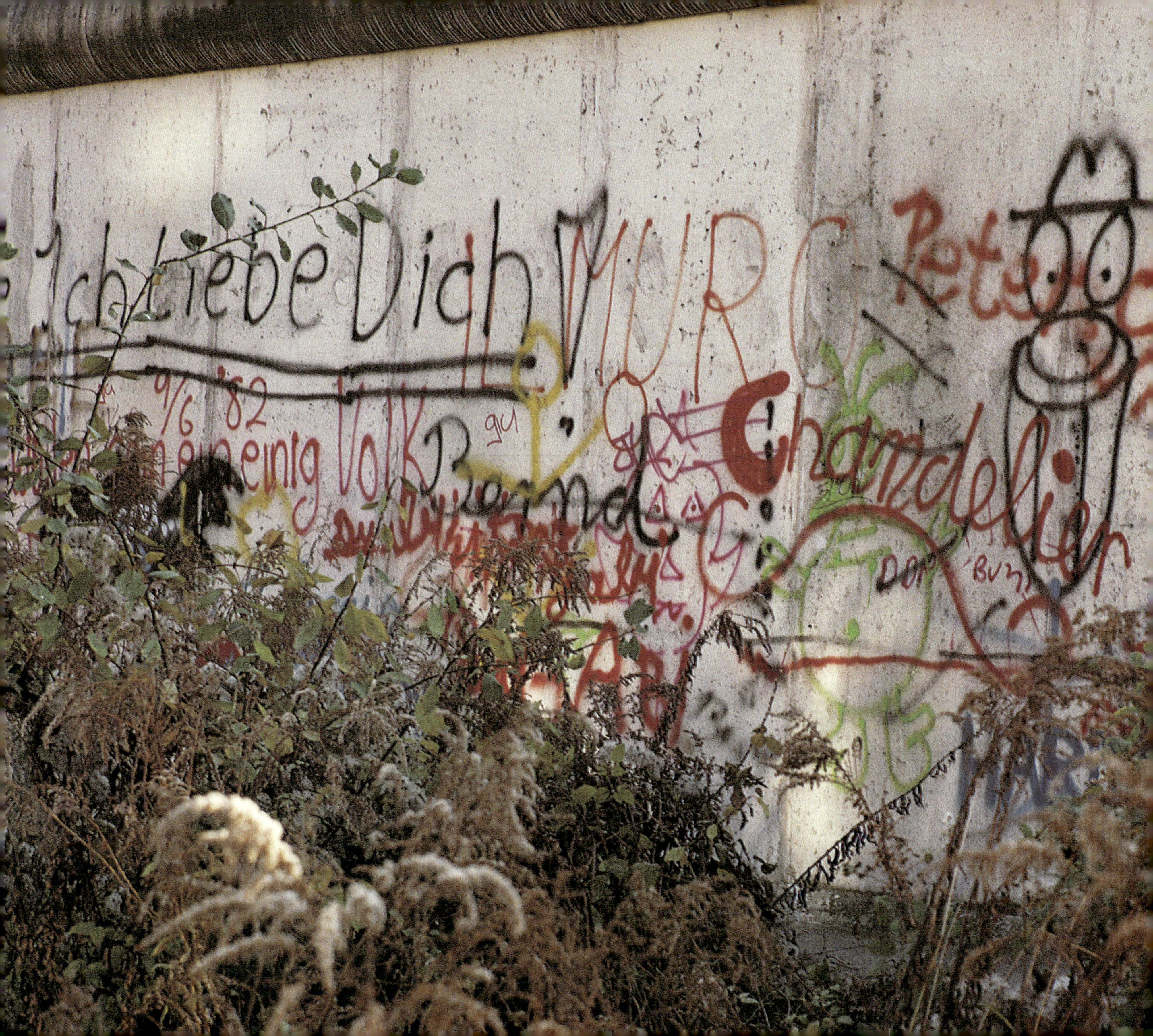
Ich Liebe Dich
9/6 '82
Volk
Bernd
Chandelier

»So helft mir doch!« Peter Fechter, 18jährig, aus Ost-Berlin, verblutet am 17. August 1962 im Niemandsland zwischen Ost und West.

"So help me, please!" Peter Fechter, 18 years old from East Berlin, bleeds to death on August 17th, 1962 in the no-mans-land between East and West.

»Angst vor der Mauer? — Wieso?« Zwei Jugendliche vor

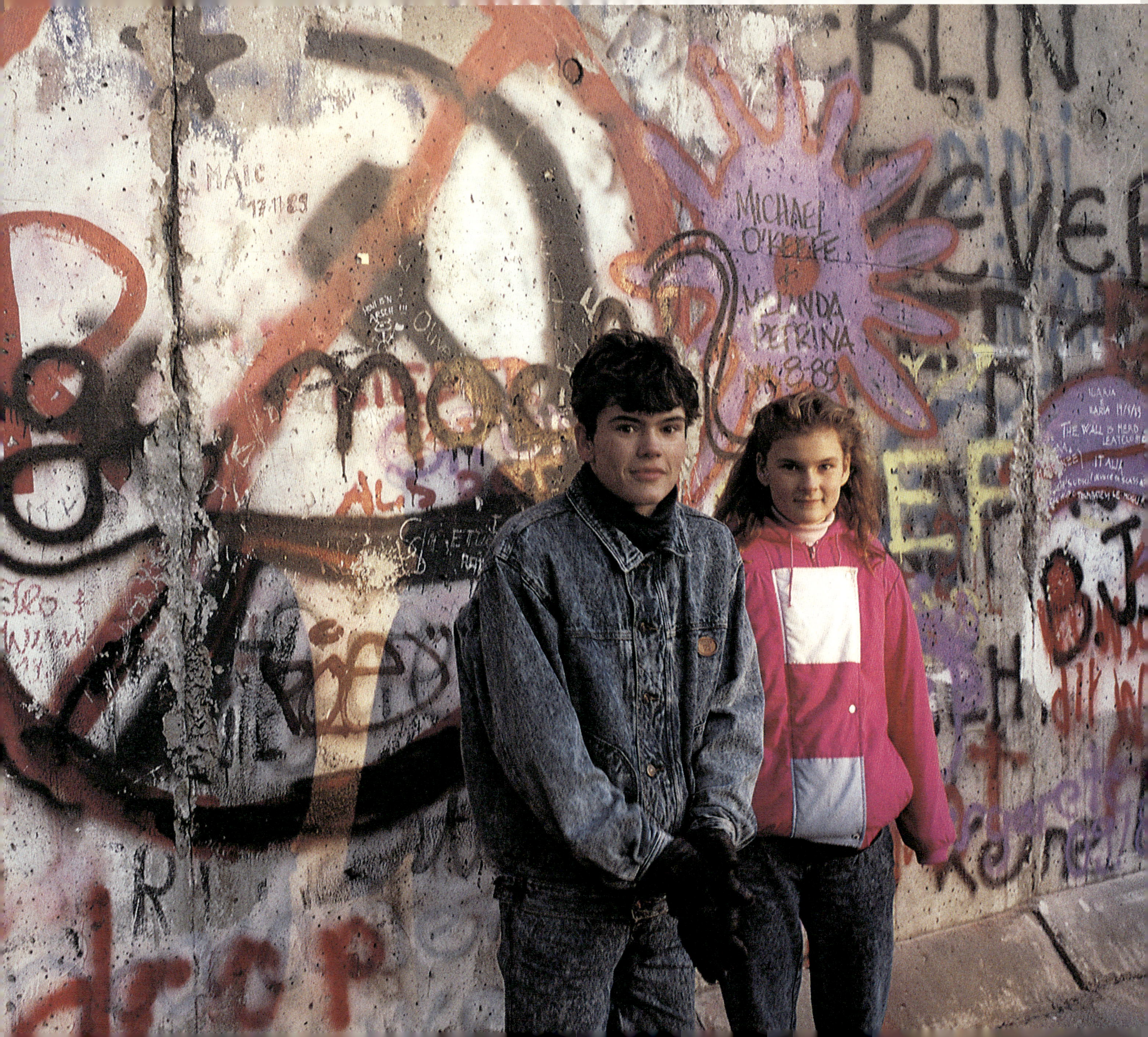
MICHAEL O'KEEFE

»Drei Personen suchen eine Zukunft!« »Mauerkieker«, zwei Männer und ein Junge blicken über die Mauer, kurz nach dem Mauerbau. Kreuzberg, Sebastianstraße.

"Three people looking for a future!" Two men and a boy glimpse over the wall shortly after its construction. Kreuzberg, Sebastianstaße.

»Bis hierher war noch Mauer — vor acht Tagen!« Zwei DDR-Grenzsoldaten am Mauerdurchbruch mit Graffito: »Fuck DDR«.

"The wall still came up to here — only a week ago!" Two GDR border guards at an opening in the wall with graffiti: "Fuck GDR".

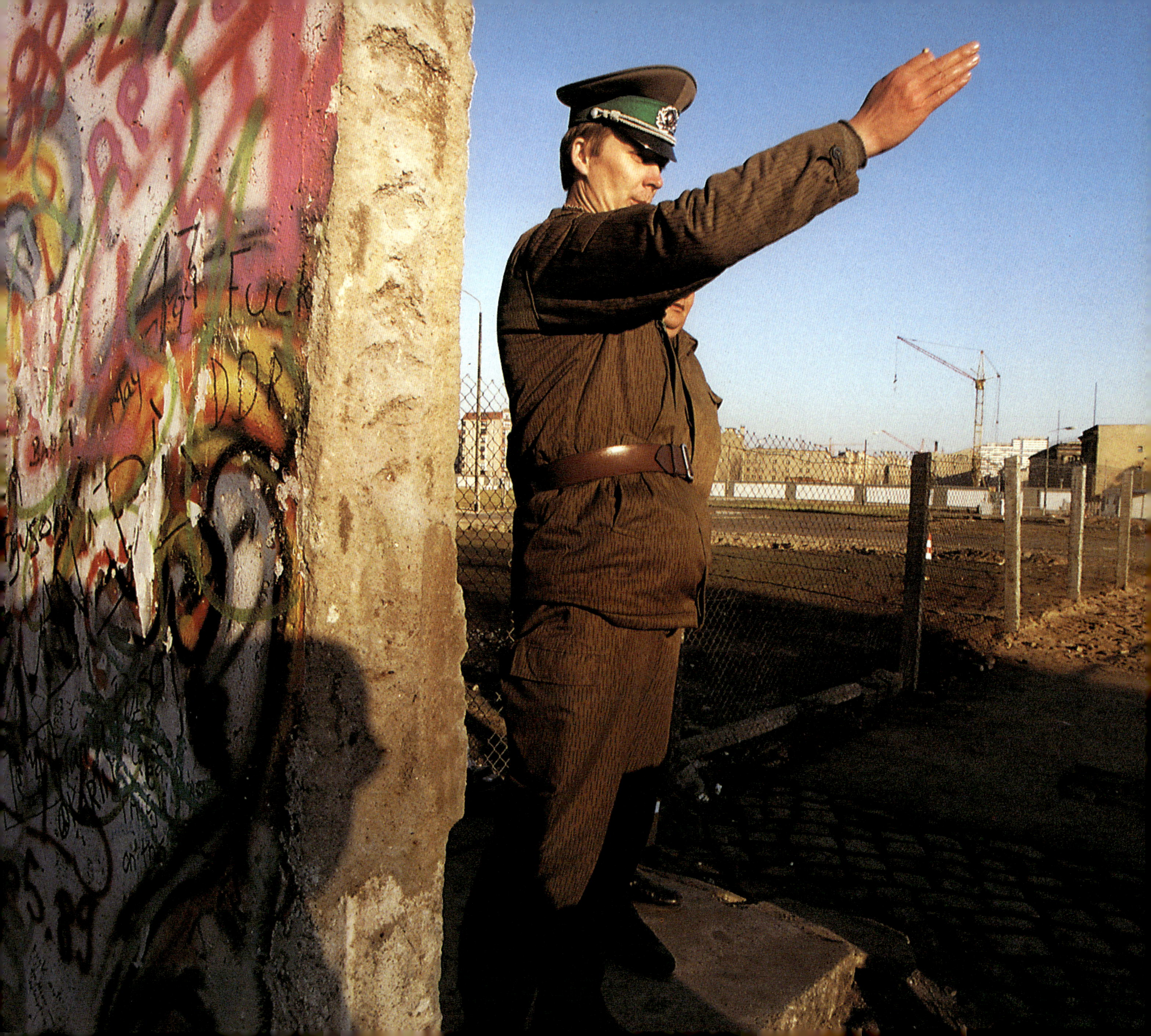
Fuck
DDR

»Ja, sehen Sie«, erklärte uns Oberstleutnant Karsch, »da mußten wir den Soldaten Kommando geben drüberzumalen ...« 6. Dezember 1989.

"Well, you see," Lieutenant-Colonel Karsch explained to us, "there we had to order the soldiers to paint over..." December 6th, 1989.

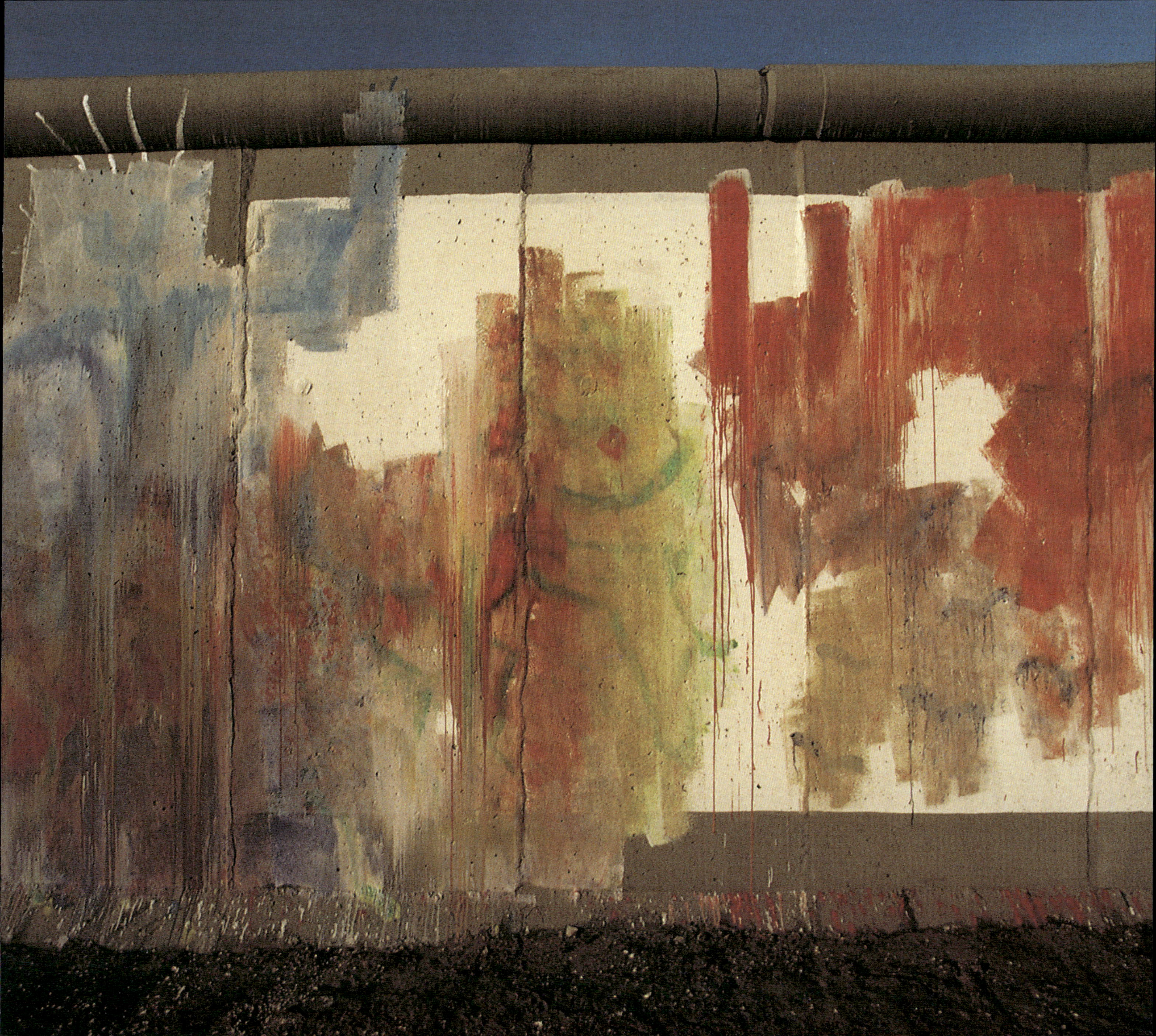

»Cocktailstunde ohne Einladung.« Menschen auf der Mauer vor dem Brandenburger Tor in der Öffnungsnacht. *Der Tagesspiegel* (Extrablatt), 10. November 1989, Titelseite.

"Cocktail hour without an invitation." People on the wall in front of the Brandenburg Gate on the night of the opening. *Der Tagesspiegel* (Special Edition), November 10th, 1989, front page.

JOY

»Pflichterfüllung statt Hilfeleistung«. Ostberliner Grenzsoldaten bergen ein totes Westberliner Kind, das in die Spree gefallen war. Bergungsversuche von Westberliner Seite wurden durch DDR-Grenzposten verhindert. Kreuzberg, 1975.

"Fulfilling a duty instead of genuinely helping". East Berlin border guards recover a dead West Berlin child who fell into the Spree. Recovery attempts from the West Berlin side were hindered by GDR border guards. Kreuzberg, 1975.

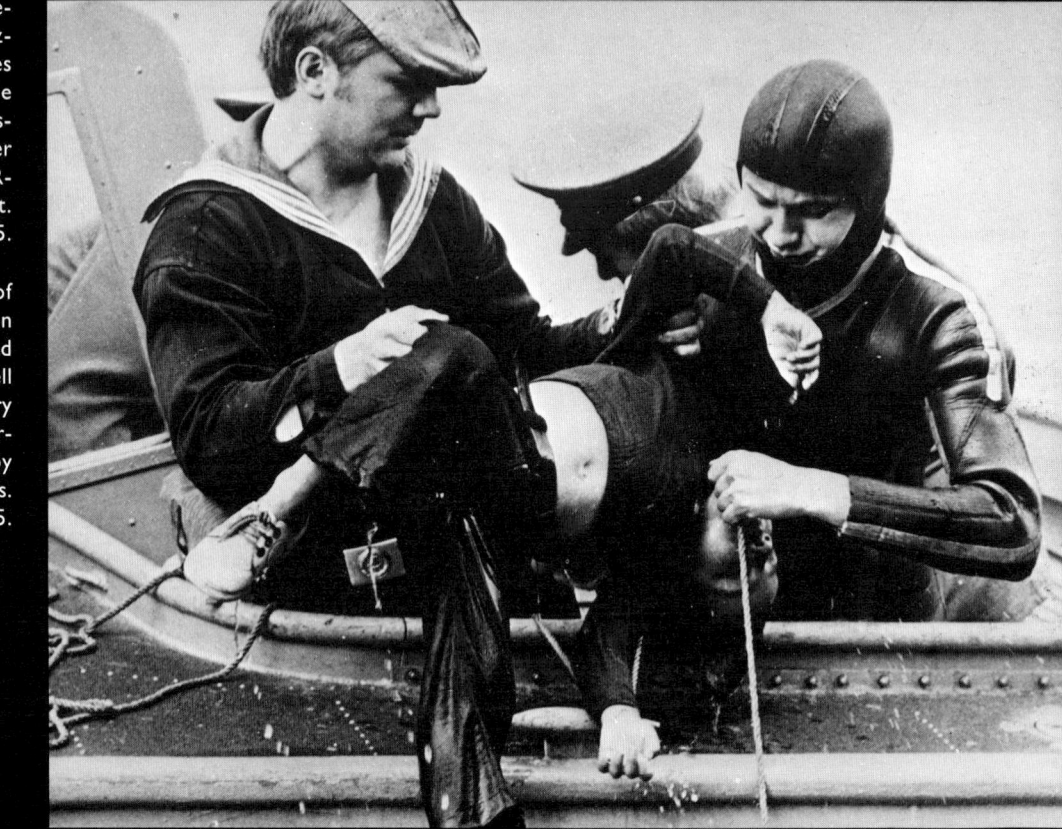

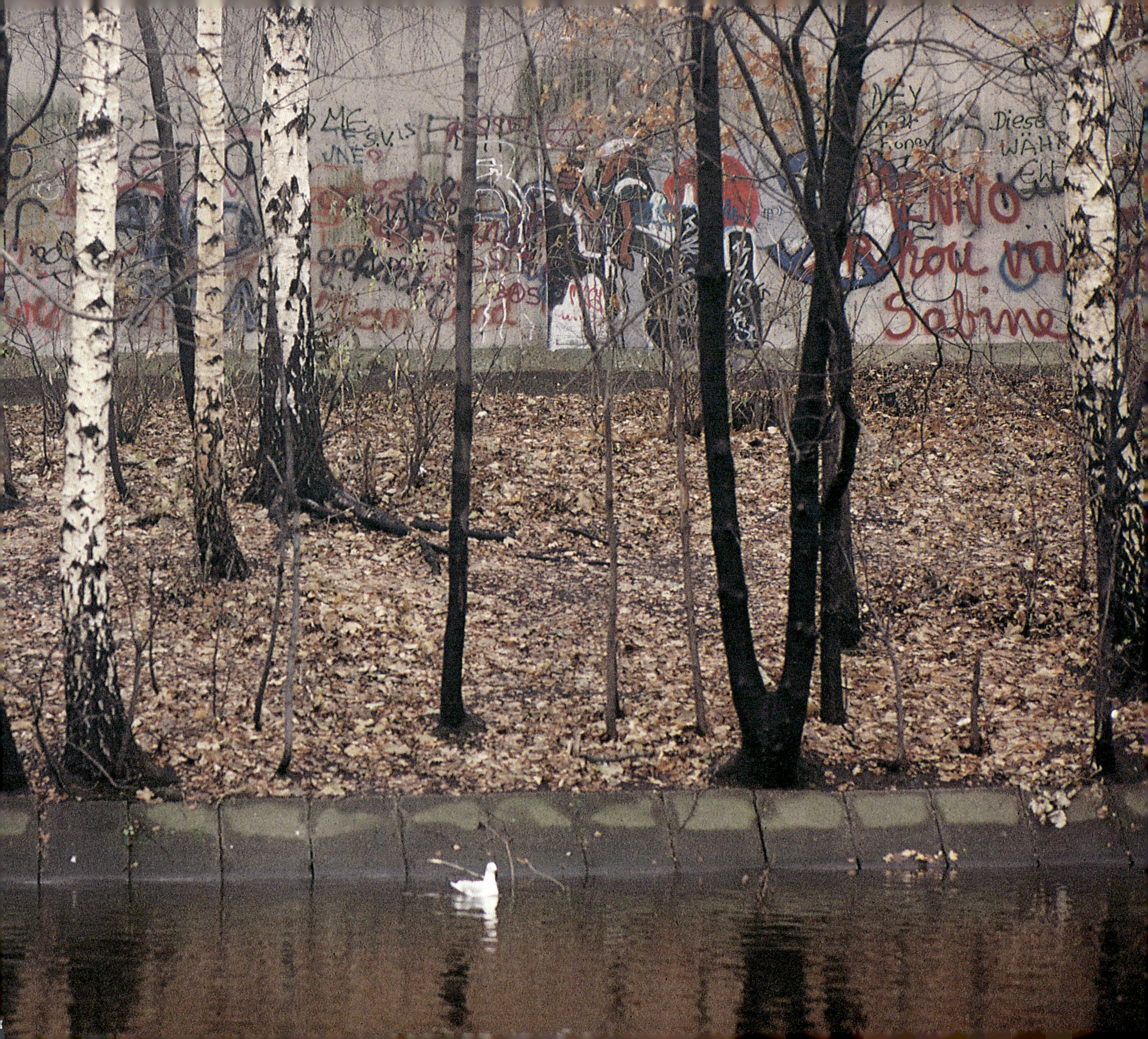
ENNO
Sabine

»Kommt noch einer durch?«
Vier Ostberliner Arbeiter
flüchteten durch dieses selbst-
geschlagene Loch in den
Westteil der Stadt.
Gartenstraße, 1963.

"Is another one coming
through?" Four East Berlin
workers fled into the western
part of the city through this
self made hole. Gartenstraße,
1963.

Nächste Doppelseite:
»Immer an der Wand lang«.
Graffito »Freedom for Lithua-
nia« auf der Mauer am
Brandenburger Tor.

Following pages:
"Always along the wall." Graffiti "Freedom for Lithuania"

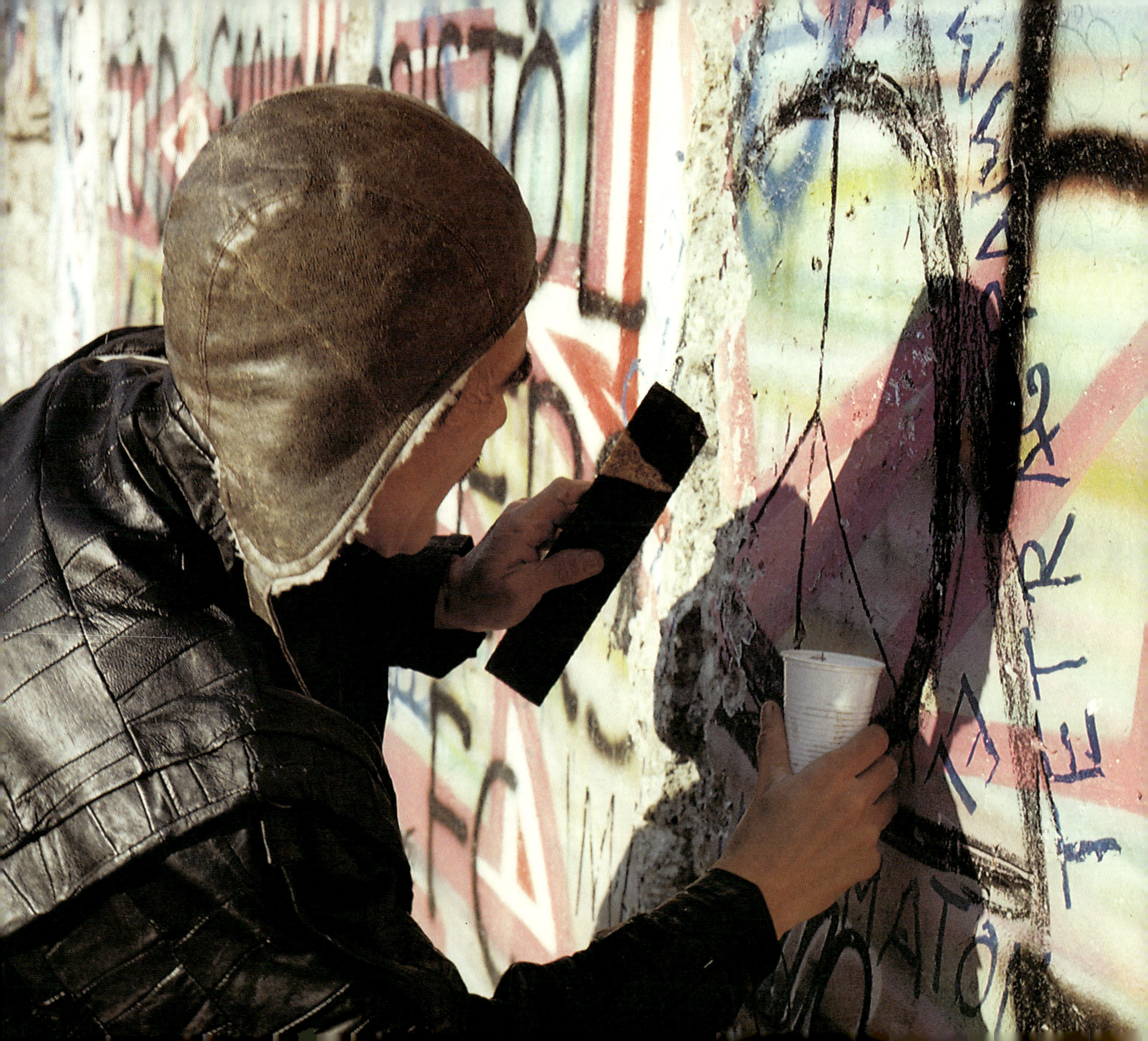

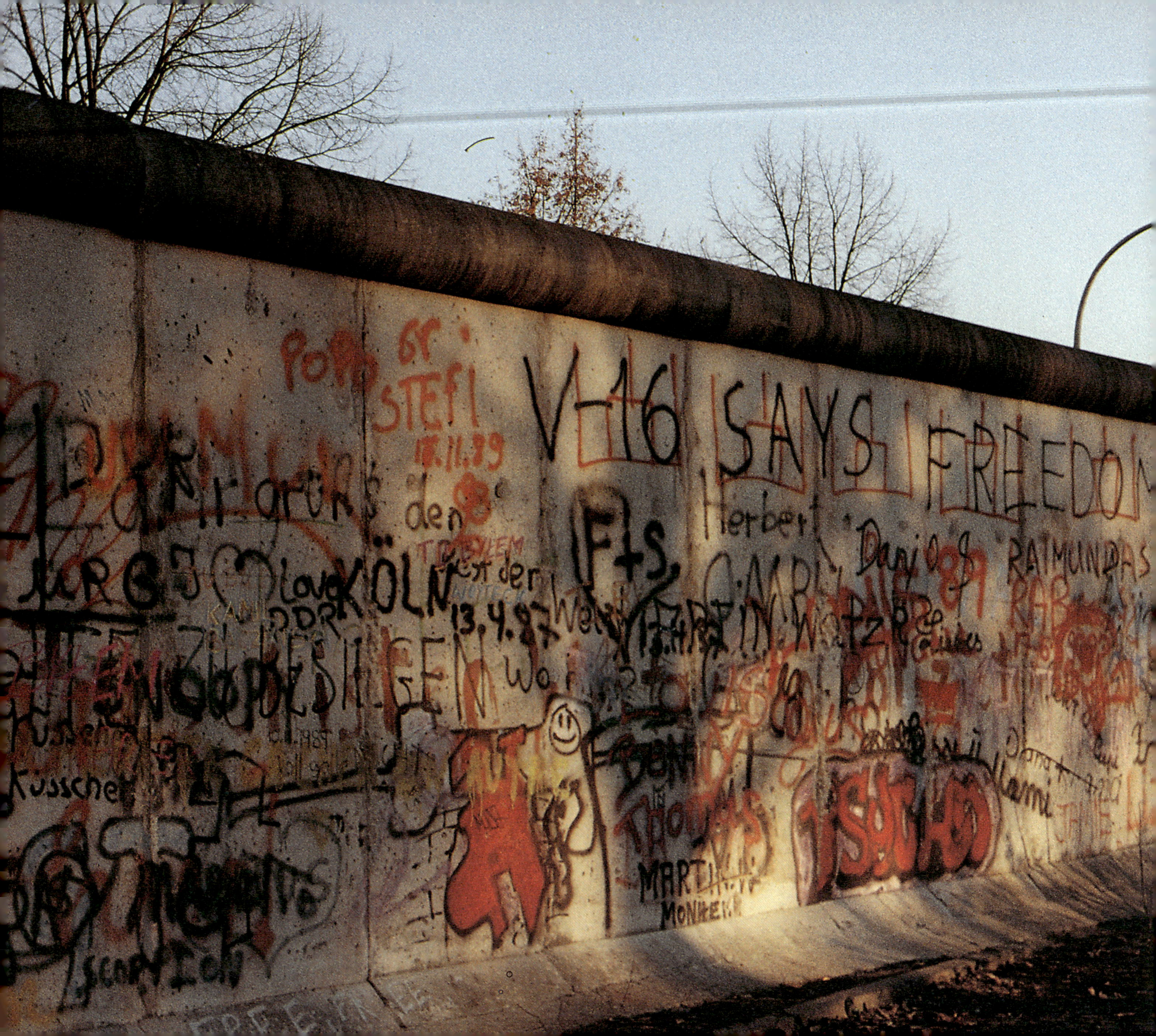

V-16 SAYS FREEDOM
STEFI
KÖLN
13.4.87
Herbert
RAIMUNDAS

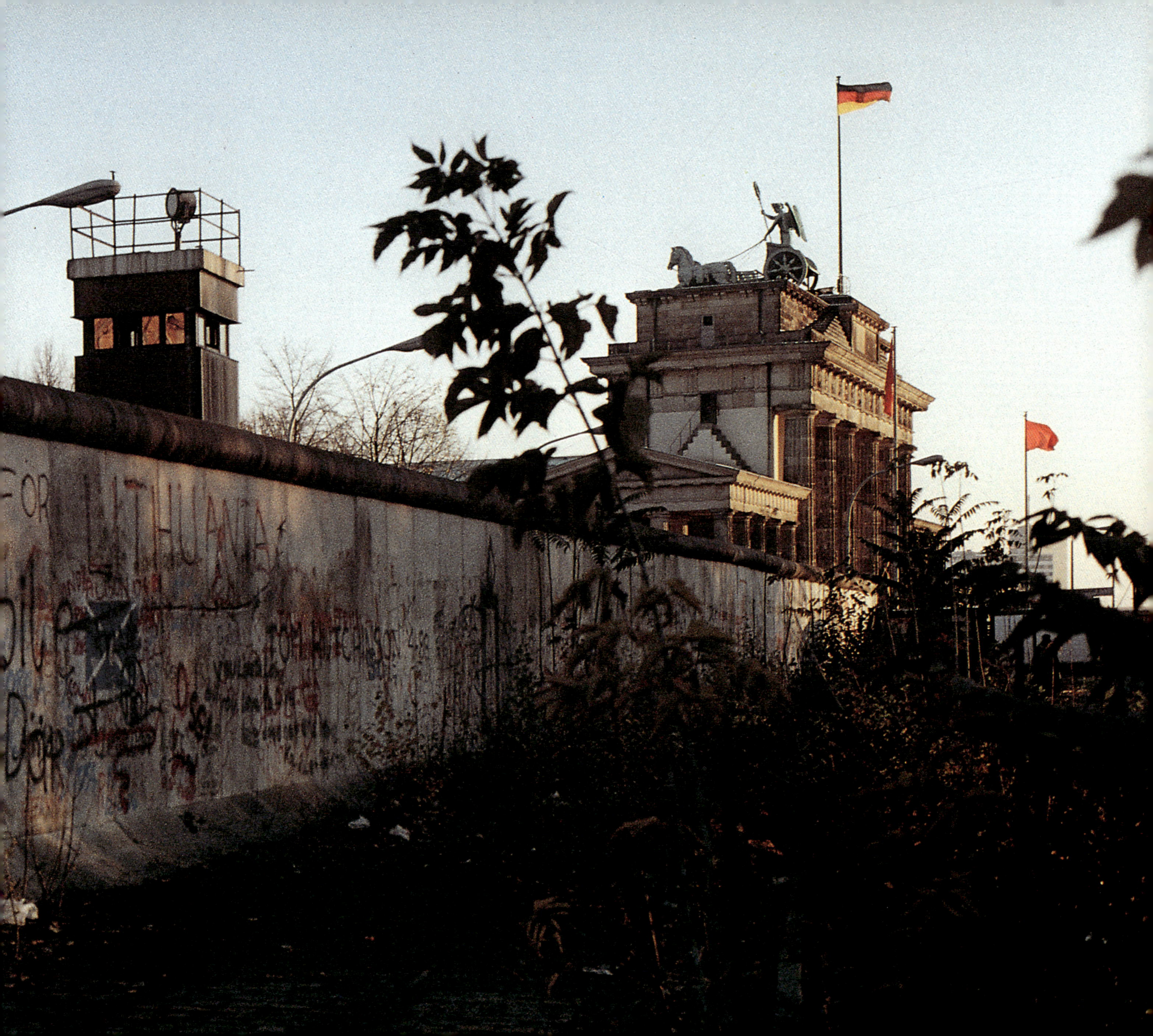
FOR LITHUANIA

»Hey, folks ...« Präsident Ronald Reagan mit Bundeskanzler Helmut Schmidt und dem Regierenden Bürgermeister Richard von Weizsäcker. Checkpoint Charlie, 1982.

"Hey, folks ..." President Ronald Reagan with West German Chancellor Helmut Schmidt and the Governing Mayor Richard von Weizsäcker. Checkpoint Charlie, 1982.

Nächste Doppelseite: »Hast du das Land ringsum beseh'n ...« Blick über die Mauer mit Todesstreifen, Wachturm und diversen »Grenzsicherungsanlagen«.

Following pages:

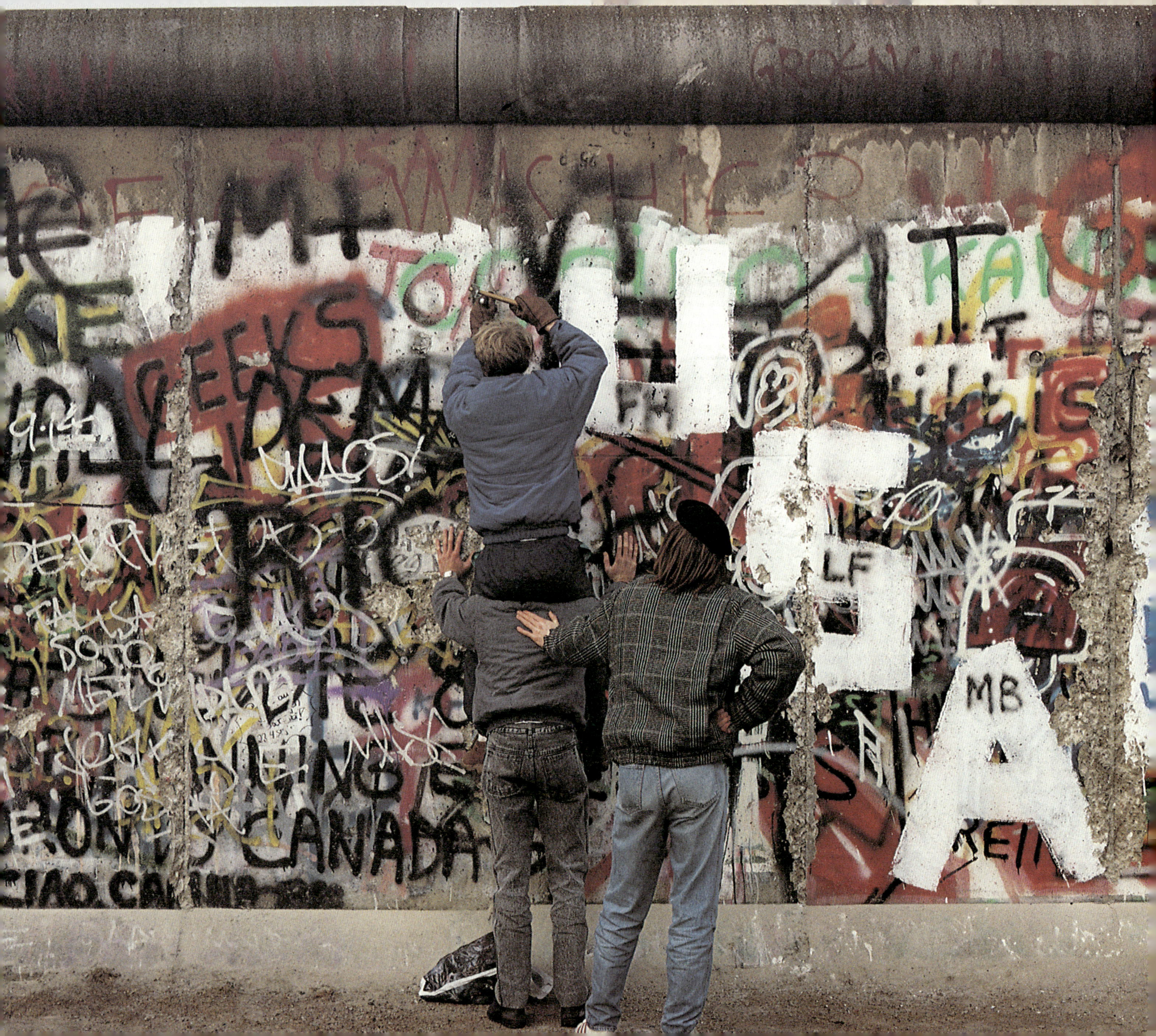
CANADA
MB
LF
FH

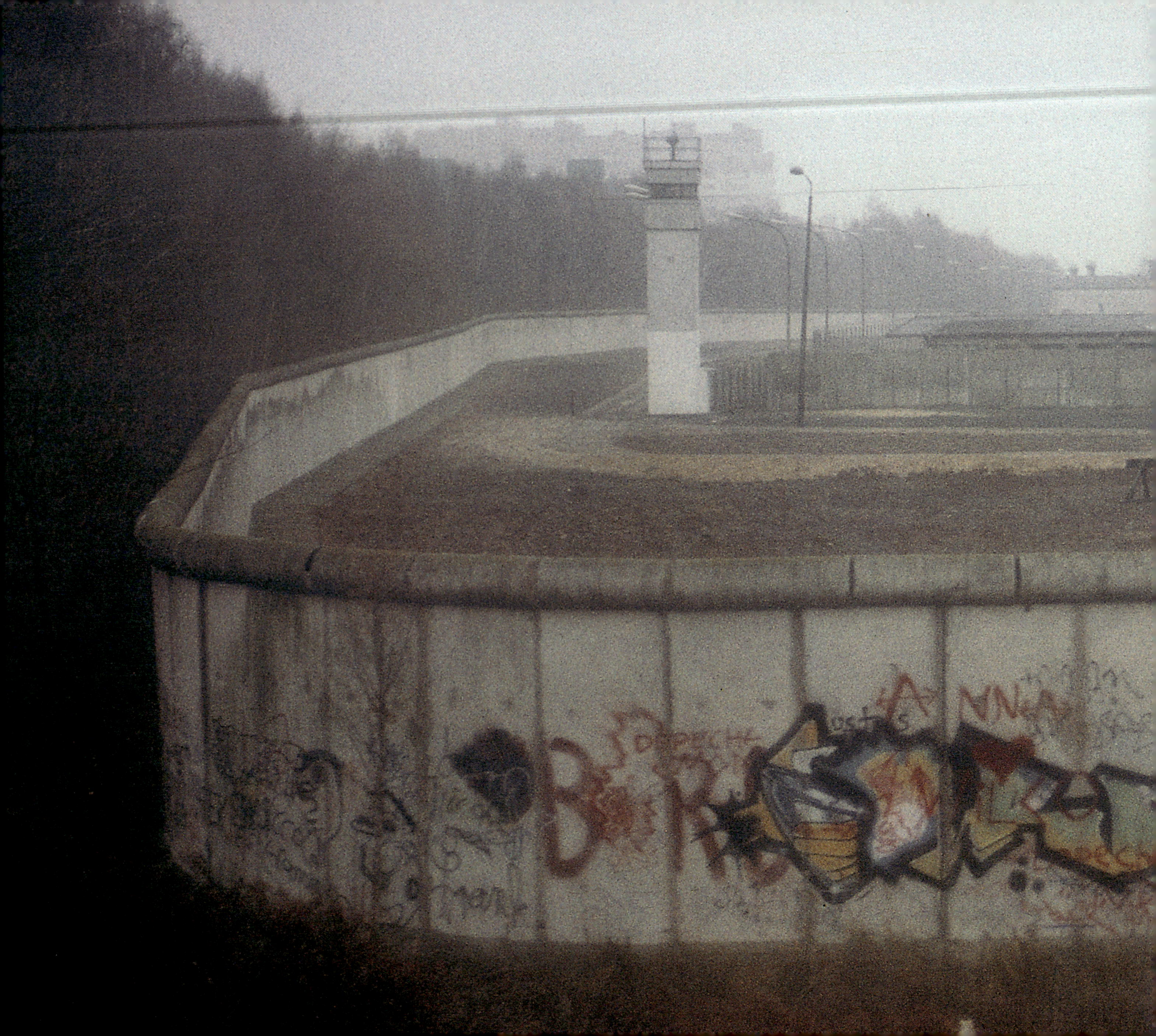

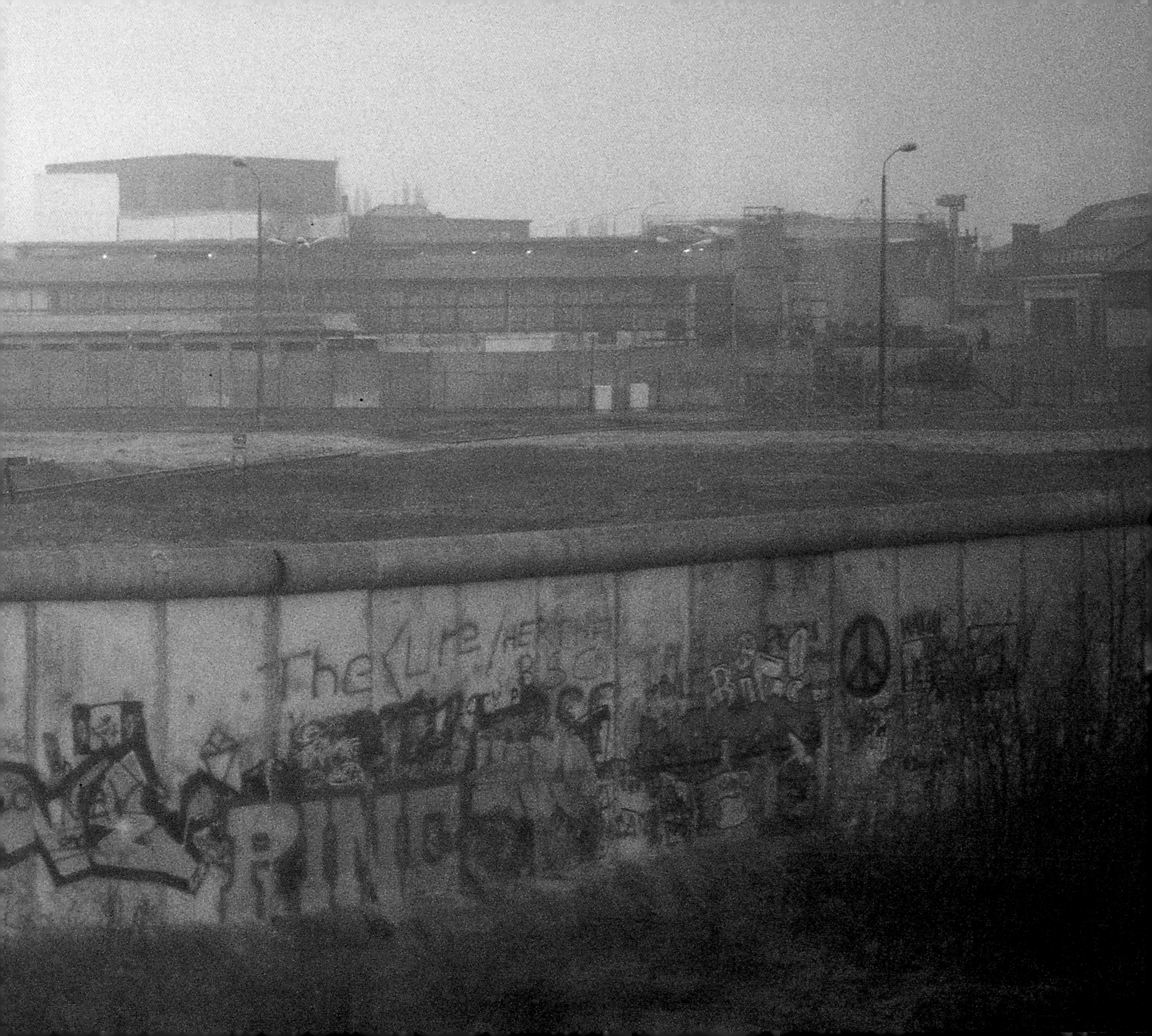
The Cure

Volksarmisten auf dem Brandenburger Tor während der Abriegelung des Tors am 14. August 1961.

People's army on the Brandenburg Gate during the closing of the Gate on August 14th, 1961.

Nächste Doppelseite (links): »Der Makel auf der weißen Weste!« Auch kleinere, nicht begehbare Maueröffnungen müssen nach dem 9. November 1989 noch auf Befehl des zuständigen DDR-Grenzkommandos wieder verschlossen werden.

Following pages (left): "The stain on the white vest!" After November 9th even smaller, impassable openings in the wall still had to be closed up again under the orders of the designated GDR border command.

Nächste Doppelseite (rechts): »Behelfsmäßige Sicherung des sozialistischen Humanismus«. Nicht genehmigte Öffnungen in der Mauer werden nach dem 9. November 1989 von den Grenztruppen mit rostigen Eisenplatten provisorisch wieder verschlossen.

Following pages (right): "Makeshift securing of socialist humanism". Following November 9th, 1990, unofficial openings in the wall were temporarily sealed up again with rusty iron plates by the border troops.

»Hindernisrennen«. Absperrzäune der Westberliner Polizei vor dem Brandenburger Tor.

Portable barricades of the

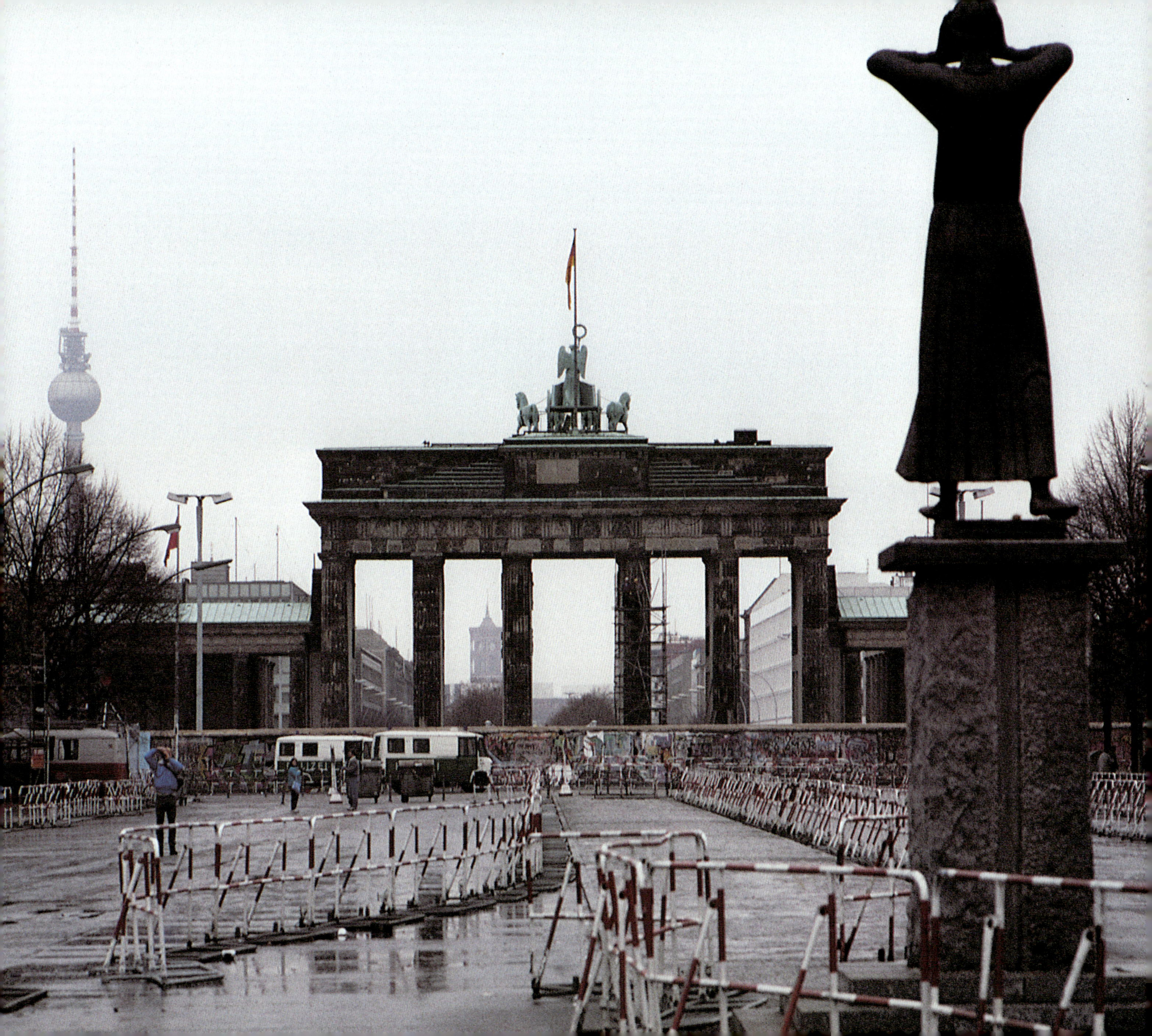

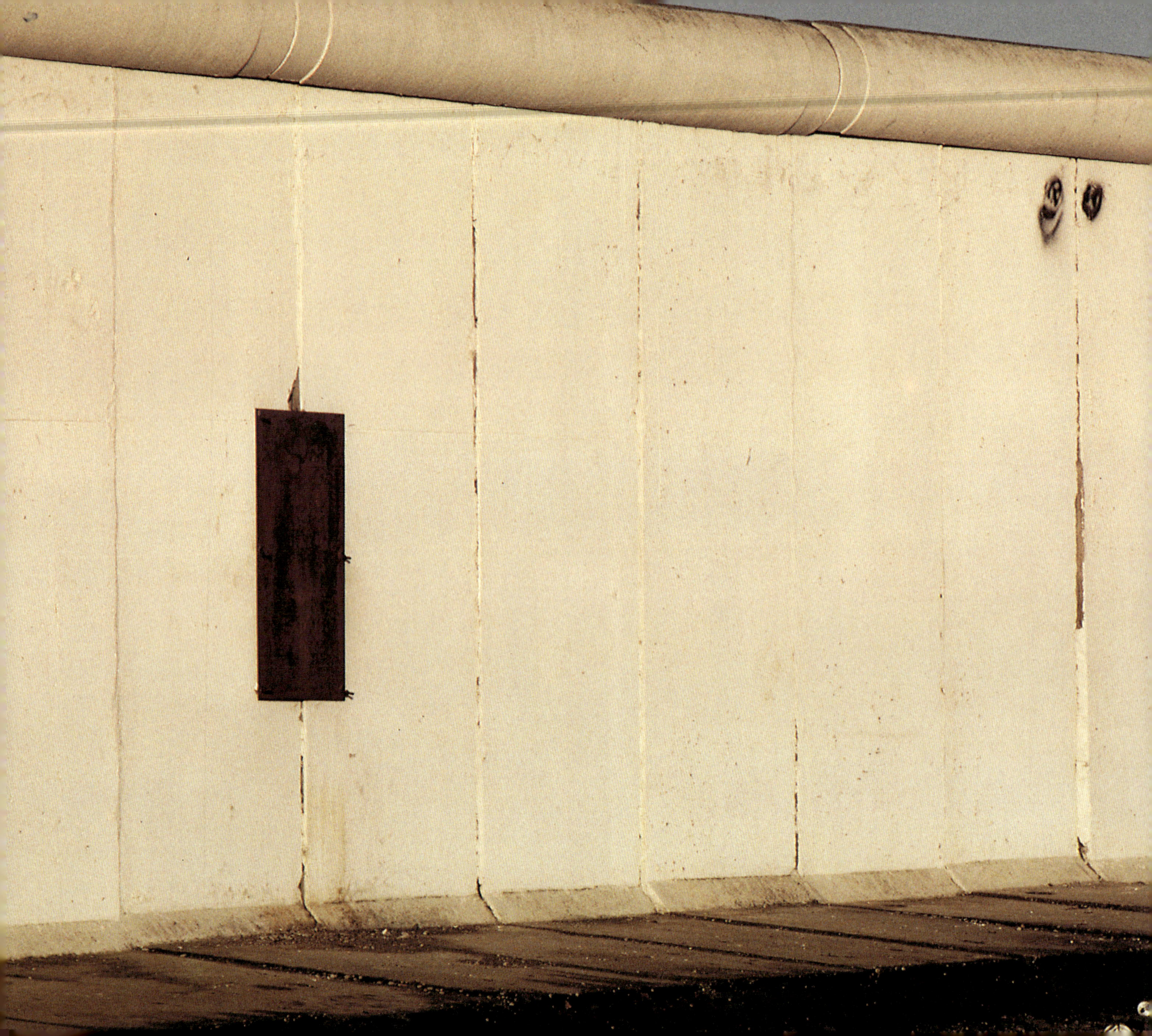

ANDY
NEWPORT
COUNTY JOE
BOOZE INFANTE
CREW   EDIE 89
89

BRIAN
BORELLO
89

FUSS
CARDIFF
CITY F.C.
BOOZE LINDEL
CREW 89 PEDERSON 89

TUT
SAW THE WALL
JEANNINE
89
J.R. WHITE
89

»Du bist gemeint!« Aufforderung an die DDR-Grenzsoldaten. Dahinter Schlagzeilen-Turm der Freien Berliner Presse. Potsdamer Platz, 1964.

"I mean you!" Directed to the GDR border guards. In the background the headline-tower of the Berlin Free Press. Potsdamer Platz, 1964.

Nächste Doppelseite (links): »Herbst in Berlin, 1989«. Mauersockel mit Graffito »Love is thicker than concrete« und Herbstlaub.

Following pages (left): "Berlin Autumn, 1989". Base of the wall with graffiti "Love is thicker than concrete" and autumn foliage.

Nächste Doppelseite (rechts): »Fenster im Beton«. Behelfsmäßige Übermalung der Ost-Graffiti durch DDR-Grenztruppen.

Following pages (right): "Window in the concrete". Makeshift painting over of East-graffiti by the GDR border troops.

»Wappentierersatz für die DDR (= Das Deutsche Raubtier)!« Graffito: Käfig und Fütterungsverbot.

Bitte nicht füttern

NICOLE

VE IS THICKER THAN CONCR

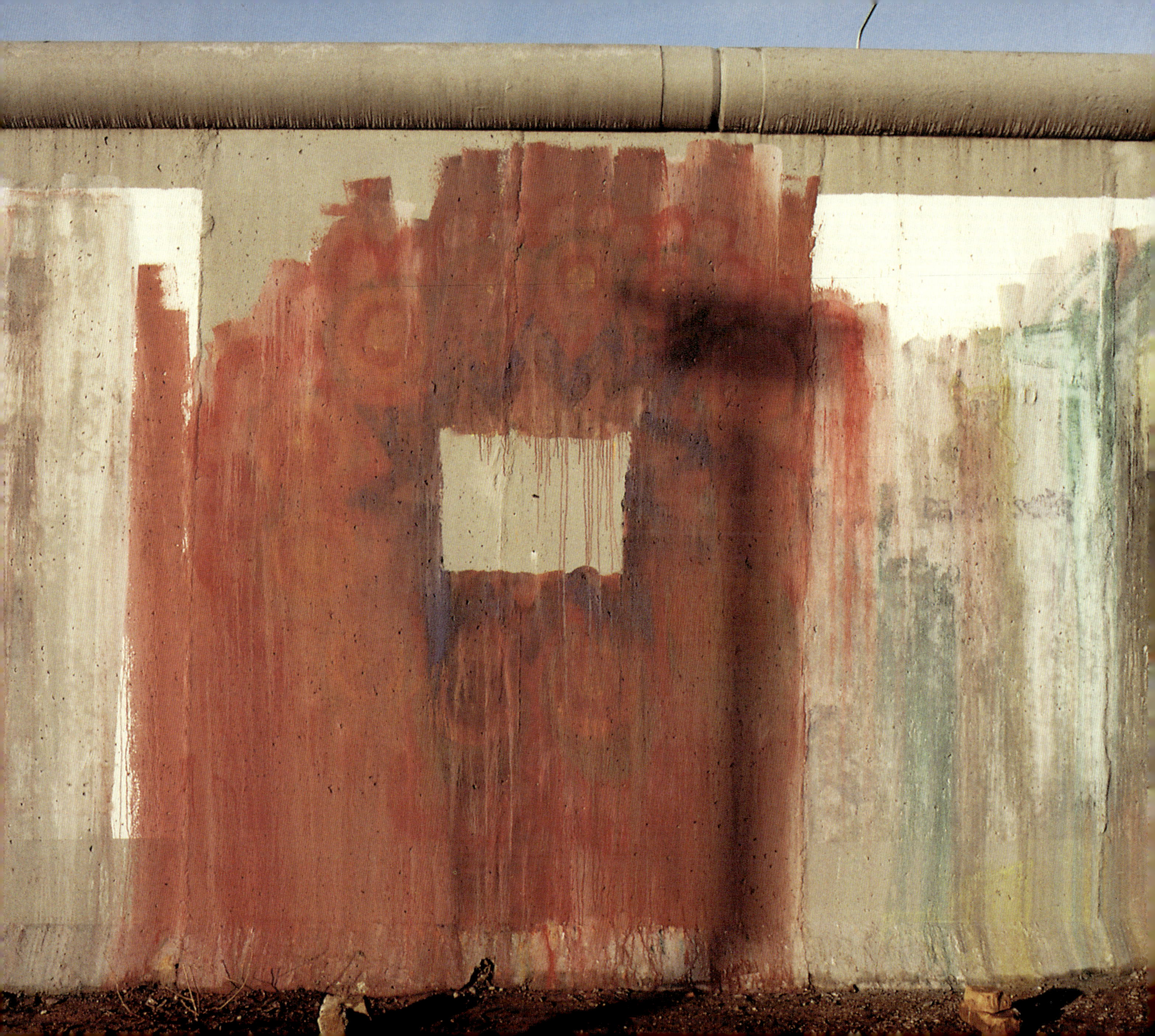

»Untergrundtätigkeit feindwärts«. Volkspolizisten forschen nach einem Fluchttunnel unter der Mauer. Harzer Straße, 1962.

"Underground activity towards the enemy". The People's police looking for a tunnel under the wall. Harzer Straße, 1962.

»Nein, eine Grenze hat Tyrannenmacht!« (Friedrich Schiller in Wilhelm Tell,

ept. 1939

GRUND-STEIN-
Legung
50 JAHRE

»Auf Friedenspatrouille«. Grenzsoldat mit Gewehr vor spanischen Reitern und DDR-Emblem. Bösebrücke, 1961.

On "peace patrol". Border guard with rifle in front of spanish horsemen and the GDR emblem. Bösebrücke, 1961.

DDR - die Bastion des Friedens in Deutschland

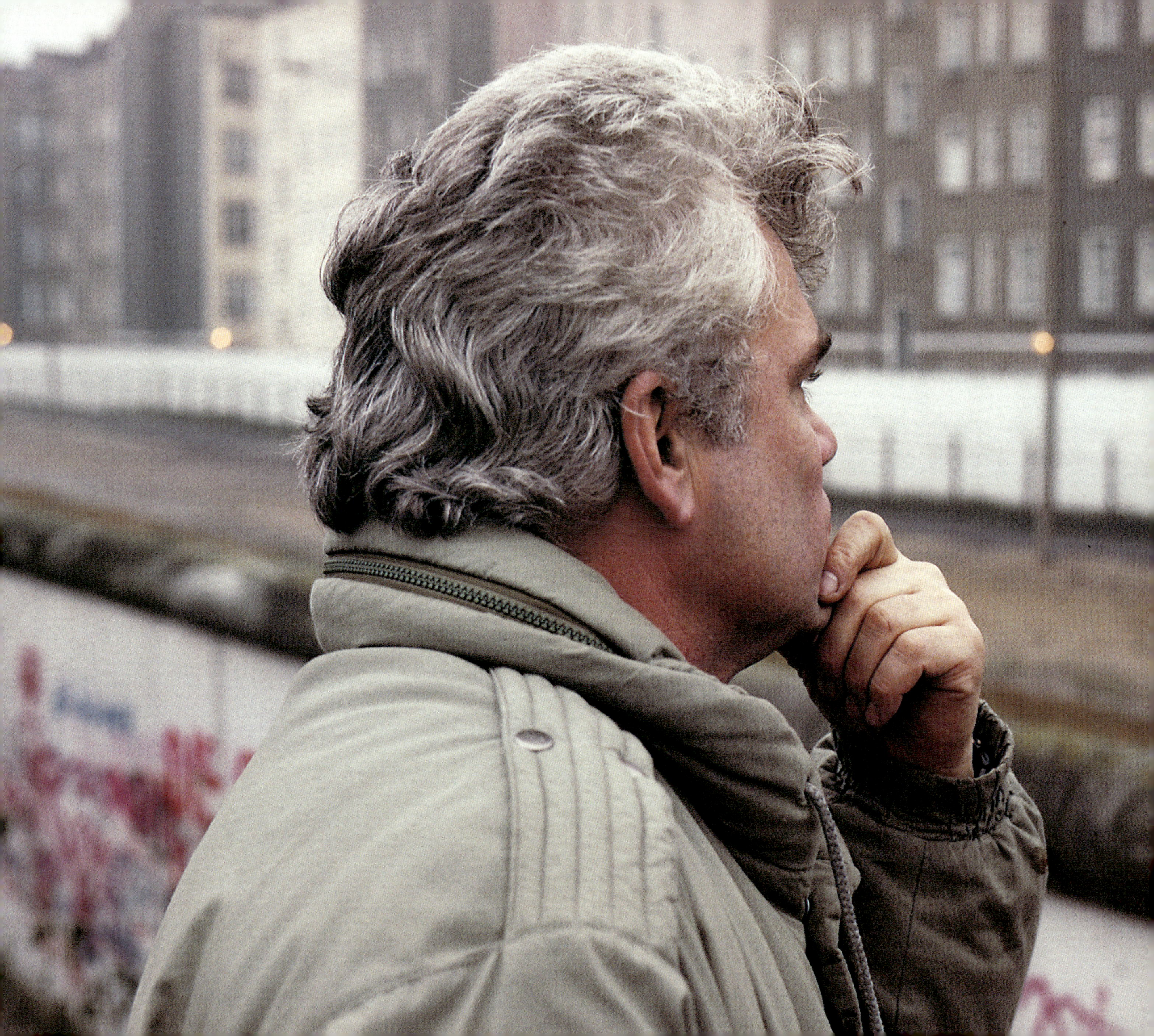

»Spuren einer Flucht«. Kleiderfetzen eines Flüchtlings im Stacheldraht nach Feuergefecht zwischen DDR-Grenzsoldaten und Westberliner Polizei während eines Fluchtvorgangs. Kreuzberg, 1964.

"Traces of an escape". A fugitive's ripped pieces of clothes caught in the barbed wire after an exchange of fire between GDR border guards and West Berlin police during an escape. Kreuzberg, 1964.

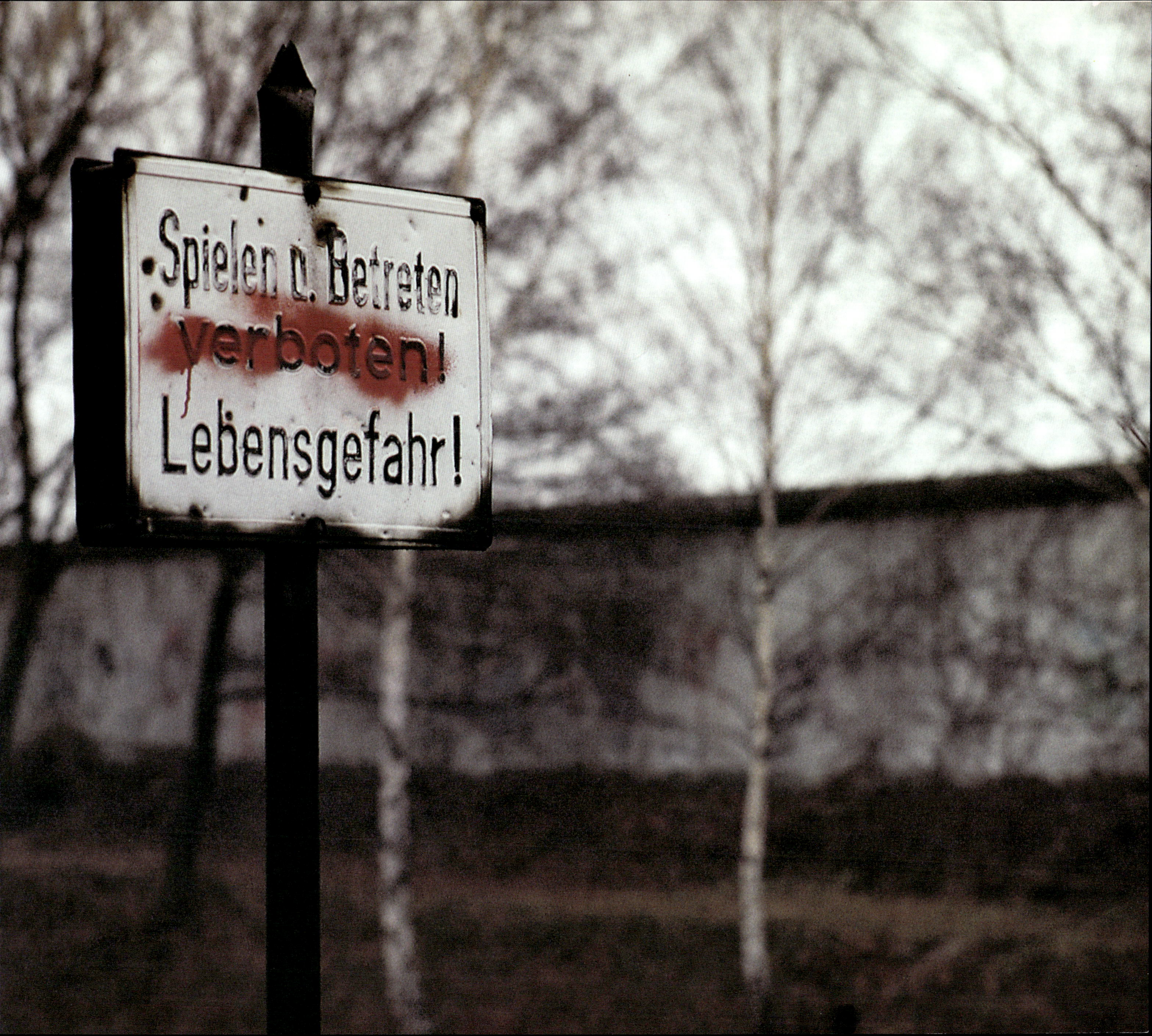
Spielen u. Betreten
verboten!
Lebensgefahr!

»Ich liebe die Mauer«, soll Nikita Chruschtschow am 29. Juni 1963 vor 500 Arbeitern der Ostberliner Maschinenfabrik Marzahn gesagt haben.

"I love the wall," Nikita Khrushchov supposedly said on June 29th, 1963 to 500 workers of the East Berlin machine company, Marzahn.

N. S. Chruschtschow, Vorsitzender des Ministerrates der UdSSR und Erster Sekretär der KPdSU, erklärte am 29. Juni 1963 vor 500 Arbeitern der Berliner Maschinenfabrik Marzahn.

Ich liebe die

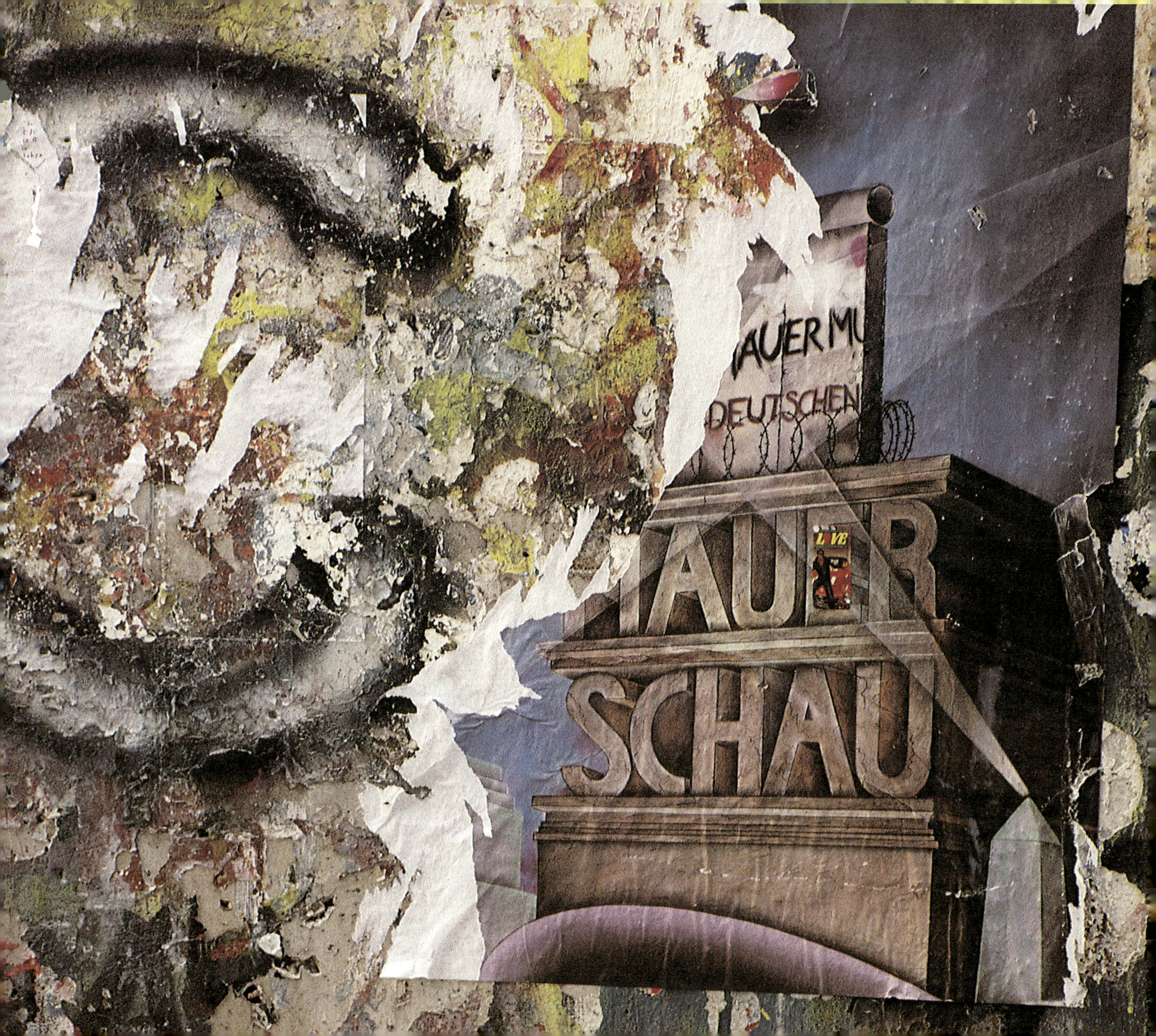
AUER MU
DEUTSCHEN
AUER
SCHAU

»Man muß die Feste feiern, wie sie fallen.« DDR-Sondermarke zum zehnjährigen Bestehen des »antifaschistischen Schutzwalls«.

"You have to celebrate when you can." GDR special print to mark the 10 year existance of the "antifacist wall of protection".

Nächste Doppelseite: »Den Wendehälsen ins Stammbuch geschrieben«.

Following pages: "For the turncoats' souvenir album".

»Üb' immer Treu' und Redlichkeit«. Kuh mit schwarzem Fellfleck, der die Form der Landkarte des geteilten Deutschlands hat. Die Kuh hält eine Stange mit dem Eisernen Kreuz und einem schwarz-rot-goldenen Wimpel.

"Always practice truth and honesty." Cow with a black spot in the shape of a map of the split Germanys. The cow holds a staff with the iron cross and a black, red and gold flag.

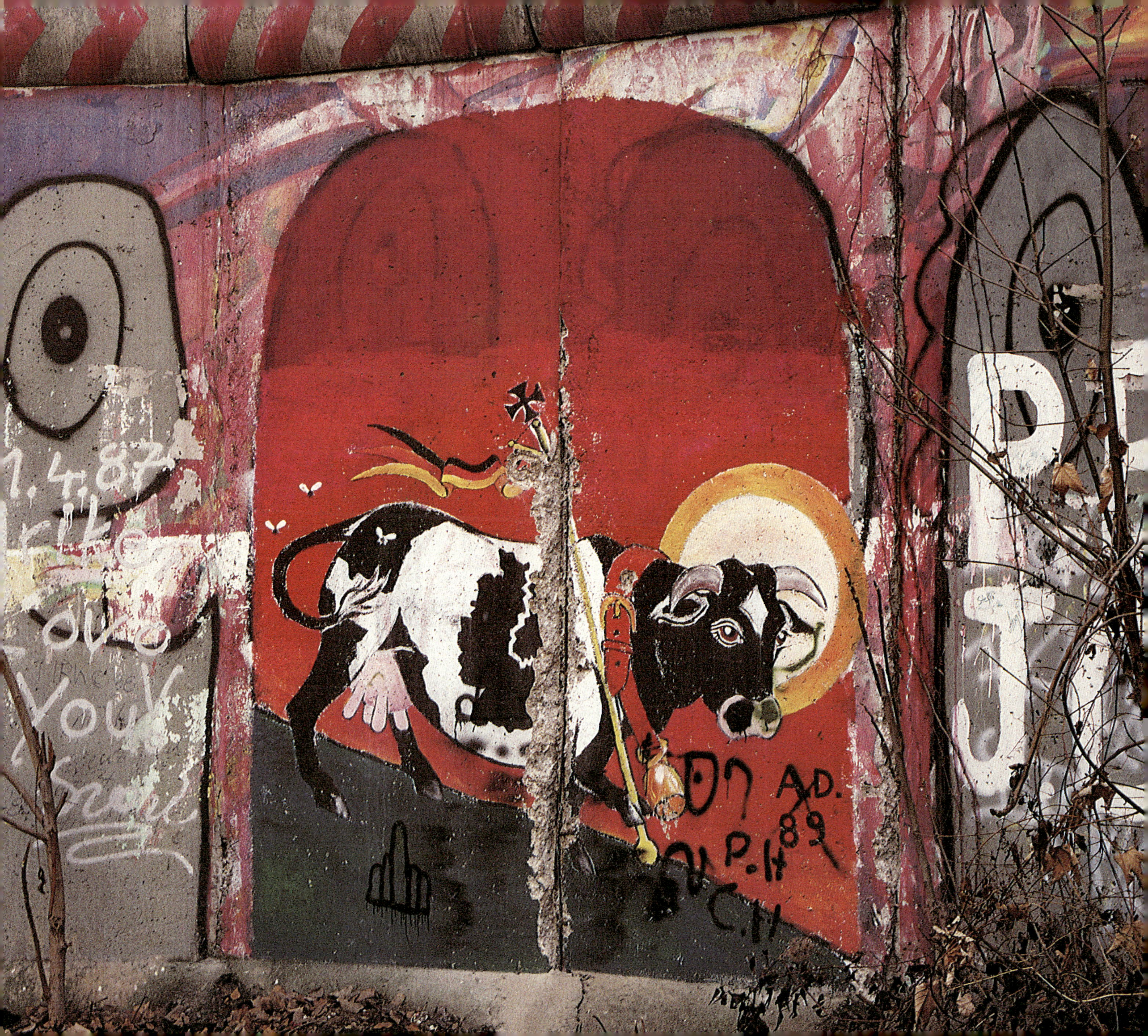
AD.
89

DIE MAUER IST KEIN HEILIG
SONDERN EIN SCHRECKLIC

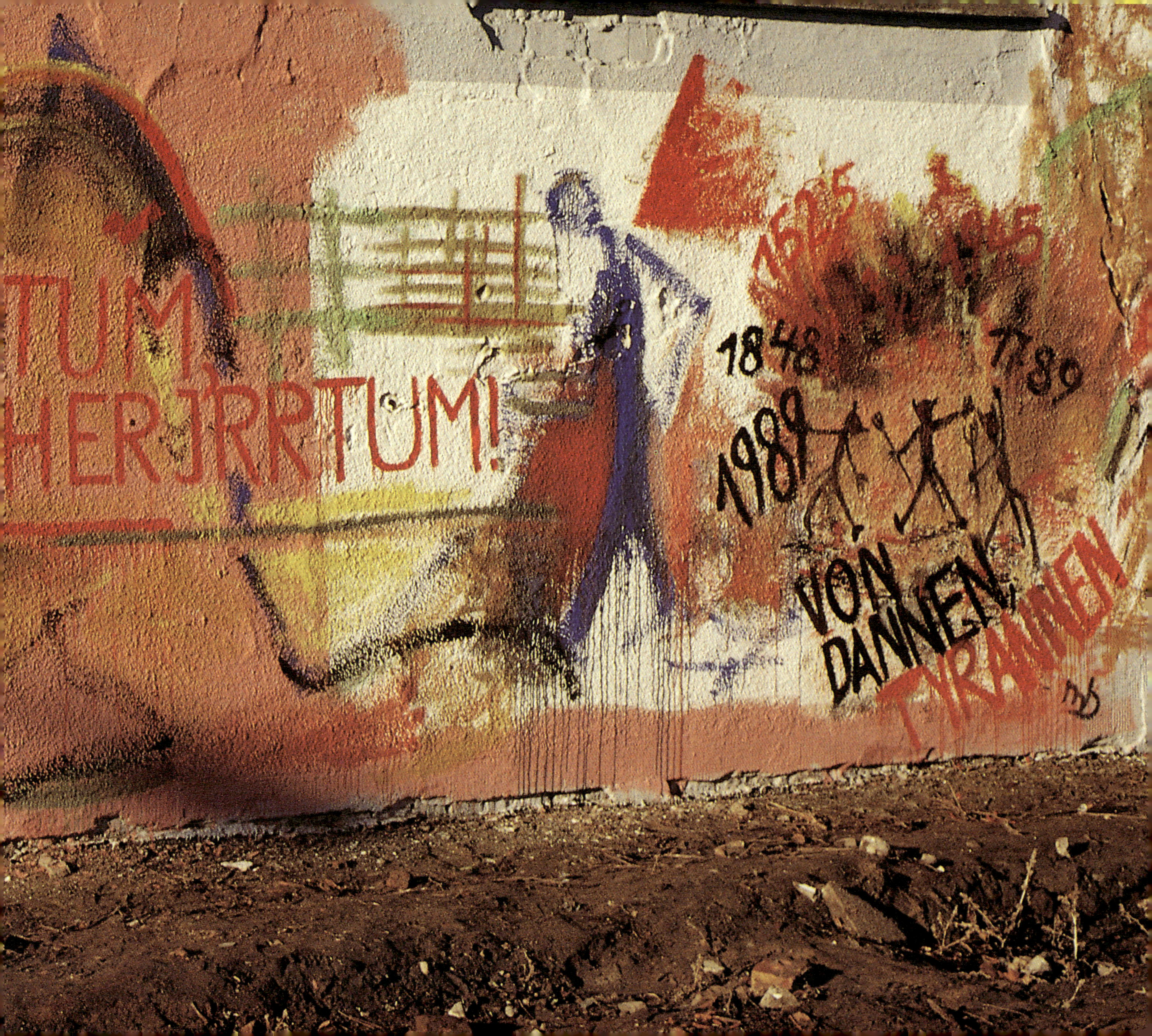
TUM
HERJRRTUM!
1525
1848
1789
1989
VON DANNEN
TYRANNEN

»Wenn's noch kommt, 100 Jahr...« *BZ*, 20. Januar 1989, Titelseite.

100 years at the most". *B.Z.*, January 20th, 1989, front page. Erich Honecker destroys any spark of hope: "The Berlin wall will stay another 100 years!"

Erich Honecker zerstört jeden Funken Hoffnung:
Die Berliner Mauer bleibt noch 100 Jahre!

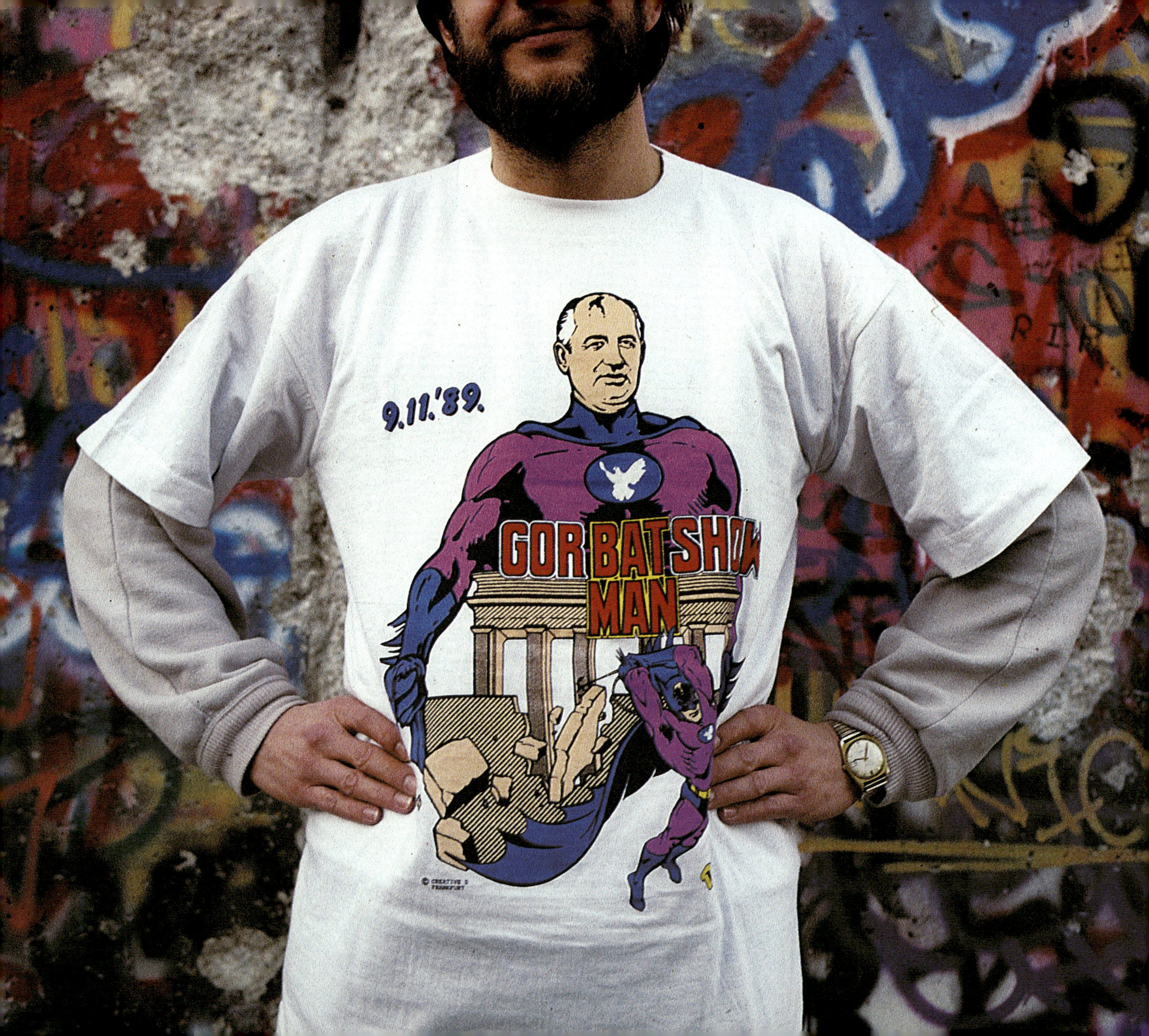
9.11.'89.
GORBATSHOW
MAN

»... und was ewig sich verbindet«. Hochzeitsgesellschaft an der Mauer. Sechziger Jahre.

"... until death do us part." Wedding guests in front of the wall in the sixties.

»Spieglein, Spieglein an der Wand ...«

"Mirror, mirror on the wall ..."

Riß in der Optik

»Aus einer Strafkolonie«. Schematischer Plan der Grenzanlagen (3. Generation): Betonplattenwand, Kontrollstreifen, Hundelaufanlage, Beobachtungsturm, Scheinwerfer, Signalgerät usw.

"From a penal colony". Schematic plan of the border construction (3rd generation): Wall of concrete plates, control strips, watch dog tracks, observation towers, flood lights, alarms, etc.

› Moderne Grenze ‹

1 Betonplattenwand mit oder ohne Rohr
2 Metallgitterzaun
3 Kontrollstreifen [K S]
4 Beleuchtungsanlage
5 Kfz-Graben
6 Linie der vorderen Begrenzung des Grenzpostens
7 Kolonnenweg
8 Hundelaufanlage
9 Signalgerät
10 Scheinwerfer
11 Beobachtungsturm
12 Schutzbunker
13 Kontaktzaun
14 Wildfangzaun

Gebiet der Grenzsicherungs- oder Pioniertechnischen Anlagen

Siehe Kapitel „Moderne Grenze" Seite 6

Nächste Doppelseite: »Punkt, Punkt, Komma, Strich — ist das nicht ein Fluchtgesicht?« Schlangestehendes Strichmännchen, bereit zum Flug über die Mauer — eines der ersten Mauerfreskos auf der »anderen Seite«.

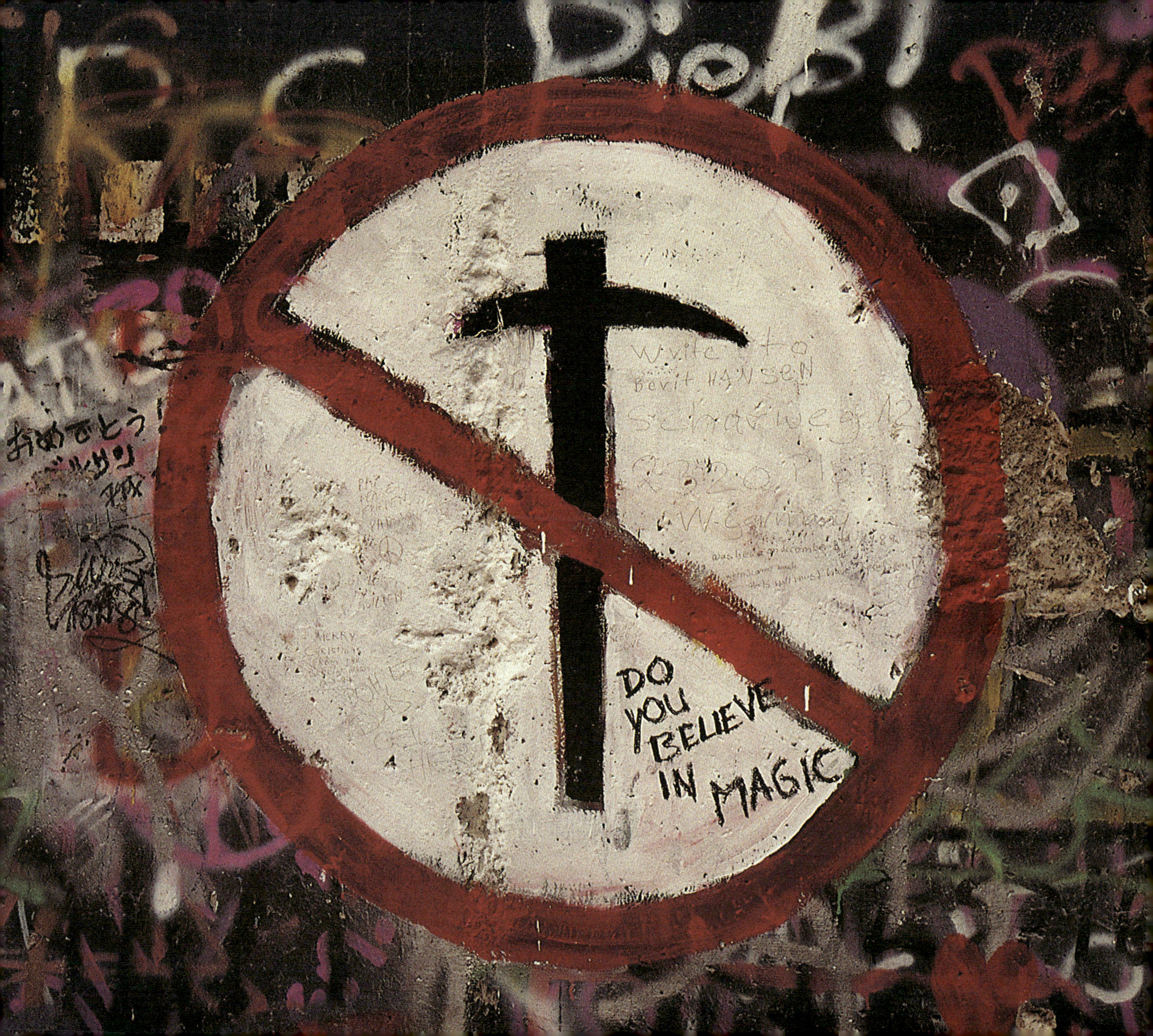
DO
YOU
BELIEVE
IN MAGIC

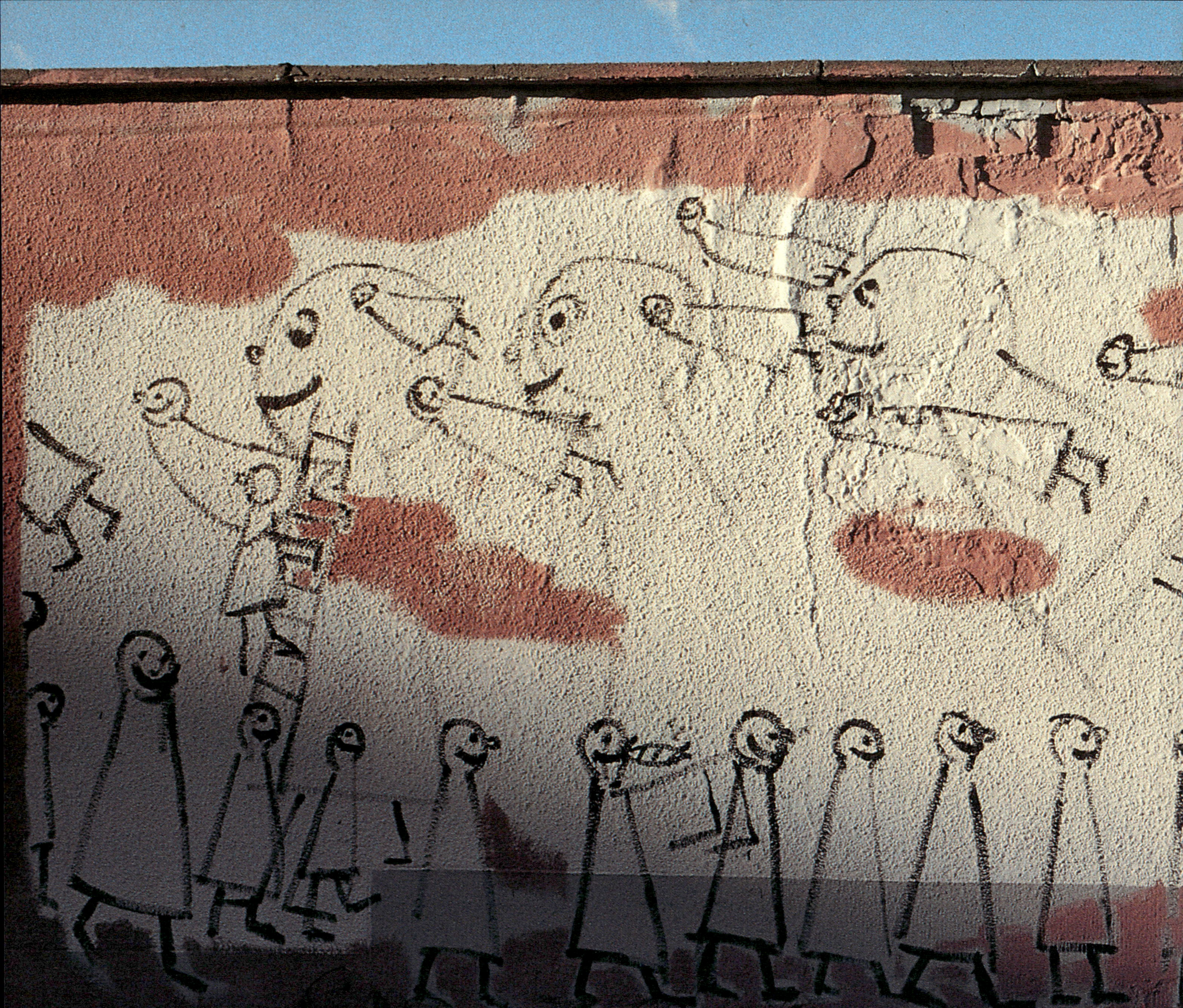

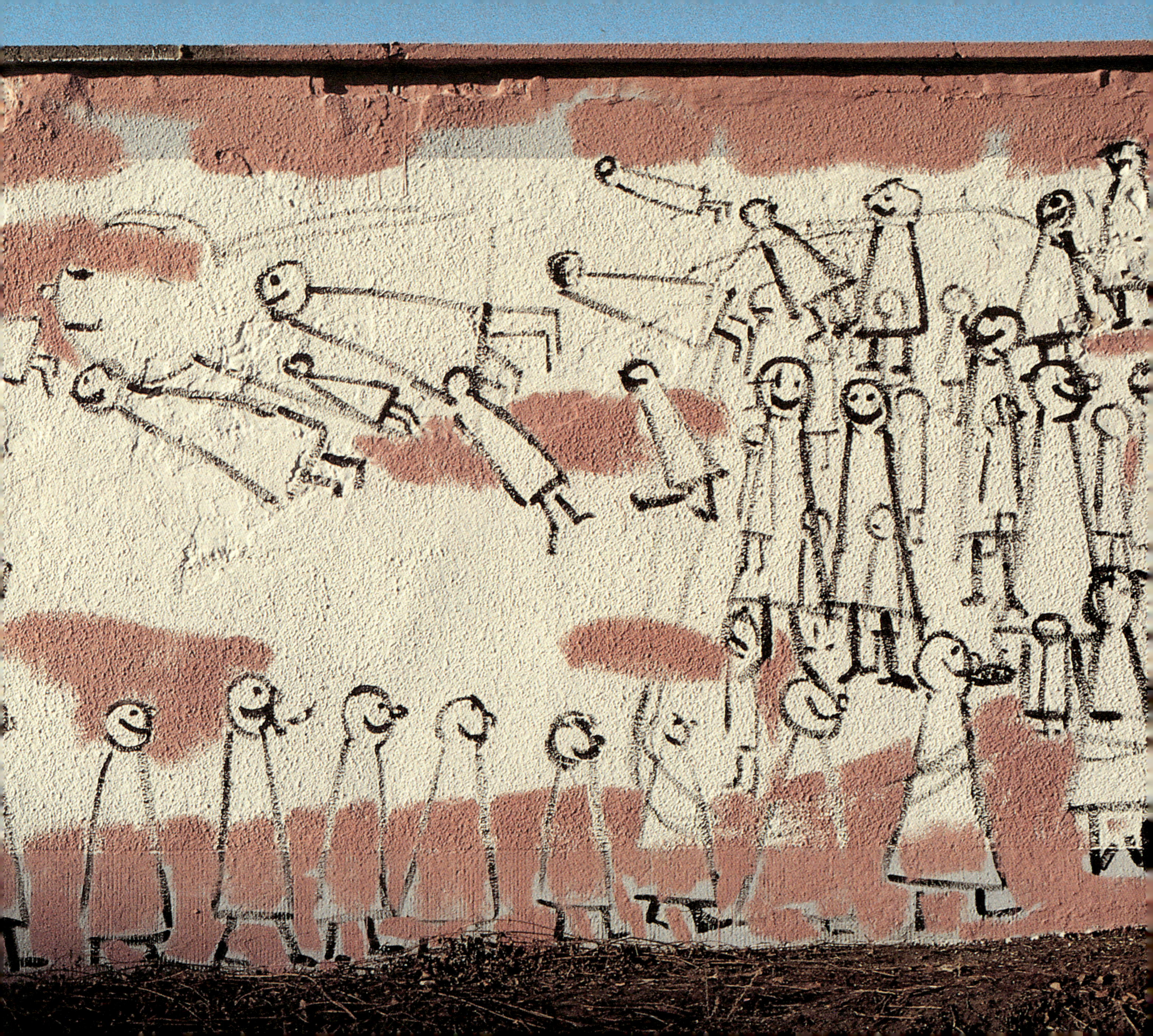

»Ihr da oben, wir da unten«, scheint dieser Ostberliner zu sagen, der aus seiner unmittelbar an der Mauer gelegenen Wohnung durch das Schutzzaungeflecht in den Westen schaut. Bernauer Straße, 1961.

"Hey, you up there, we're down here!" this East Berliner from his apartment right on the wall looking through the protecting fence into the West appears to say. Bernauer Straße, 1961.

HAZ REVOLUCION

»Ich bin ein Berliner!«
Präsident John F. Kennedy mit
dem Regierenden Bürgermeister Willy Brandt und Bundeskanzler Konrad Adenauer an
der Mauer, 1963.

"I am a Berliner!" President
John F. Kennedy with the
Governing Mayor Willy
Brandt and the West German
Chancellor Konrad Adenauer
at the wall, 1963.

Nächste Doppelseite:
»Was gibt's denn da noch zu
verzollen?« Westberliner
Zollbeamter, Ostberliner
Grenzsoldat und Westberliner
Polizist (v.r.) »kommen
zusammen«.

Following pages:
"Do you have anything else
that needs to be declared?"
West Berlin Customs officer,
East Berlin soldier from the
border troops and West Berlin Police "coming together".

»Zur Freiheit, zur Freiheit ...«
(L. v. Beethoven, Fidelio, Arie
des Florestan). Graffiti der
französischen Maler
Christophe Bouchet und
Thierry Noir.

"Towards freedom, towards
freedom ..." (Beethoven,
Fidelio, Florestan's Aria)
Graffiti by the French painters
Christophe Bouchet and
Thierry Noir.

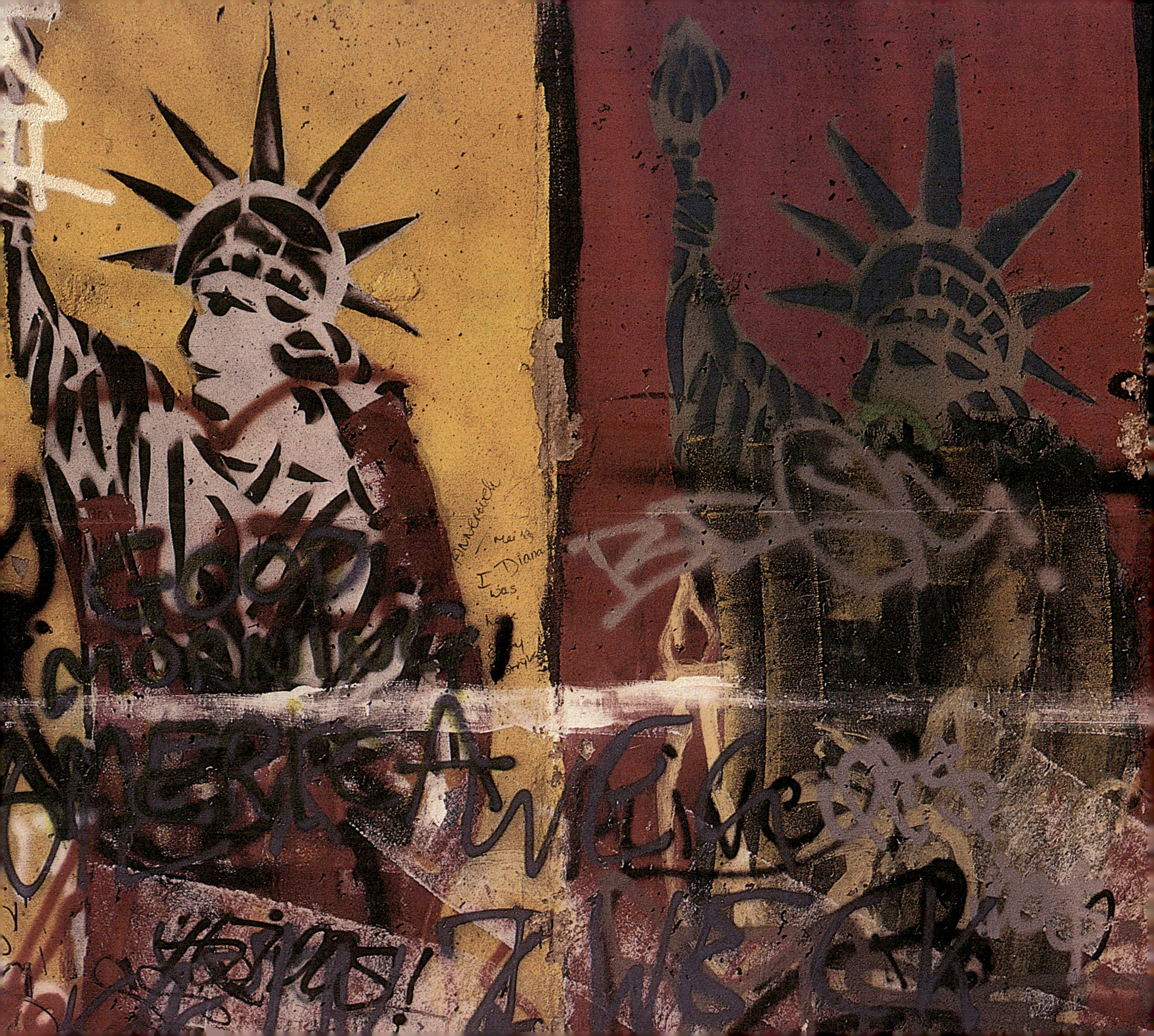

COME TOGETHER

NICHA

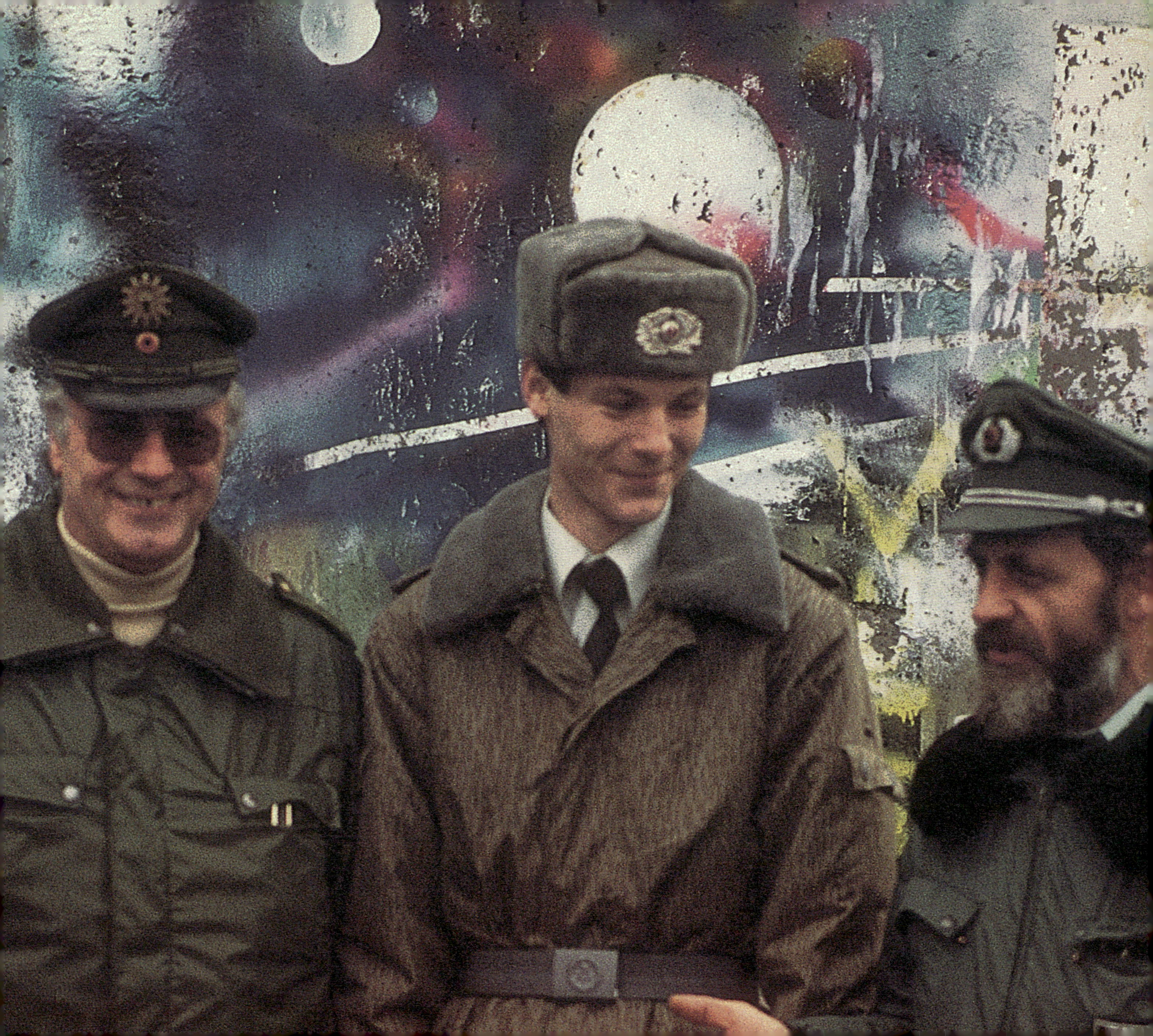

»Sackgasse«. Absperrgitter in einem Kanalisationsschacht, um die strafbare Republikflucht auch unterirdisch zu verhindern. Gleimtunnel im Bezirk Wedding, 1962.

"Deadend". Barricades in a canalisation shaft to prevent the unlawful fleeing of the country from underground. Gleimtunnel in the district of Wedding, 1962.

Nächste Doppelseite (links): »Zwei Herzen im Dreivierteltakt«. Zwei rote Herzen mit gemalten Augen und Inschrift.

Following pages (left): "You are my heart's delight". Two red hearts with eyes painted in and scription.

Nächste Doppelseite (rechts): »Angst?« Eines der ersten Graffiti auf der Ostseite der Mauer nach dem 9. November.

Following pages (right):

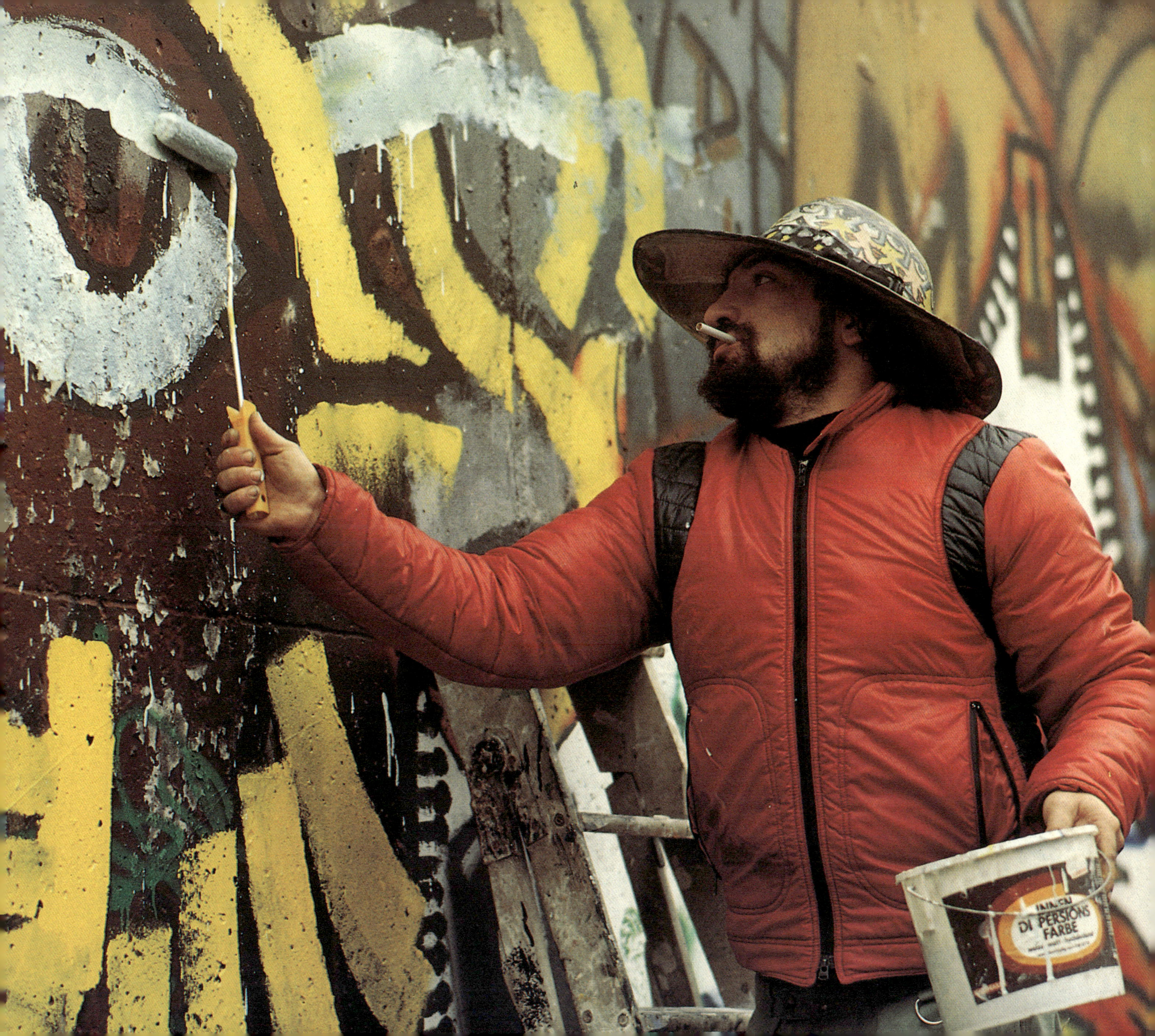
DI PERSIONS
FARBE

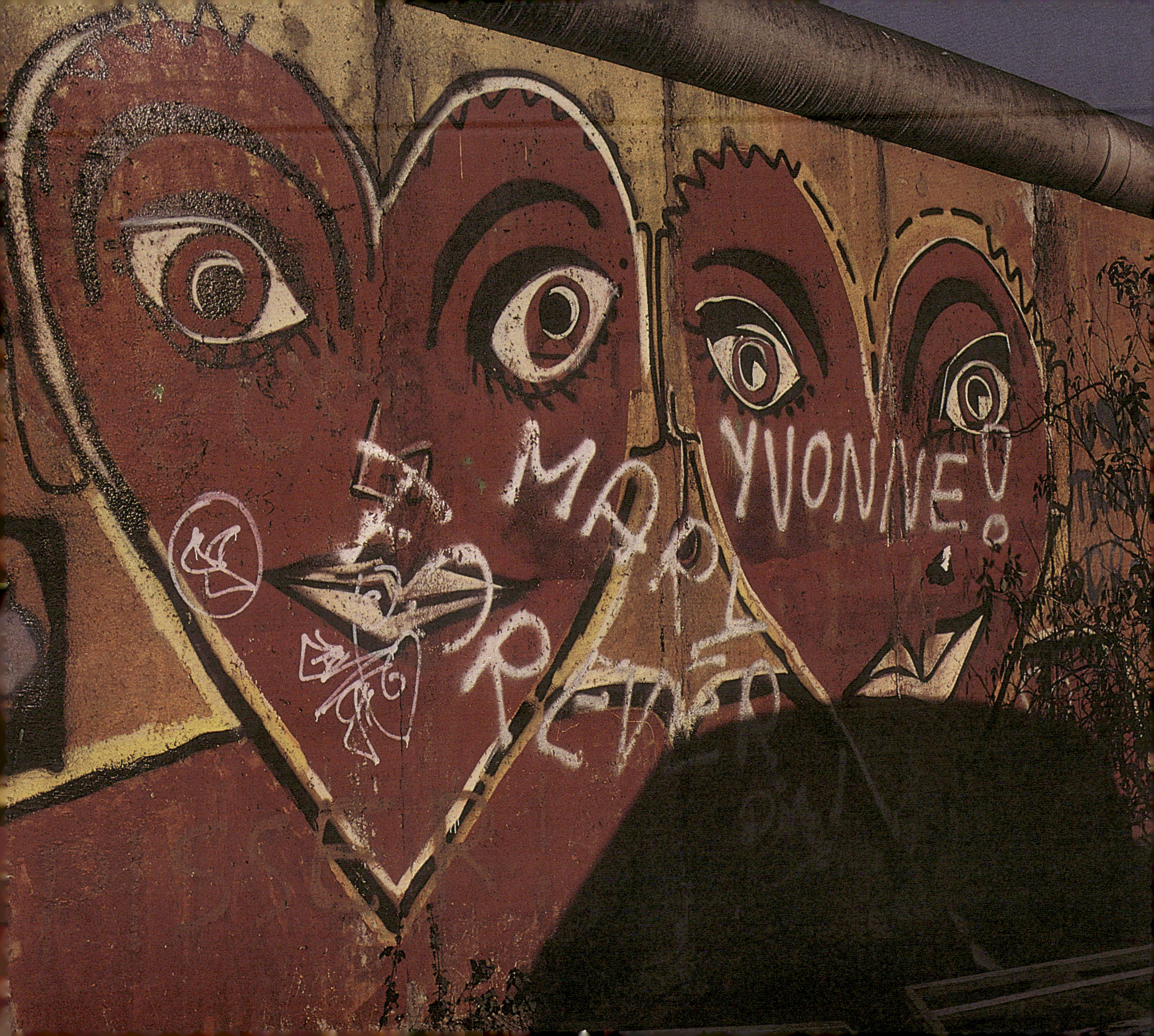
YVONNE

17 Millionen, Egon!

Berliner Stadtplan mit genau
kartographiertem Mauer-
verlauf.

Berlin city map with the exact
cartography of where the wall
runs.

Nächste Doppelseite:
»Weg damit!« Aufforderung
zur wahrhaft volksnahen
»Pionierfreundschaft«
zwischen Neu-Ost und
Alt-West.

Following pages:
"Away with it!" Encouraging
"pioneer friendship" between
the New-East and the
Old-West.

»Sehen Sie die Fahne da
drüben«, sagt Oberstleutnant
Uwe Karsch zu mir und
deutet auf die bundes-
deutsche Fahne, die vom First
des Reichstagsgebäudes unter
der kalten Dezembersonne im
Wind flattert, »die ist nämlich
ungesetzlich!« Wachablösung
an der Mauer vor dem
Brandenburger Tor,
6. Dezember 1989.

"See the flag over there,"
Lieutenant-Colonel Uwe
Karsch says to me and points
to the West German flag
waving in the wind beneath a
cold December sun from the
Reichstag (parlament build-
ing), "that is unlawful!"
Changing of the guard at
the wall in front of the
Brandenburg Gate,
December 6th, 1989.

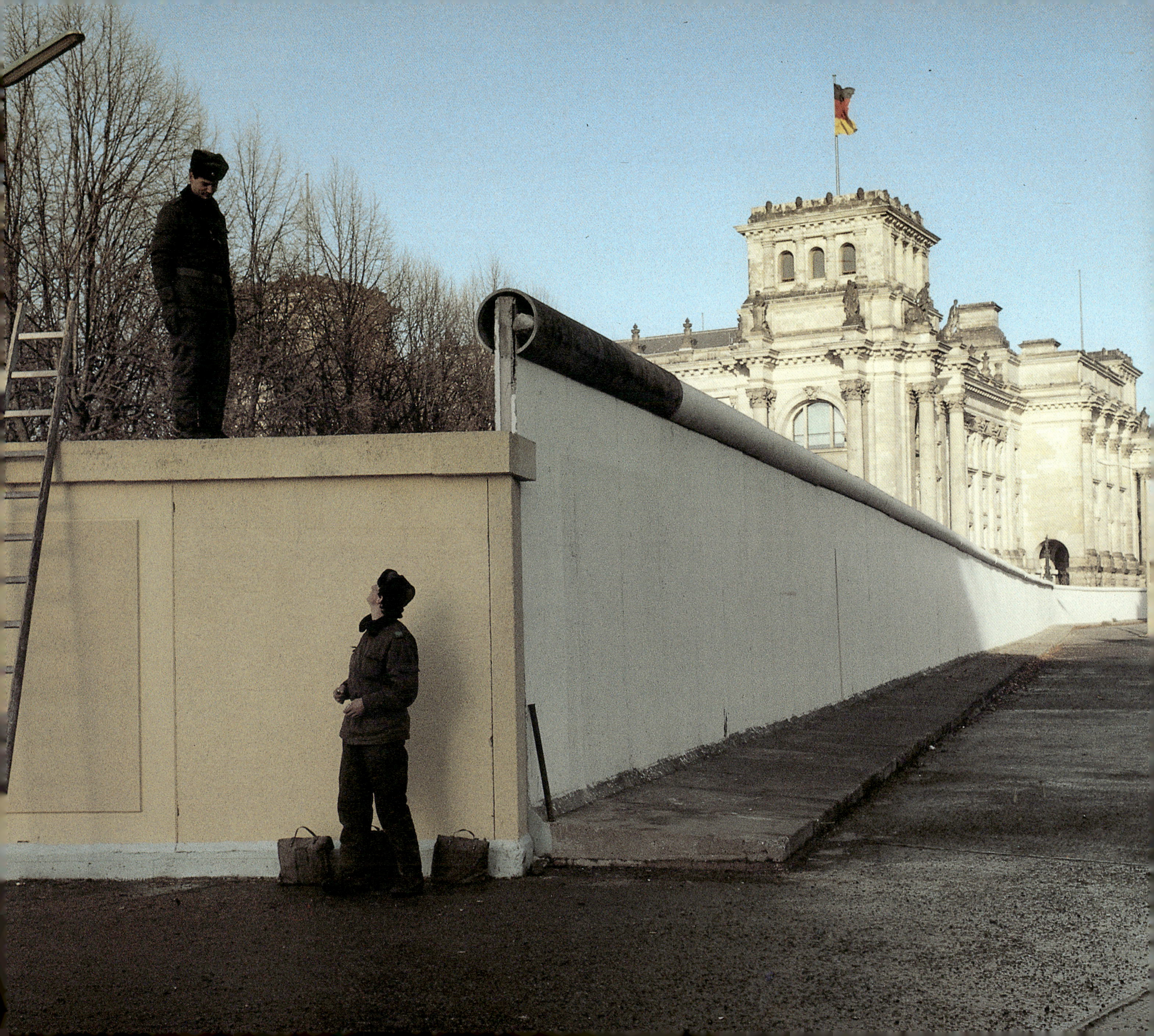

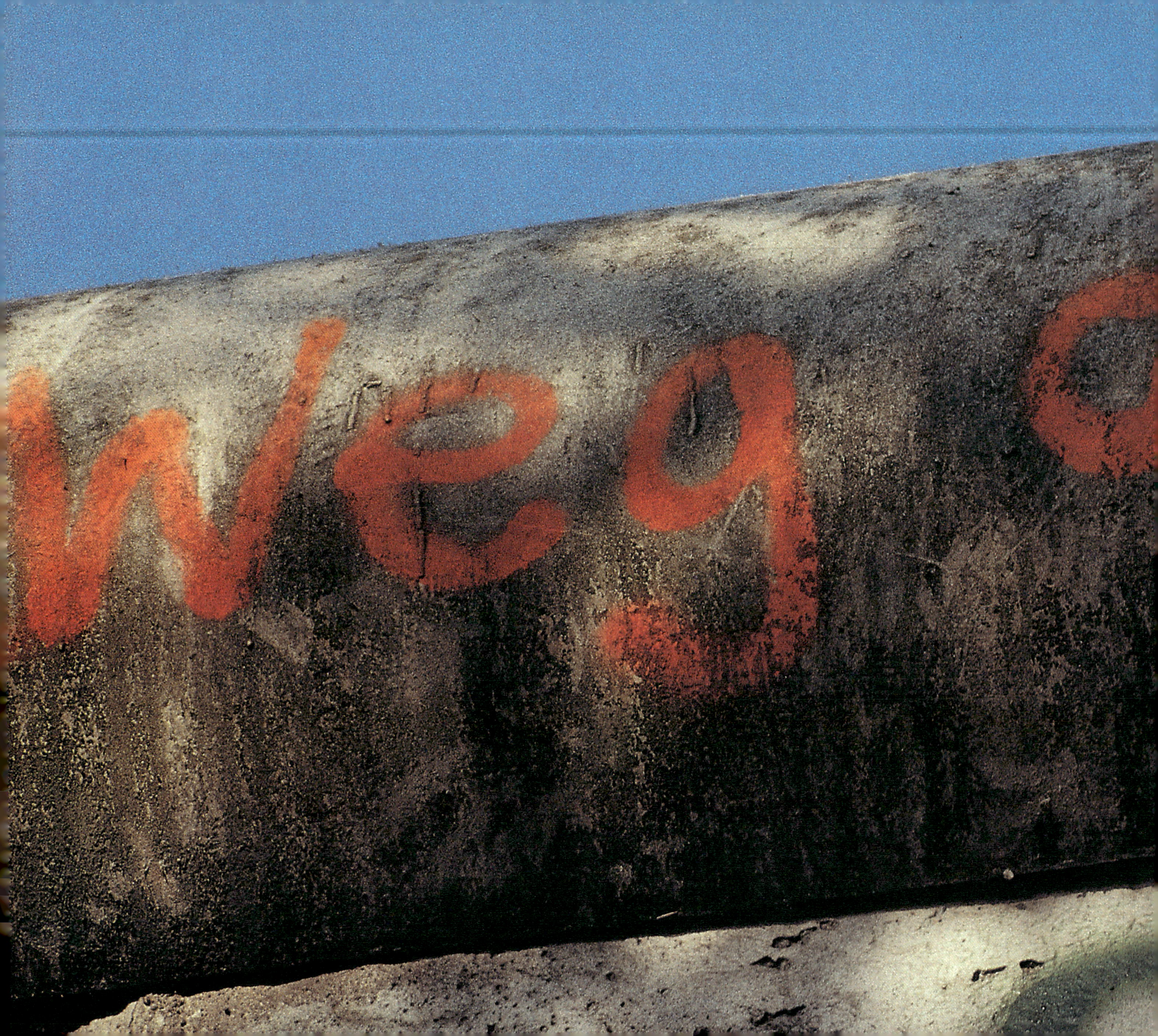

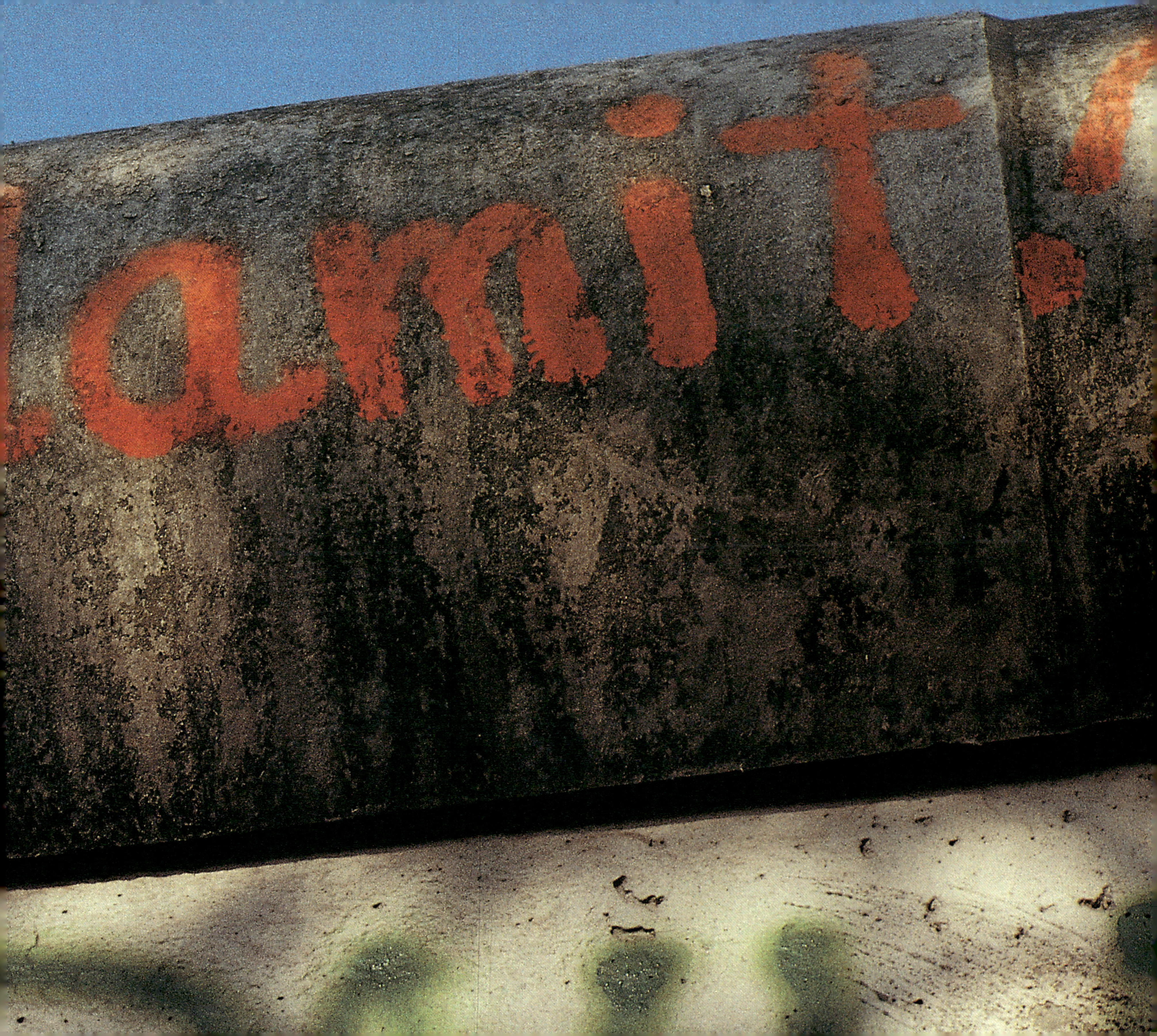

Endstation Sehnsucht«. Der Eiserne Vorhang als Betonmauer quer über den Potsdamer Platz.

"A Streetcar named Desire." The iron curtain as concrete wall straight through Potsdamer Platz.

Nächste Doppelseite: »Wir sind die Tiere!« Giraffen, Frösche und Fabeltiere der Phantasie feiern ihre »pluralistische Existenz«.

Following pages: "We are the animals!" Giraffes, frogs and ficticious animals celebrate their "pluralistic existance".

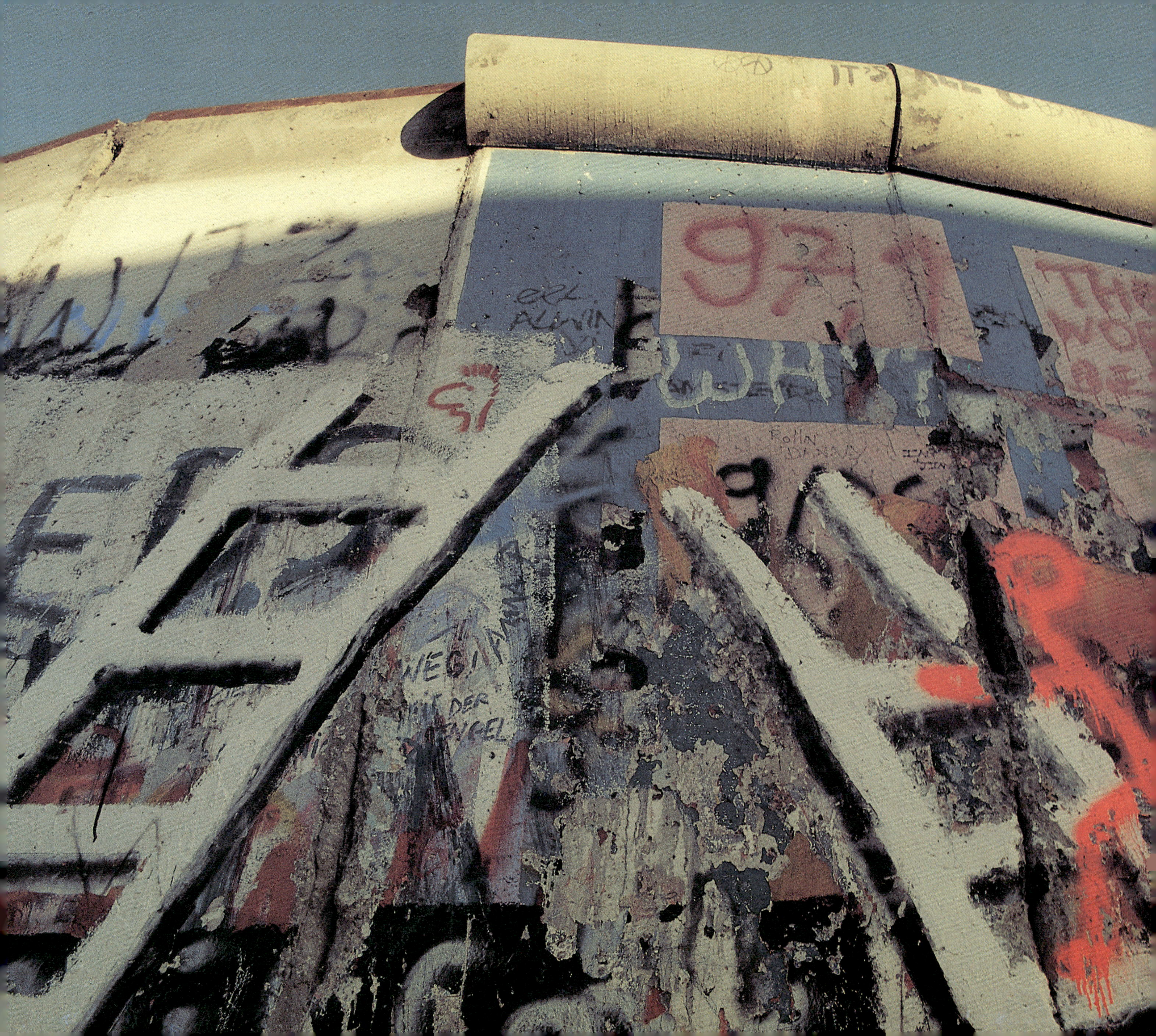
WHY

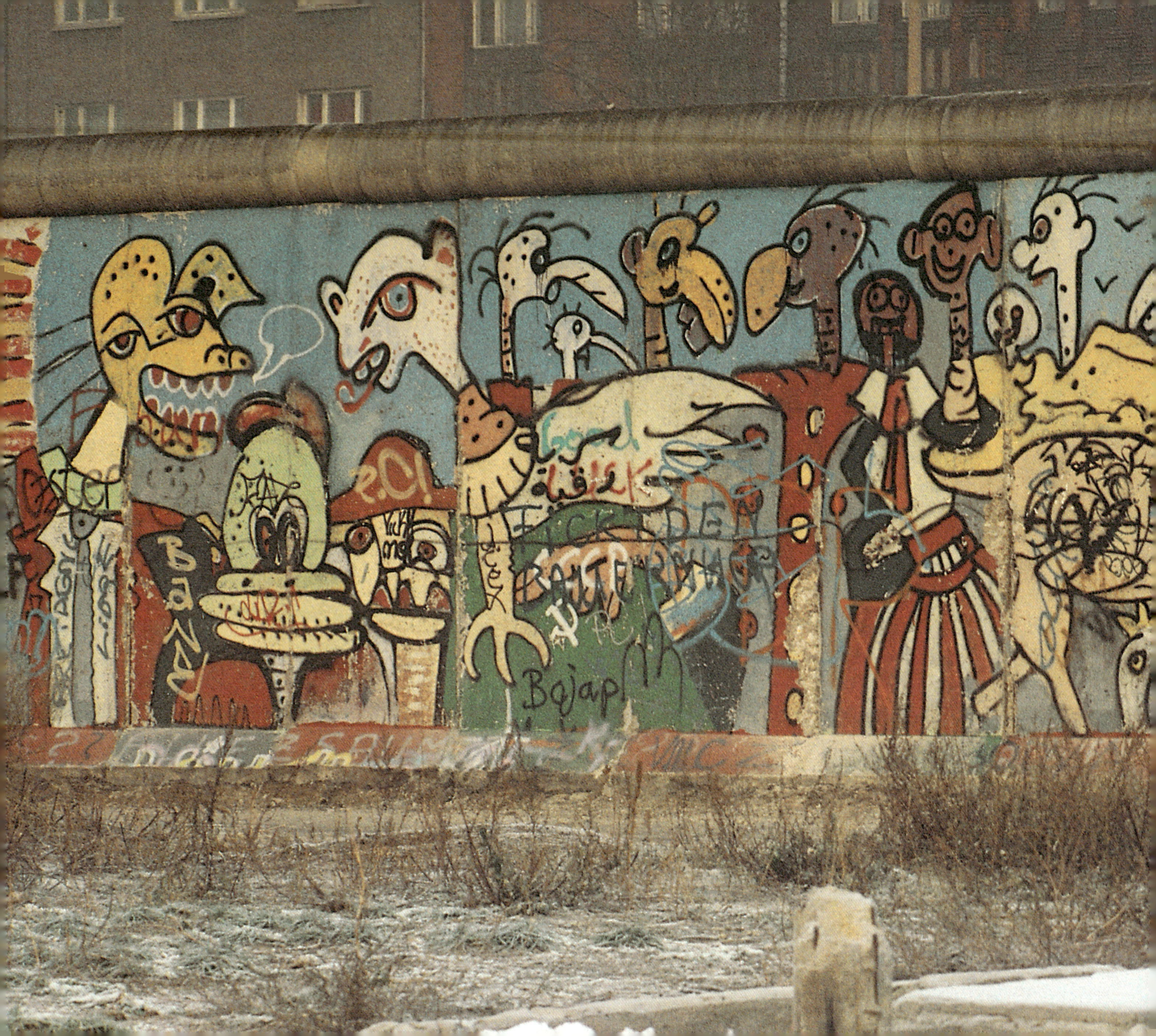

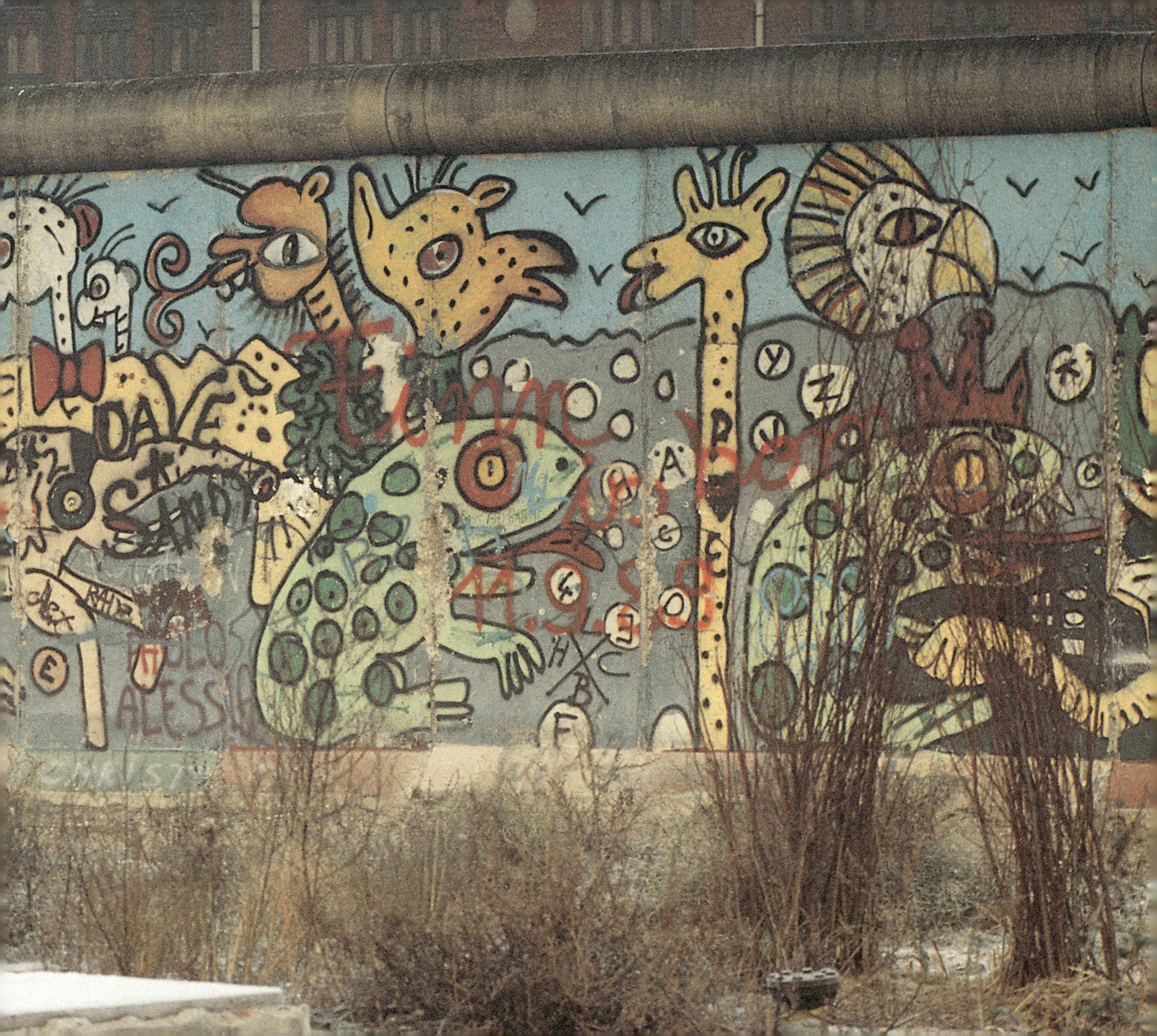
DAVE

»Kommunistischer Morgengruß«. DDR-Transparent hinter Stacheldraht. Wilhelmstraße, 1961.

"Communist morning greeting". GDR banner behind barbed wire. Wilhelmstraße, 1961.

Nicht frech werden, Herr Brandt, wir sind gute Schützen.

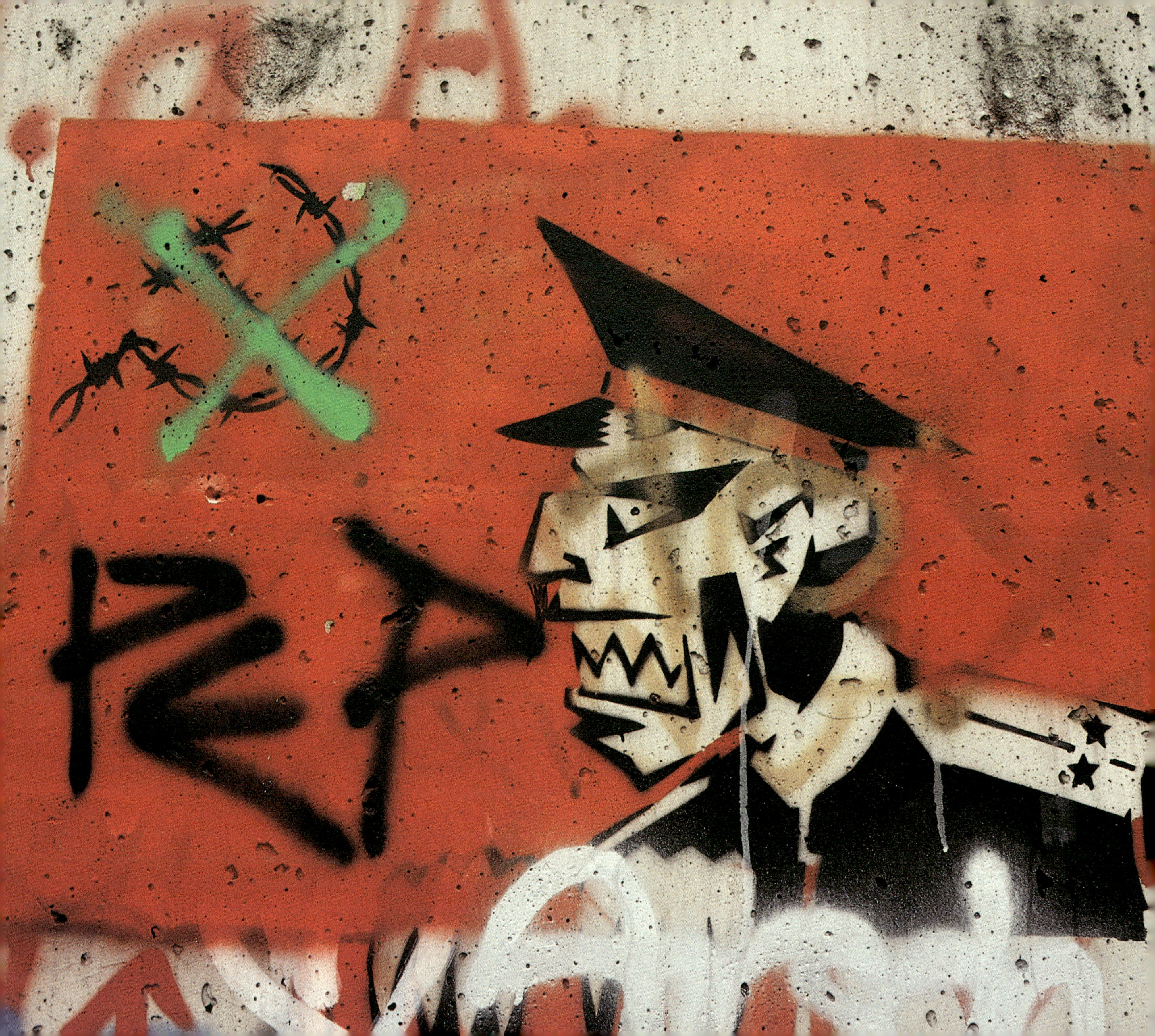

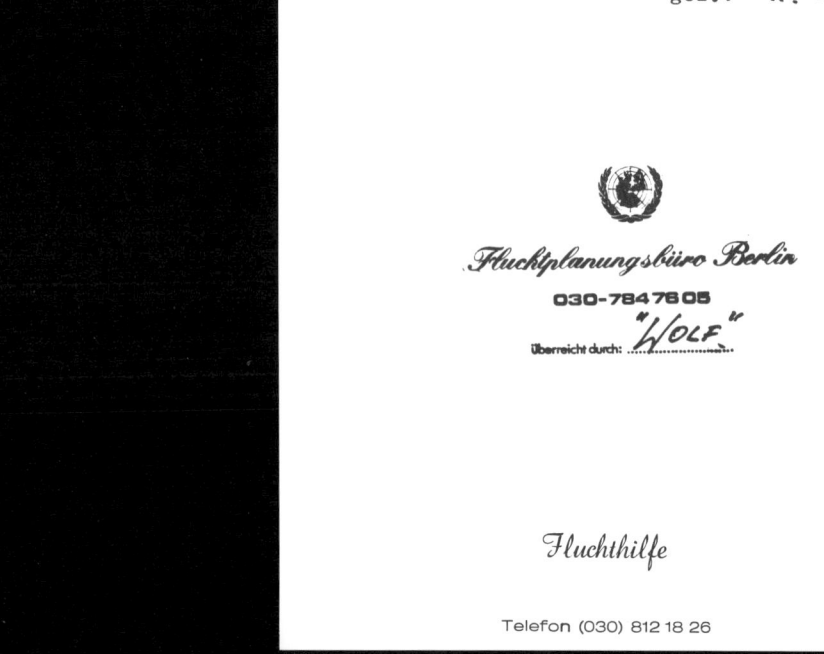

| »Fluchthilfe«. Kommerzielle Fluchthelfer bieten fluchtbereiten DDR-Bürgern bzw. deren westlichen Helfern ihre Dienste an. |
| "Escape assistance". Commercial escape — people offer their services to GDR residents who are ready to flee the country and to their western helpers. |

LIBERTAS OMNIBUS HOMINIBUS!

H. WILL
1 Berlin 62
Postfach 208

Sehr geehrter Herr, Frau Doktor!

Betr.: Familienzusammenführung von Ost nach West.

Wir sind ein renommiertes und seriöses Unternehmen mit zehnjähriger Erfahrung. Die uns erteilten Aufträge werden korrekt und diskret durchgeführt. Auf Wunsch stehen Ihnen Reverenzen zur Verfügung. Bitte empfehlen Sie uns gegebenenfalls auch Ihren Verwandten und Freunden. Teilen Sie uns Ihre Adresse oder Rufnummer mit, wir setzen uns mit Ihnen umgehend in Verbindung.

gez.: H. Will

Fluchtplanungsbüro Berlin
030-78 47 60 05
Überreicht durch: "WOLF"

Fluchthilfe

Telefon (030) 812 18 26

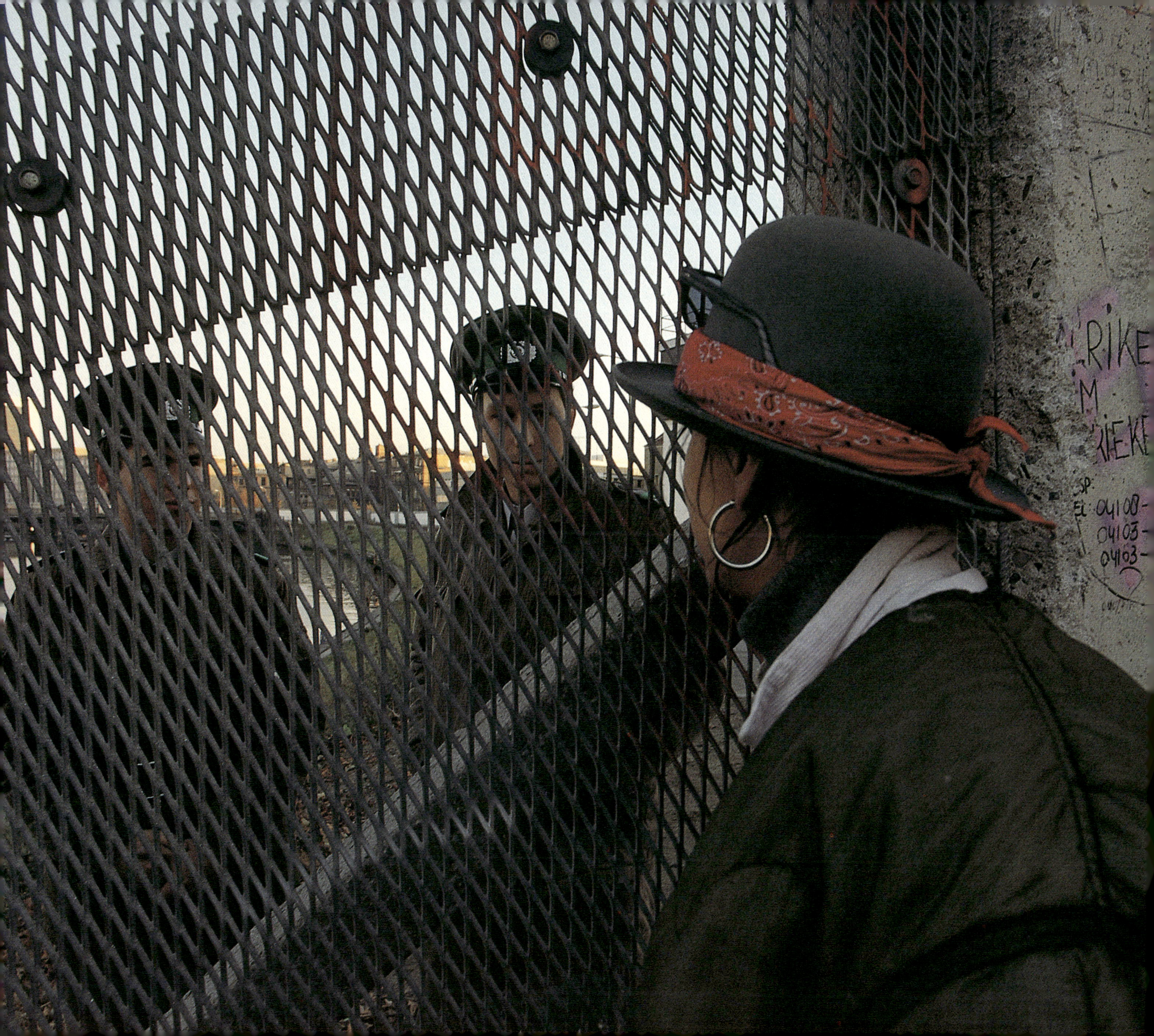

»Anruf — Warnschuß — Zielschuß!« Gedenkkreuz für zwei Ostberliner, die am 16. Oktober 1961 beim Durchschwimmen der Spree von DDR-Grenzsoldaten erschossen wurden; das Mahnmal ist auch vom östlichen Ufer aus gut lesbar.

"Verbal warning — Warning shot — Target shot!" Memorial cross for two East Berliners who, on October 16th, 1961 were shot to death by GDR border guards as they tried to swim across the Spree. The monument is also easily readable from the Eastern bank.

Nächste Doppelseite: »Bier der frommen Denkungsart«. Taube mit Inschrift: Bier.

Following pages: "Doves are good for you!" Dove with inscription: beer.

»Ich liebe dich, my best friend, Moskau ...!« Graffiti mit den im Titel collagierten

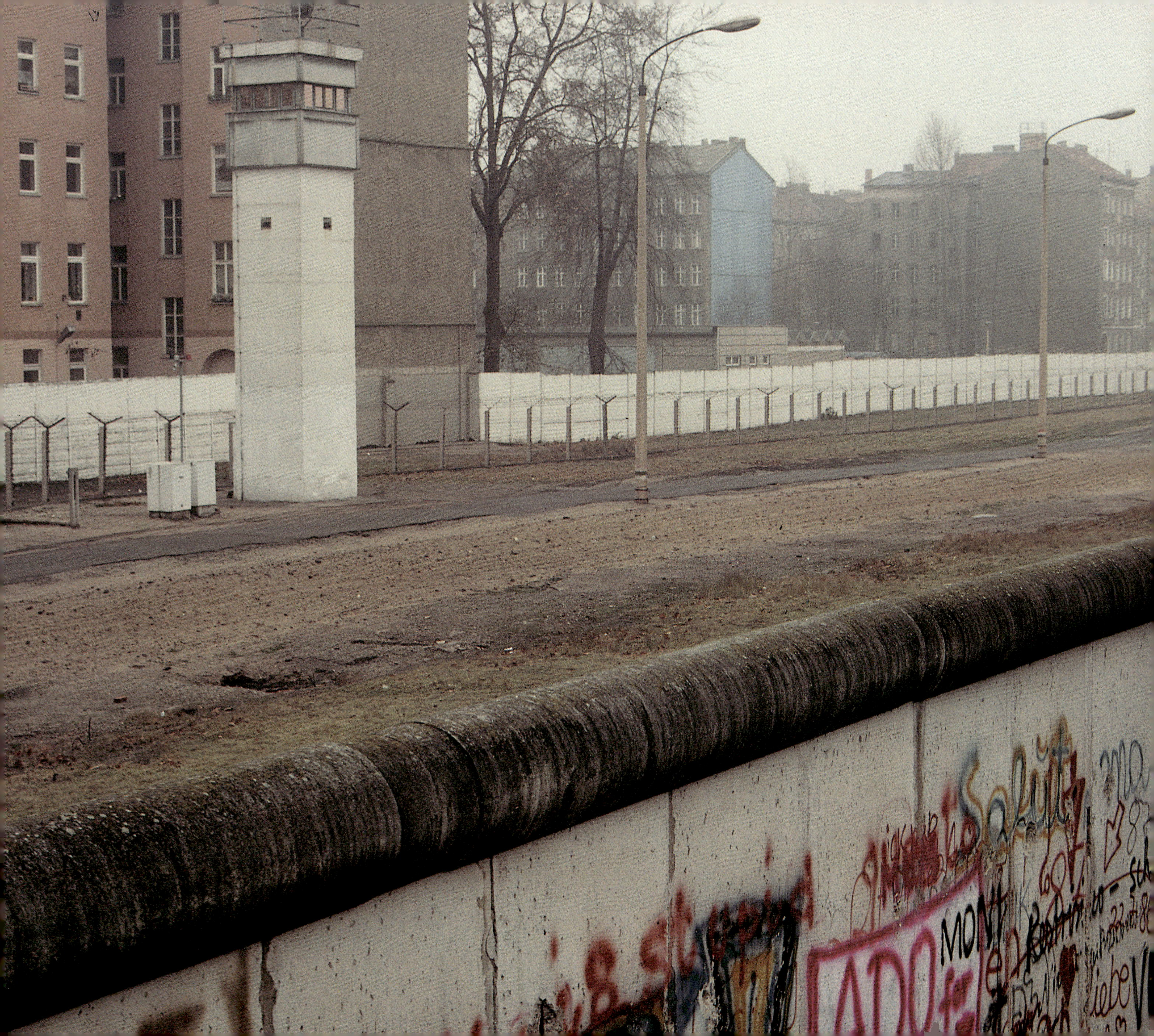
MONT

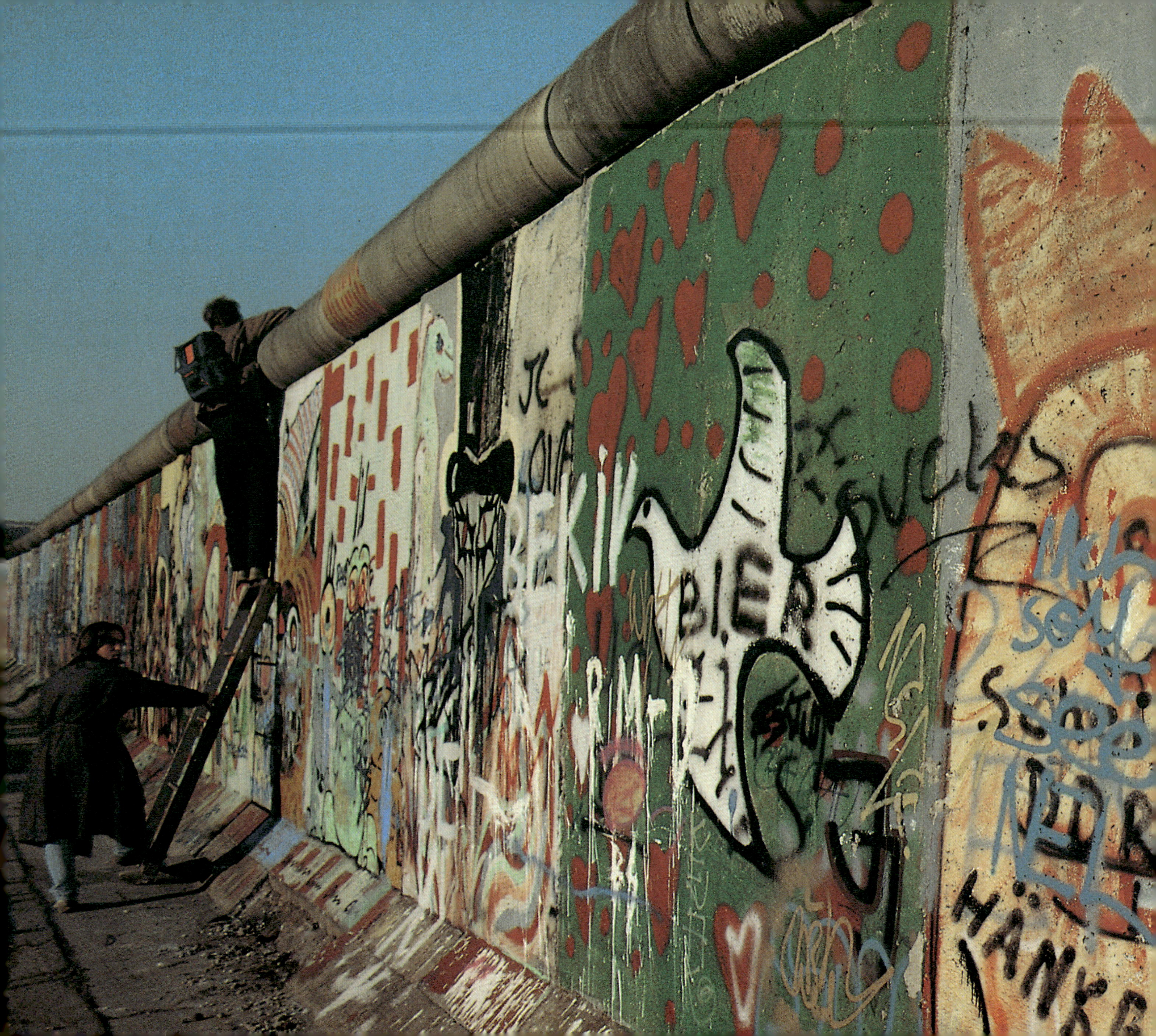
BIER

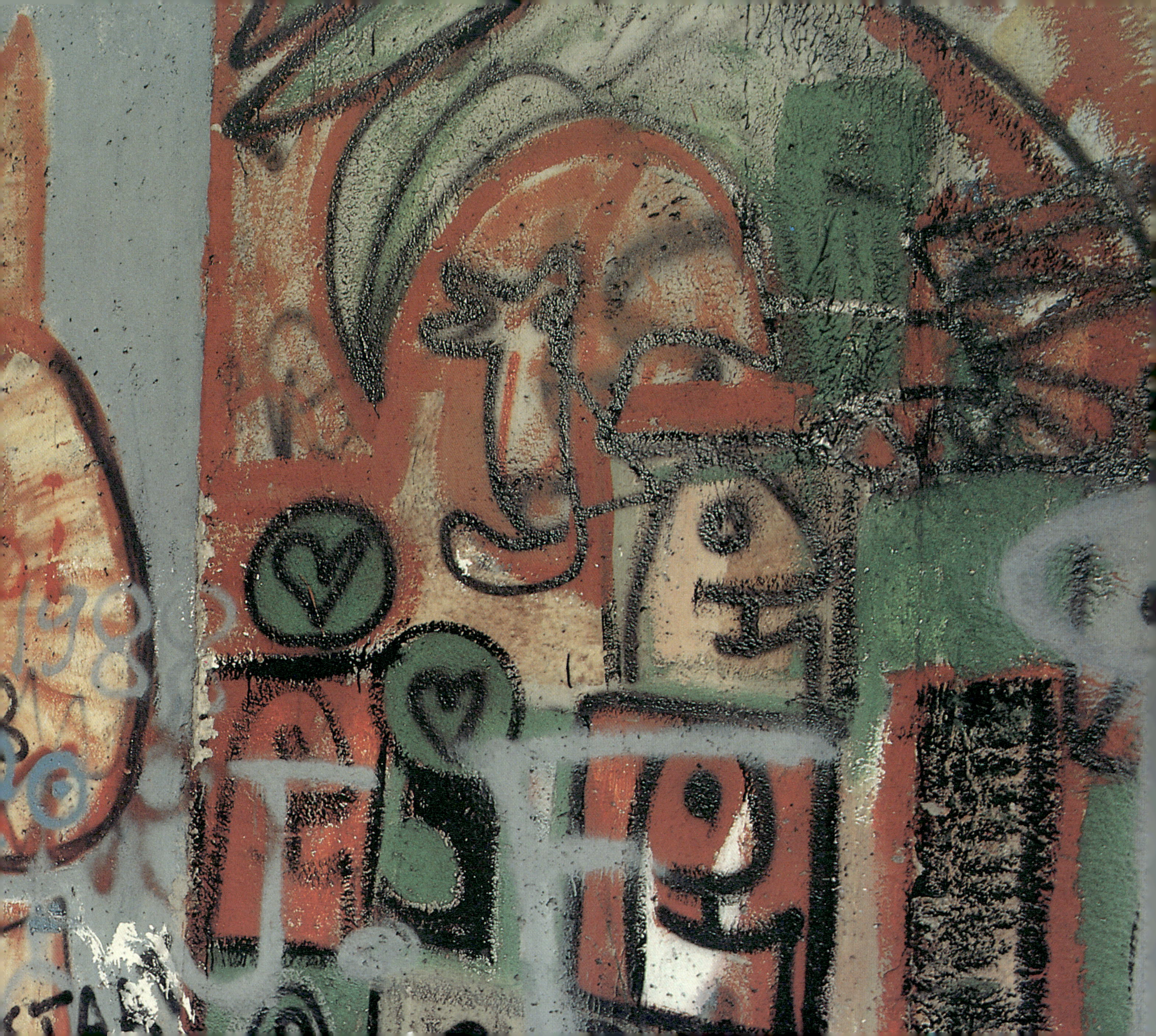

»Die Schmerzen hielt ich fast nicht mehr aus, Druck auf Hände und Füße, Atembeschwerden!« Liane Sündermann über ihre 55 Fluchtminuten im Gestänge des Beifahrersitzes eines Austin Mini. Fluchtauto mit Gliederpuppe in Fluchtstellung, befindet sich jetzt im Museum Haus am Checkpoint Charlie.

"I almost couldn't stand the pain anymore, with pressure on my hands and feet, and the breathing difficulties!" Liane Sündermann talking about the 55 minutes of her escape hidden inside the passenger seat of an Austin Mini. The escape car with a marionette in Sündermann's escape position can now be seen in the Haus am Checkpoint Charlie museum.

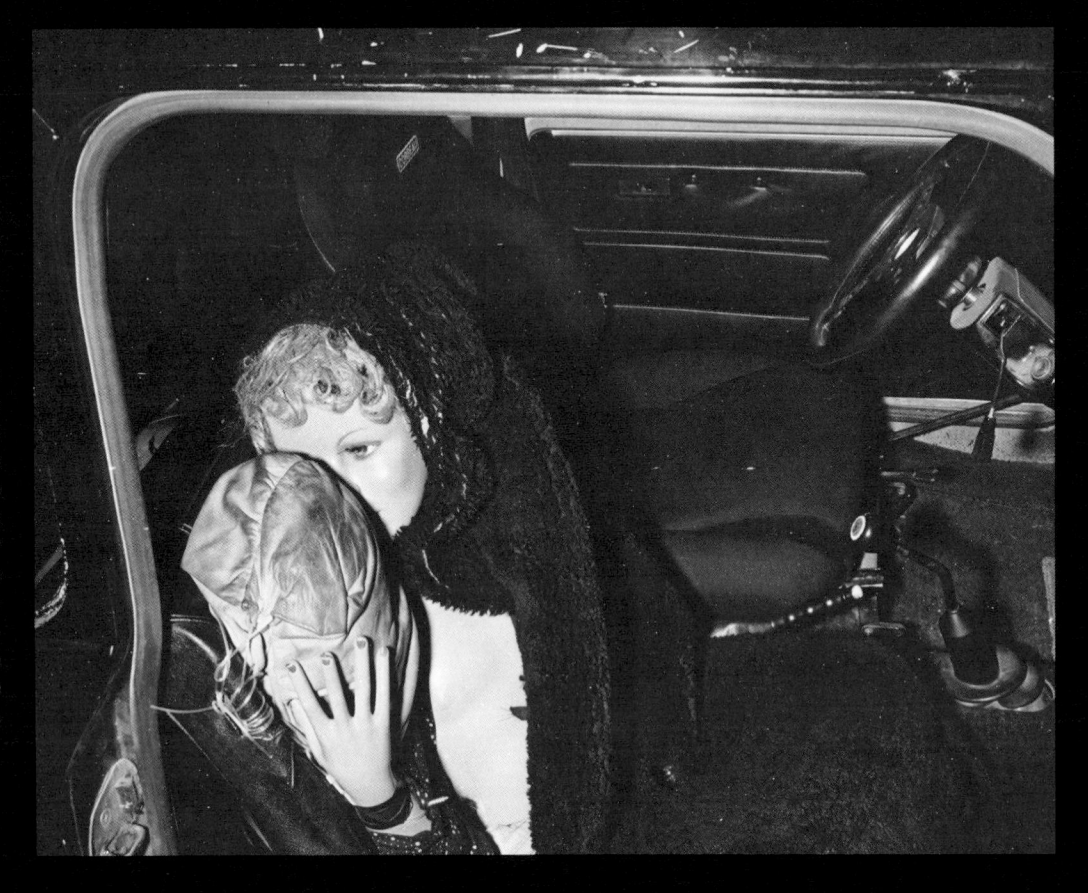

»‚Schatz, zieh dich schwarz an!' sagte mein Freund Georg zu mir, das war am 28. Mai 1988, unserem Fluchttag«, berichtet Liane Sündermann. Schwarz als Tarnfarbe passend zu den Schonüberzügen des Beifahrersitzes im Austin Mini, in dessen ausgehöhltem Sitzgestänge Liane versteckt wurde. Liane am Fluchtort, Grenzübergang Invalidenstraße, am 6. Dezember 1989, bei leichtem Schneegestöber und 18 Monate nach »Grenzübertritt«.

"'Dear, dress yourself in black!' my friend George told me. That was on May 28th, 1988, our day of escape," reported Liane Sündermann. Black camouflage was a fitting colour for the dark upholstery in the Austin Mini, in whose hollowed out passenger seat Liane was hidden. 18 months after her "border crossing", Liane, during light snow flurries on December 6th, 1989, stands at Checkpoint Invalidenstraße where she escaped.

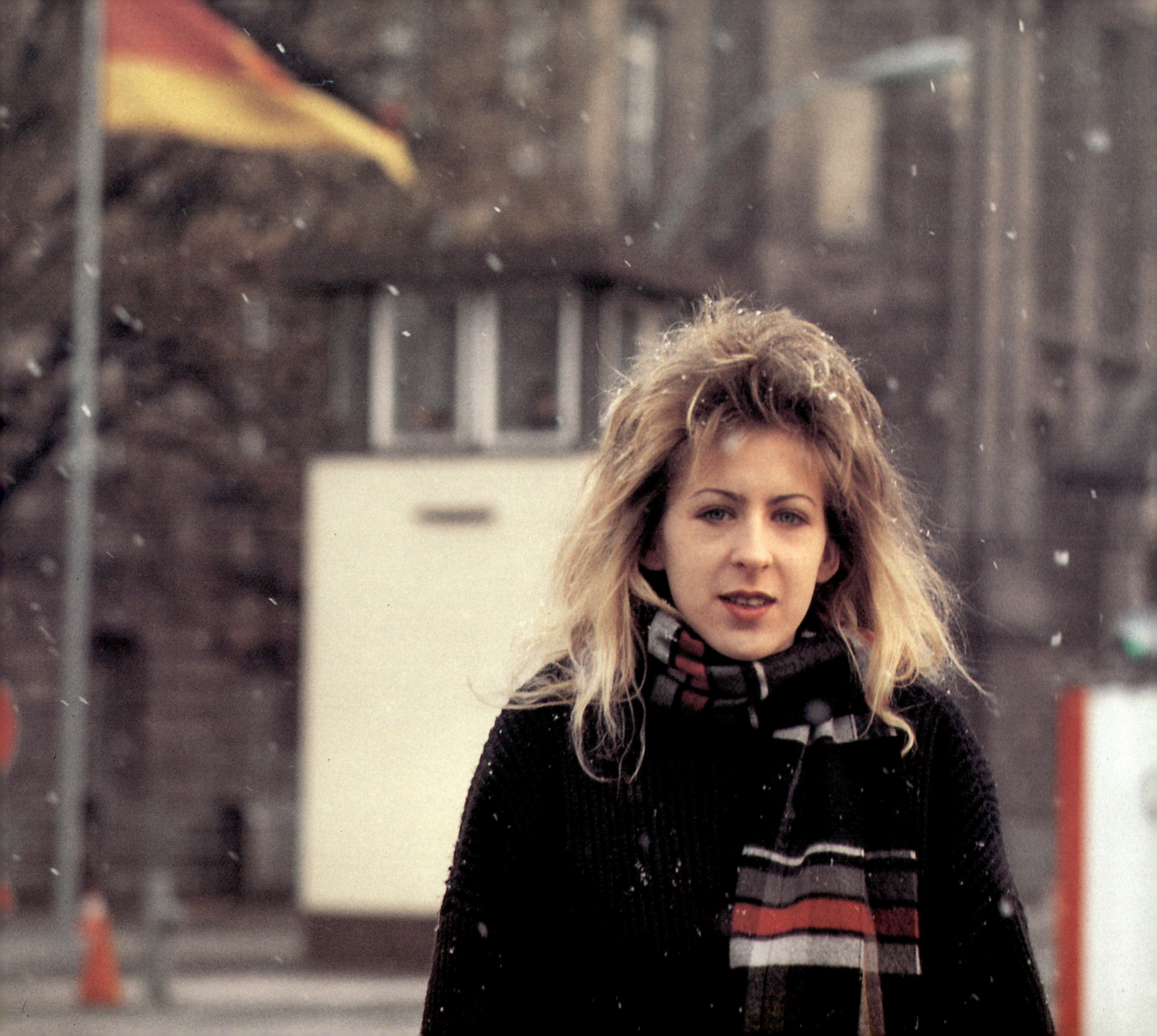

»Hommage à Kafka: Balkone für das Nichts«. Vermauerte Ostfassaden, davor Gedenkkreuz für Maueropfer. Bernauer Straße, 1961.

"Homage to Kafka: Balconies for nothing". Walled up Eastern façades. In front, the memorial crosses for victims of the wall. Bernauer Straße, 1961.

Nächste Doppelseite: »Fahnen im Wind«. Historischer »Austausch des Flaggengrußes« zwischen der DDR-Fahne am Brandenburger Tor und der bundesdeutschen Fahne am alten Reichstagsgebäude, aus der Fernsicht kein Unterschied!

Following pages: "Flags in the wind". Historical "exchange of flag salutes" between the GDR flag at the Brandenburg Gate and the West German flag at the old Parliament building; from a distance there's no difference!

»Ritze, Ratze ...« Jugendliche »Mauerspechte« bei der

Kommunistische Widerstands-
kämpferin, 1944 im KZ
Ravensbrück ermordet.

Niederkirchnerstraße

8 - 9

Wilhelmstraße

98-107

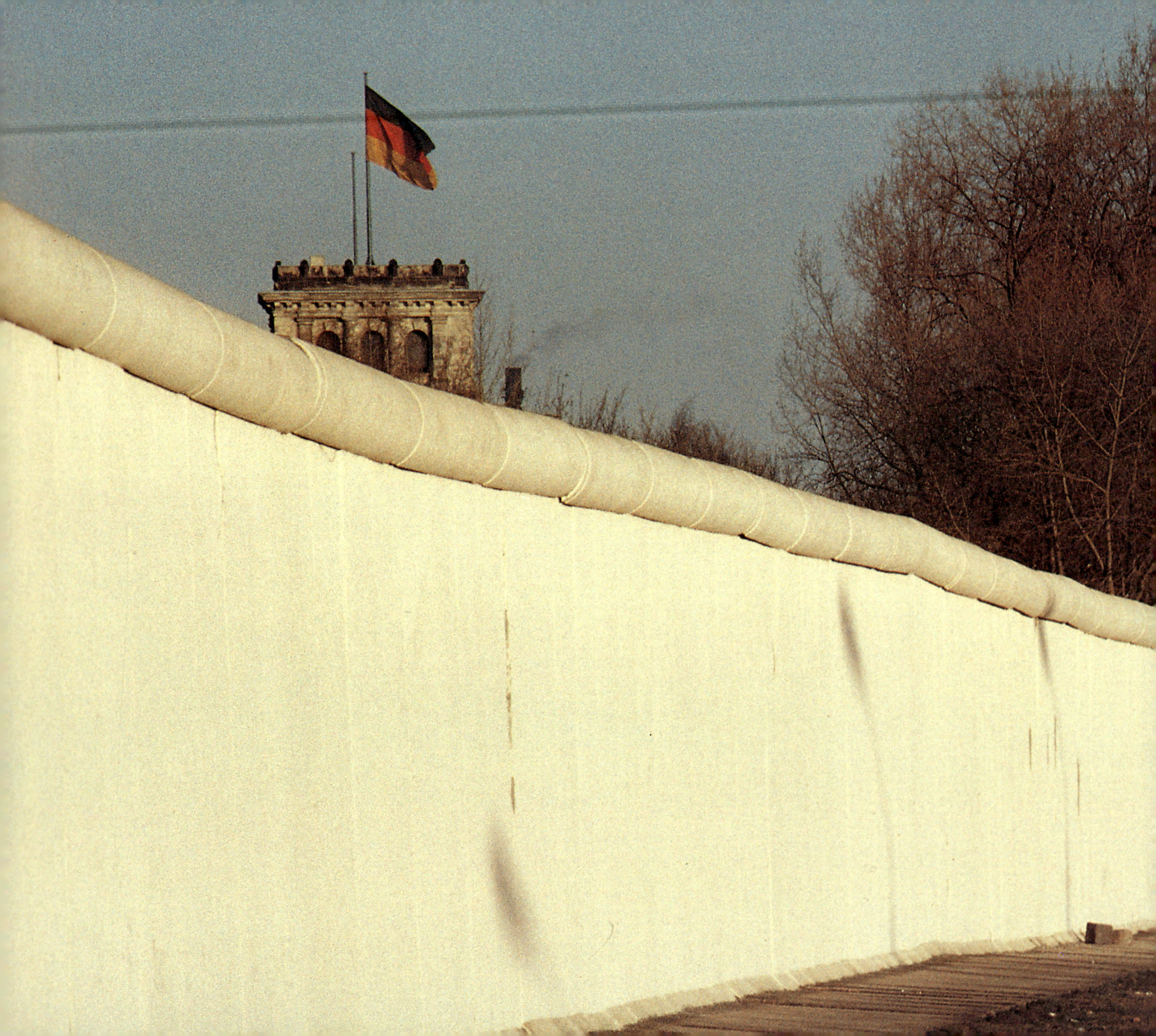

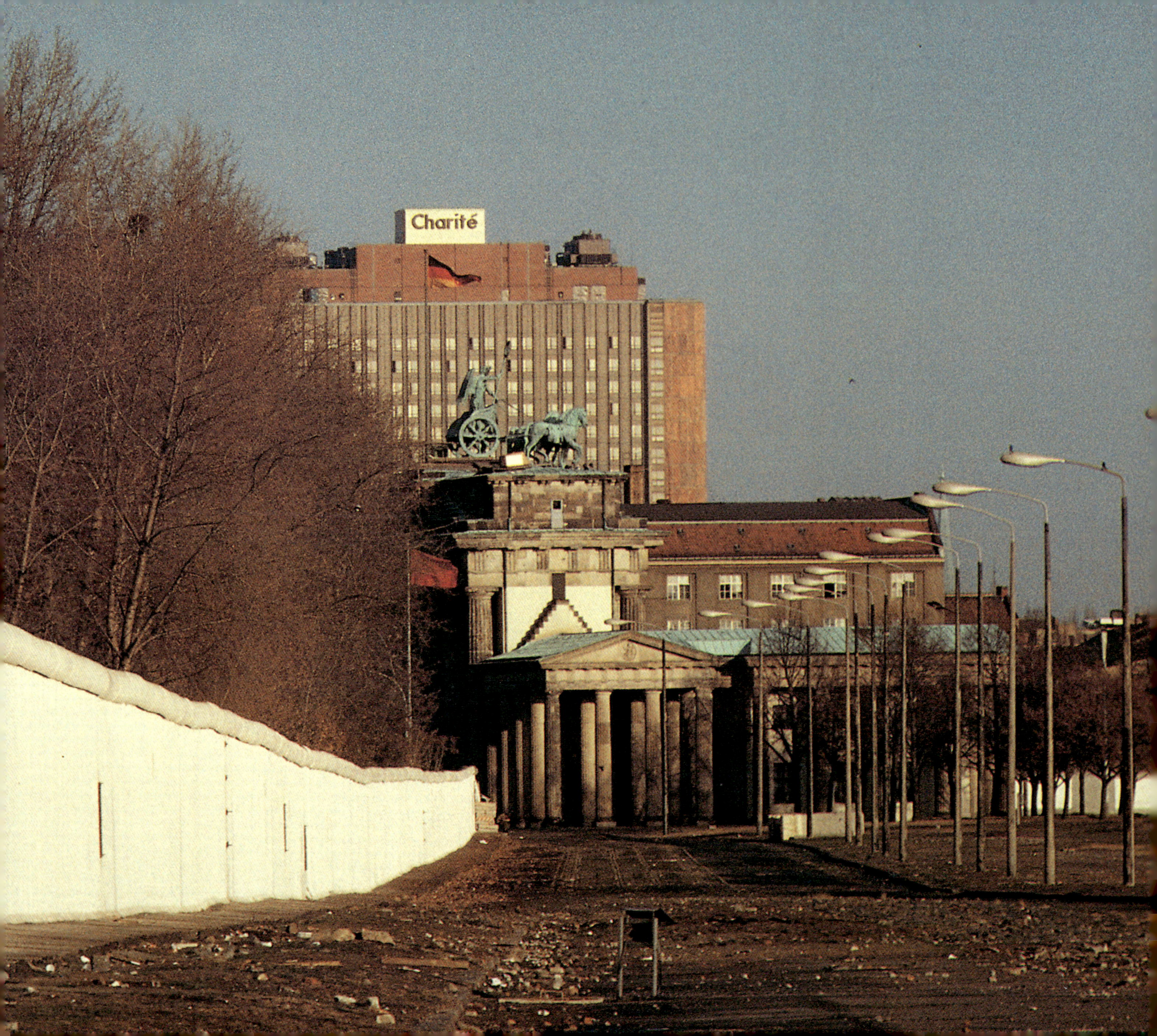
Charité

Mit diesen Plakaten demonstrierte das Ehepaar Karin und Werner Nuthmann auf dem Ostberliner Alexanderplatz. Nach kurzzeitiger Festnahme gestattete man ihnen die Ausreise nach West-Berlin, wo dann dieses Bild entstand. 1974.

Karin and Werner Nuthmann demonstrated with these placards at Alexanderplatz in East Berlin. After a short arrest they were given permission to go to the West, where this photograph was made. 1974.

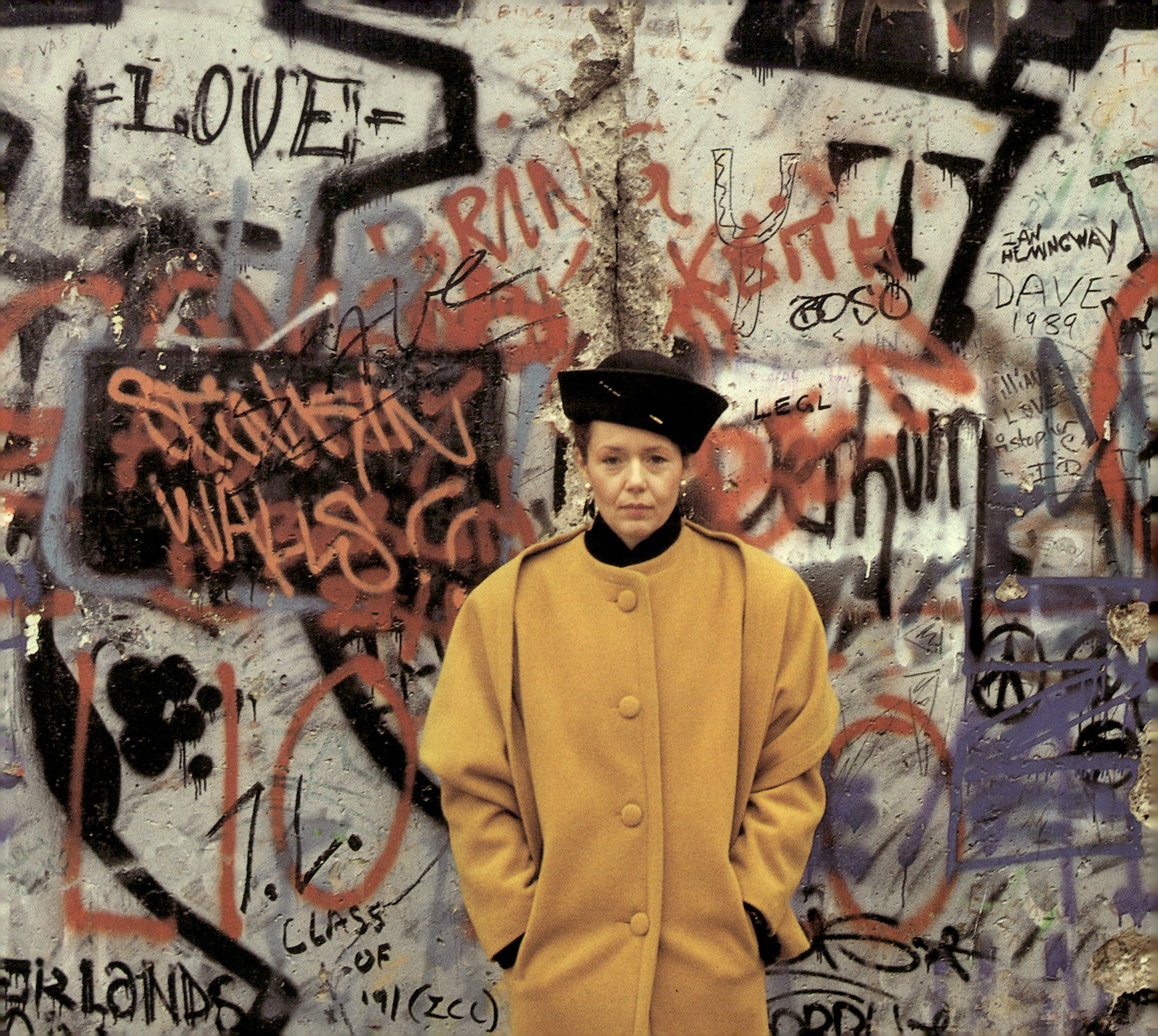
LOVE
KEITH
IAN HEMINGWAY
DAVE
1989
LEGL
CLASS
OF

»Verhängt das Paradies!«
Genosse Ulbricht läßt das Brandenburger Tor verhängen, um Präsident Kennedy bei dessen Berlin-Besuch Einblicke in das Arbeiter- und Bauernparadies zu verwehren. *Bild-Zeitung*, 26. Juni 1963, Titelseite.

"Cover up paradise!" Comrade Ulbricht has curtains hung behind the Brandenburg Gate so that President Kennedy, when he visits Berlin, can't see the workers' and farmers' paradise. *Bild-Zeitung*, June 26th, 1963, front page.

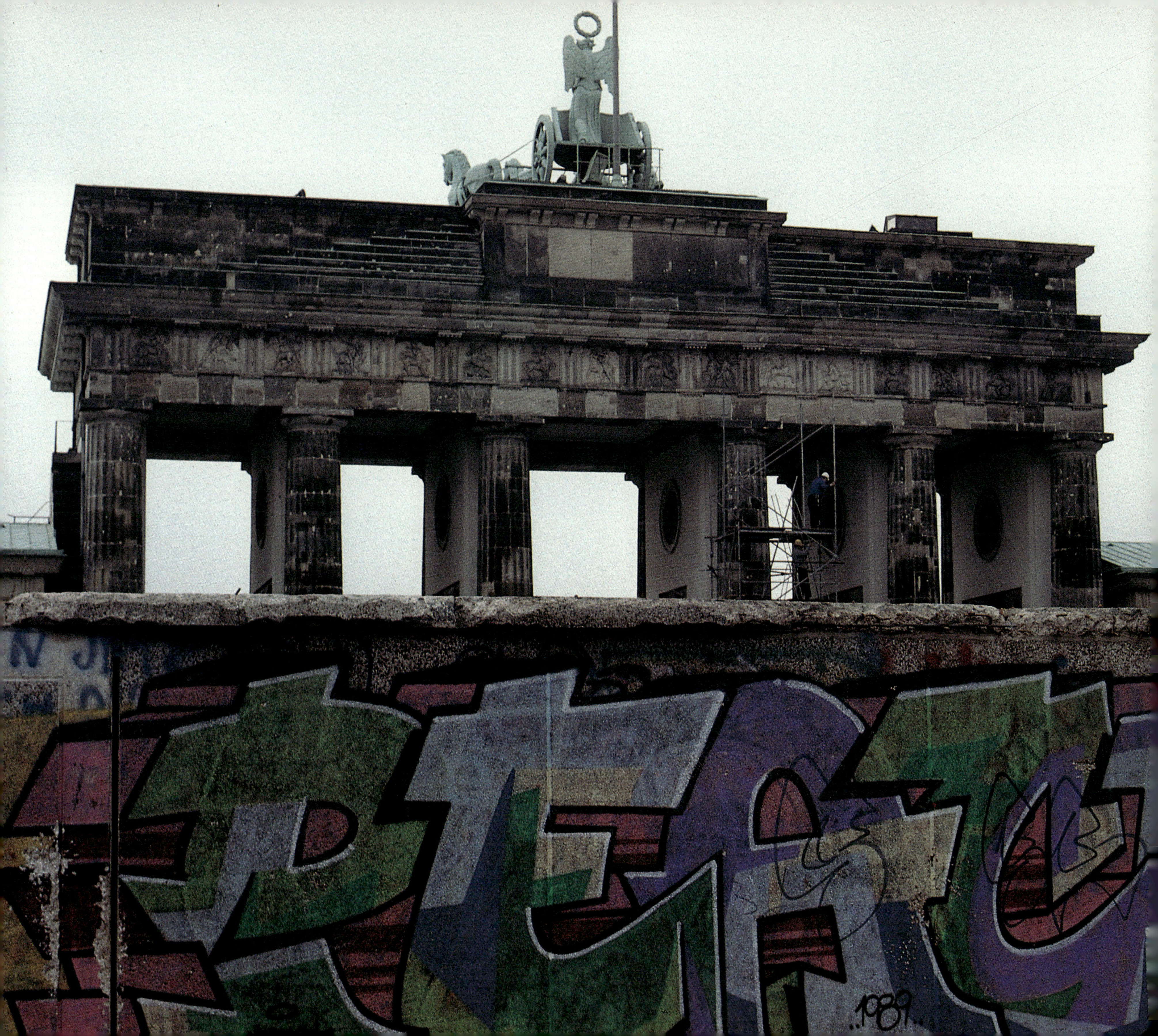
1989

Weihnachten 1963. Plakat der Gesamtdeutschen Hilfe.

Christmas 1963. Poster of the Gesamtdeutsche Hilfe asking people to send "Letters — Packages — Parcels over there."

»Bei Kerzenschein«. Blick über die Mauer auf Wachturm mit Soldat und brennender Kerze.

"By candle light". View over the wall of an observation tower with a soldier and a burning candle.

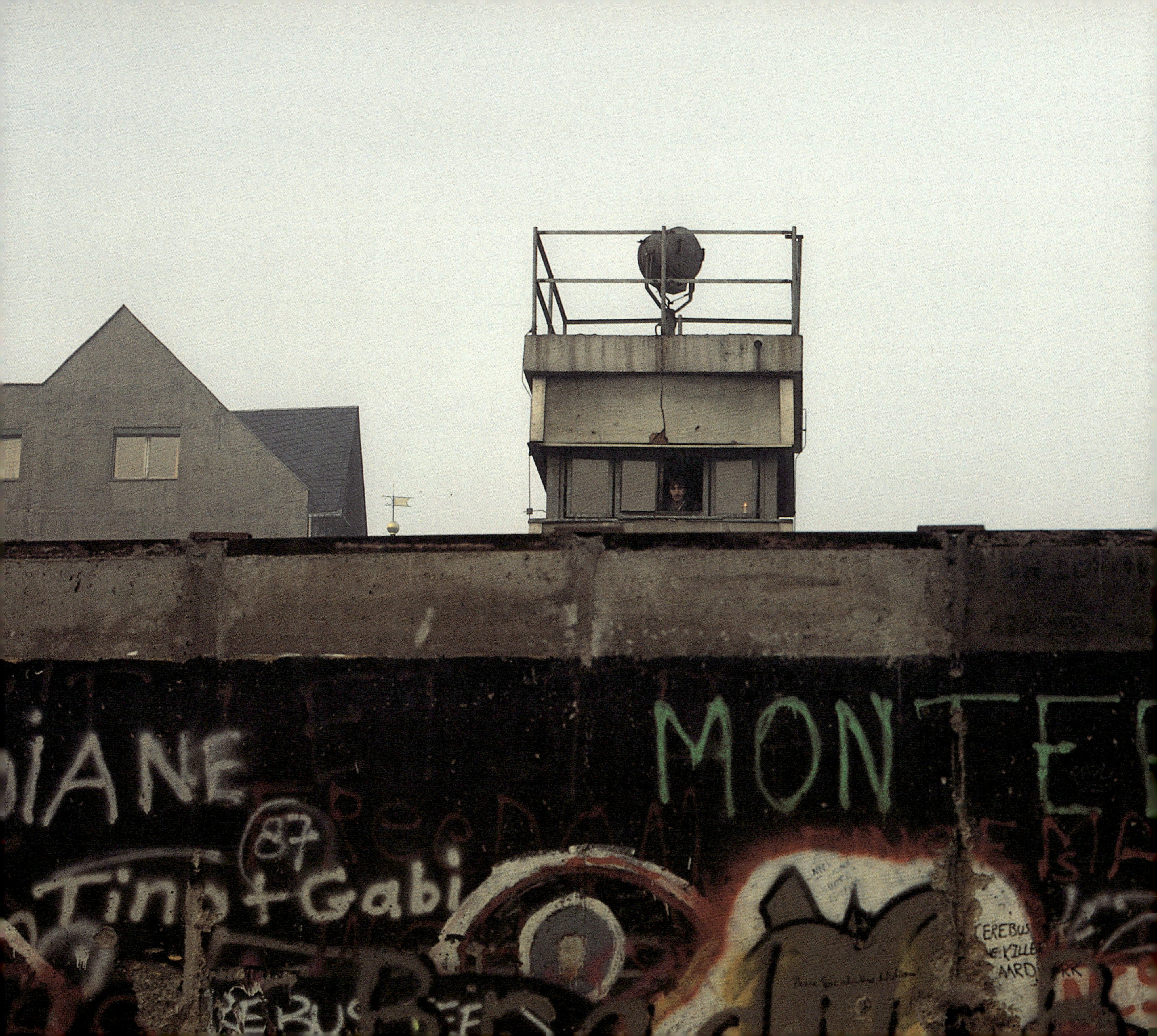
DIANE
MONTE
87
Gabi

»Zum Wohl!« Vermauerung des Portals einer Weinstube durch Soldaten der Grenztruppen. Sebastianstraße, 1964.

"To your health!" Walling up the entrance of a wine tavern by soldiers of the border troops. Sebastianstraße, 1964.

KNOCK IT DOWN

»Der Rutsch aus dem ... Paradies«. Über diese Abseilanlage, die in einen Tunnel unter ein Haus der Bernauer Straße führt, gelang 57 Personen im Oktober 1964 die Flucht in die Freiheit.

"The slide out of paradise". Over this cable construction that leads through a tunnel beneath a house on Bernauer Straße, 57 people were able to escape into freedom in October 1964.

Nächste Doppelseite: »Wird die Mauer im Nebel der Geschichte verschwinden?« Vorweihnachtsstimmung 1989 an der Mauer.

Following pages: "Will the wall disappear in the fog of history?" Christmas spirit at the wall, 1989.

»Da haben wir uns abgeseilt.« Familie Klein über dem Fluchtort in der Bernauer Straße am 5. Dezember 1989.

"There is where we slide down." The Klein family at their place of escape on Bernauer Straße on December 5th, 1989.

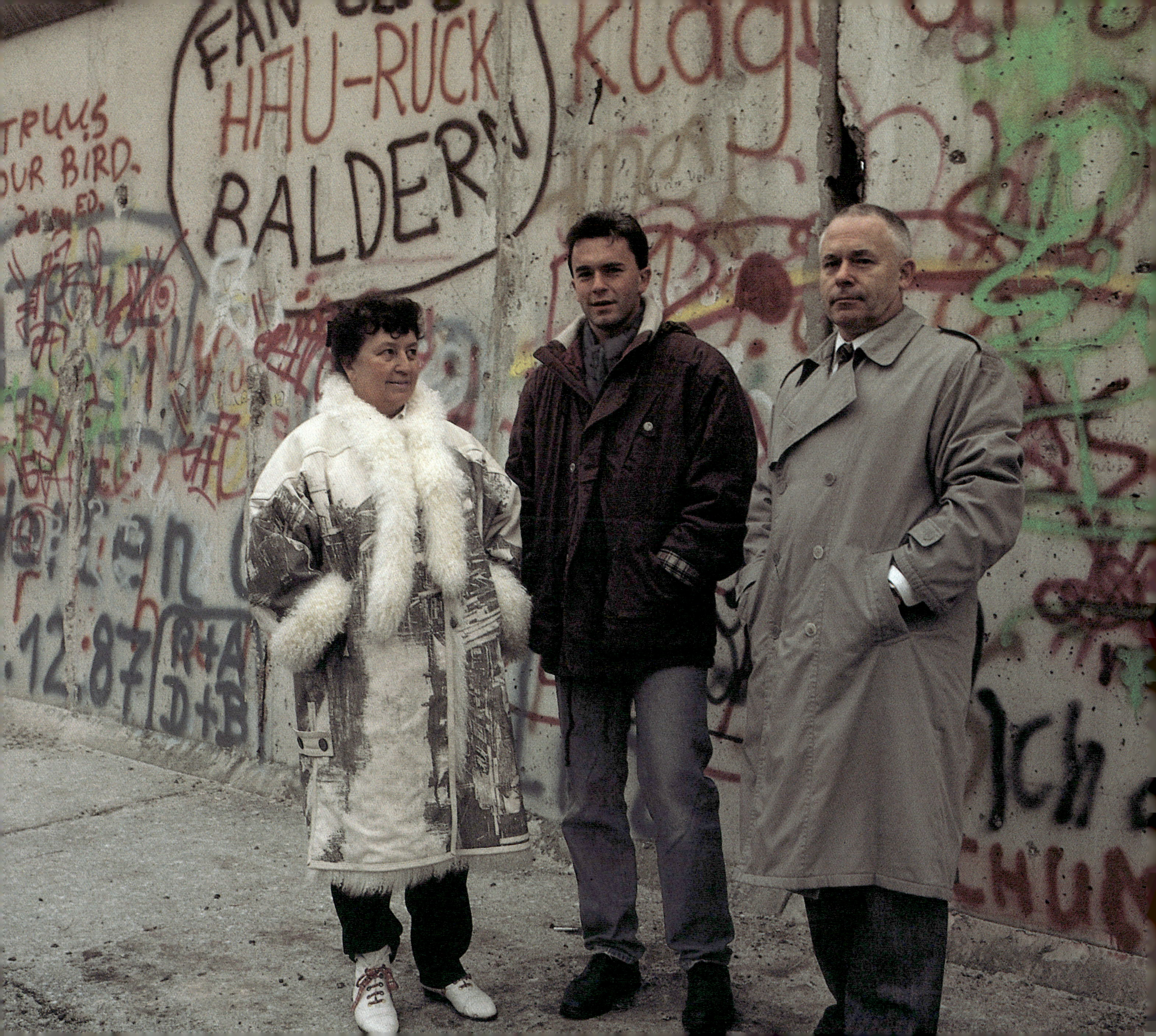
HAU-RUCK
OUR BIRD.
.12.87
R+A
D+B
Ich

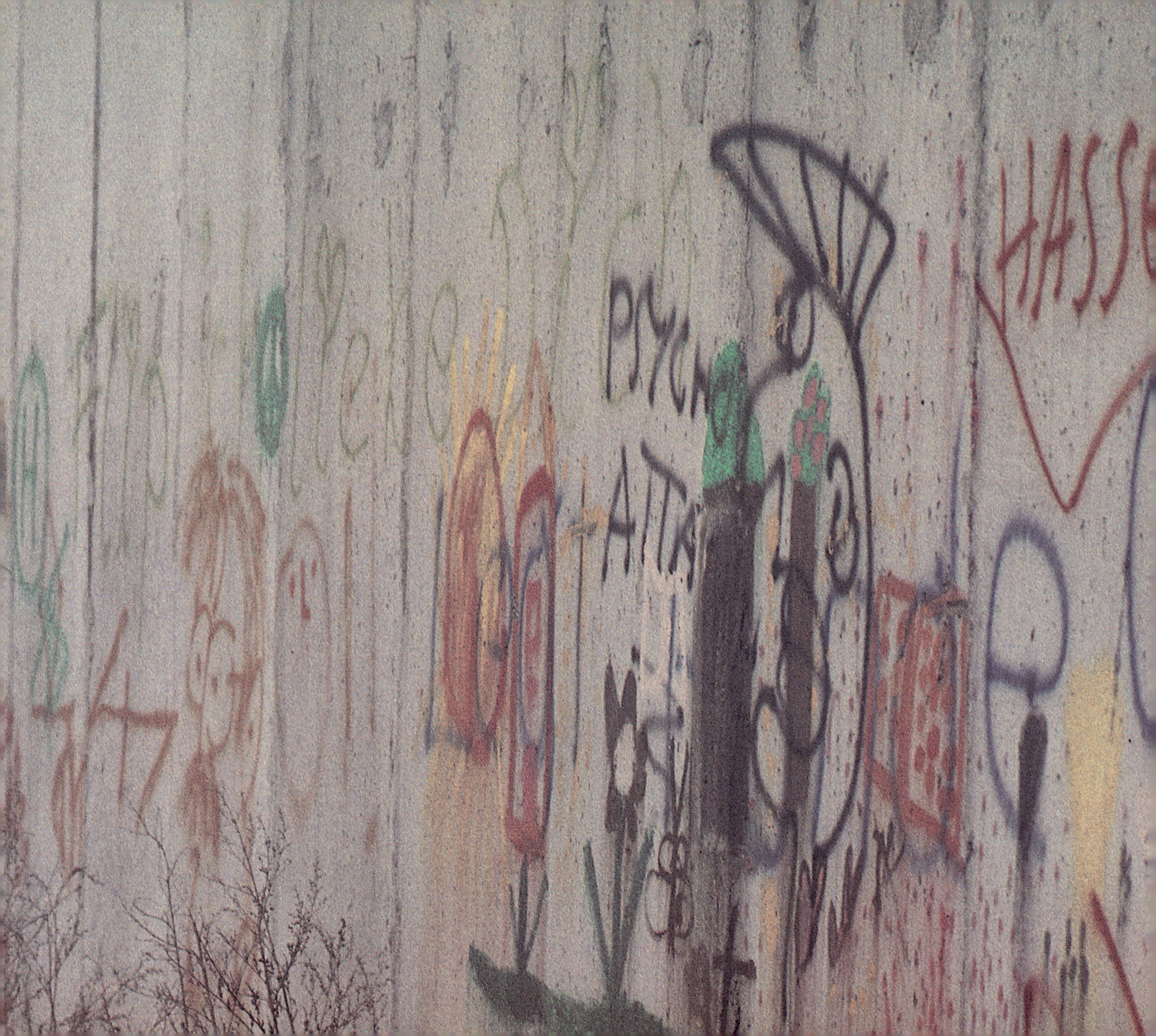

»It's bloody thick ...!!« Der Regierende Bürgermeister Willy Brandt und der US-Justizminister Robert F. Kennedy am Potsdamer Platz, 1962.

"It's bloody thick ...!" The Governing Mayor Willy Brandt and the US Minister of Justice Robert F. Kennedy at Potsdamer Platz, 1962.

»Ringel-ringel-Reihen« oder »Hinweistafel für Westberliner Kreisverkehr«.

"Ring around the roses" or "Traffic sign for circular traffic in West Berlin".

BERLINER STADT-RUNDFAHRT

»Public Relations«.
Elsenstraße, 1962.

"Public Relations".
Elsenstraße, 1962.

»Der Weg in die Freiheit ist steinig und liegt im Bereich des Schießbefehls.« Kontrollpunkt Friedrichstraße, Grenzübergang für Ausländer und Diplomaten. Blick auf Mauer der 3. Generation (einfache Betonplatten) und Todesstreifen. 1977.

"The way to freedom is rocky and puts you in danger of being shot." Checkpoint Friedrichstraße, border crossing for foreigners and diplomats. View of the wall of the 3rd generation (simple concrete panels) and the death strip. 1977.

Nächste Doppelseite (links): »Mauerdichtung: Tear down the wall, and all the others will fall.« Gereimtes Aufbegehren.

Following pages (left): "Wall poetry". Tear down the wall, and all the others will fall. Rhyming revolt.

Nächste Doppelseite (rechts): »Übermalt ...« Zitat: »Irgendwie haben sie doch gedacht, die mögen noch so schön daherkommen, aber es ist der Klassenfeind, und dem ist nicht zu trauen.« (*Der Spiegel* im Gespräch mit DDR-Dramatiker Heiner Müller.

Following pages (right): "Painted over ..." Quotation: "Somehow they thought that though seem to be nice people, they are still the enemy of the working class, and they are not to be trusted." (Der Spiegel in an interview with GDR dramatist Heiner Müller.

»Der Kater auf dem heißen Blechdach«. Falk Mühlbach, Elektronikfacharbeiter aus Lichtenberg bei Dresden, kletterte über die Dächer und flüchtete dann über den Kontrollpunkt Friedrichstraße.

"Cat on a hot tin roof". Falk Mühlbach, Electrician from Lichtenberg near Dresden, climbed over the roofs and then fled over the checkpoint at Friedrichstraße.

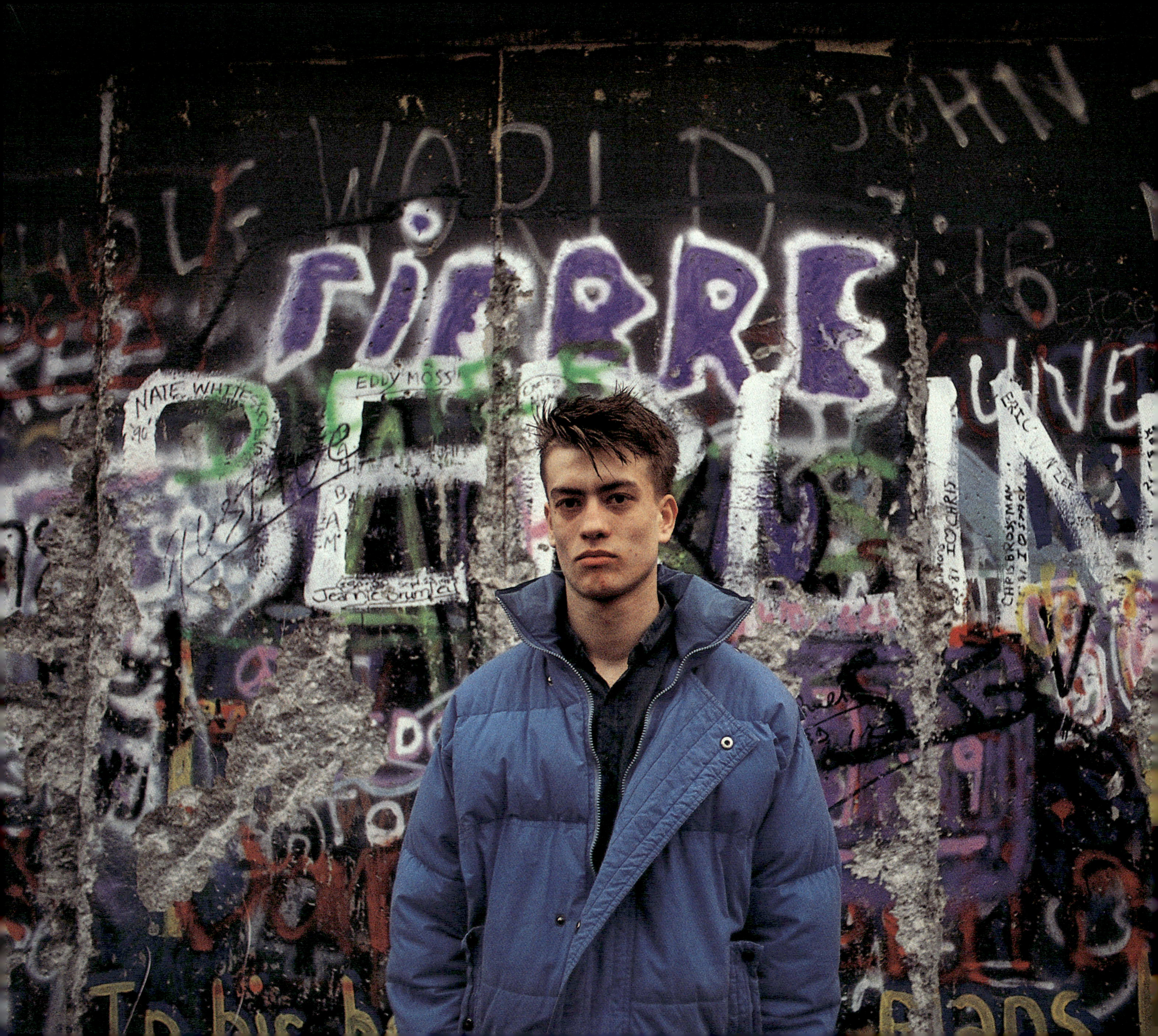
JOHN
Pierre
EDDY MÖSS
CHRIS BROSSMAN

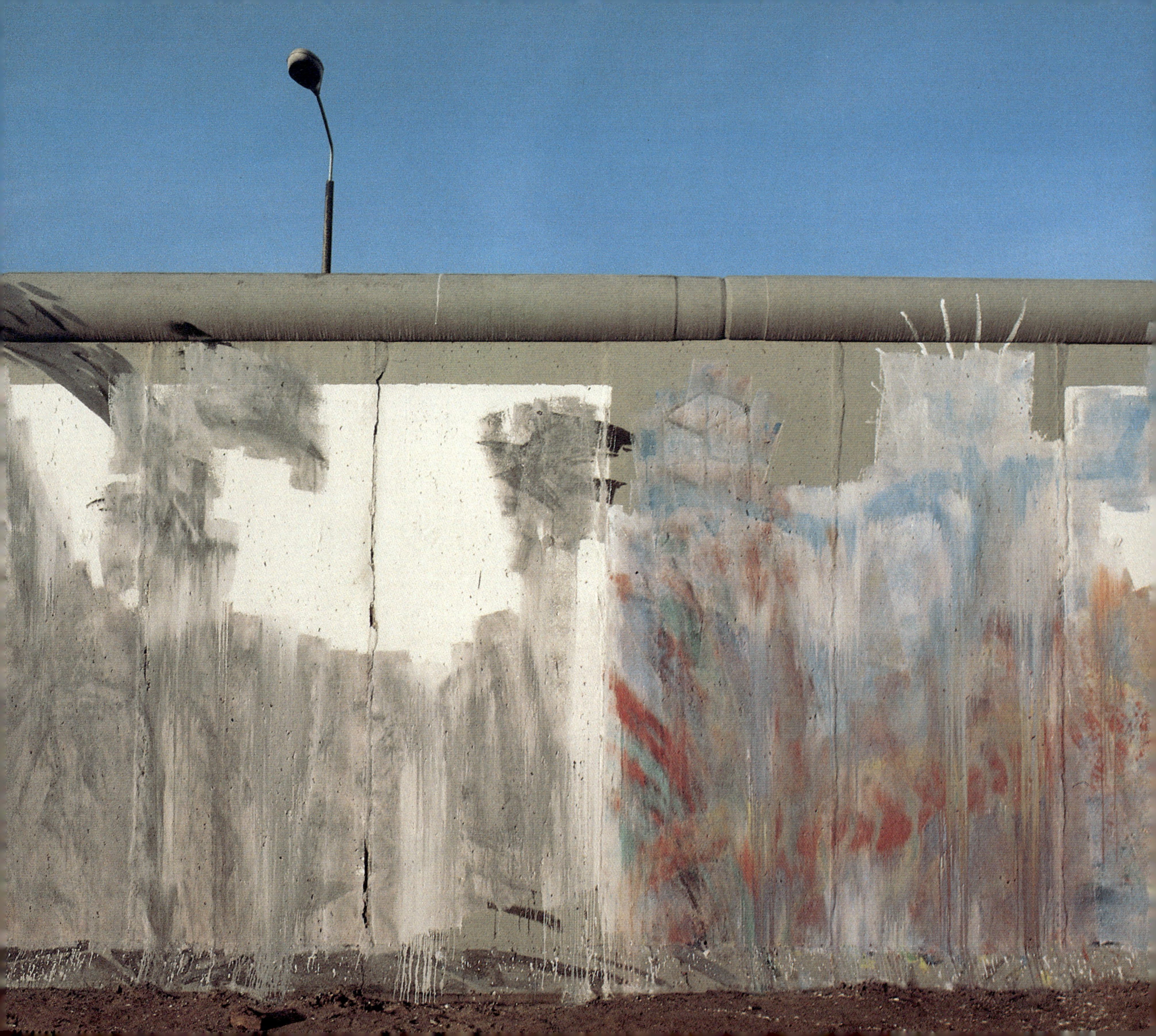

»Sie ist (fast) weg!«
BZ, 10. November 1989,
Titelseite.

"It is (almost) gone!" *B.Z.*, November 10th, 1989, headline. "The wall is gone."

Die Mauer ist weg!

JEDER darf ab sofort durch!
Deutschland weint vor Freude.
Die ersten sind schon da!
Wir reichen uns die Hände!

B.Z.

Nr. 263/45 · 113. Jahr / Freitag, 10. November 1989 · A 2032 A
Die größte Zeitung Berlins

60 Pf

Berlin ist wieder Berlin!

Alle DDR-Grenzen zum Bundesgebiet offen – und alle Übergänge nach West-Berlin offen!

Berlin, 10. November. Die Mauer ist nach 28 Jahren symbolisch verschwunden. Die DDR öffnet ab sofort alle Berlin-Übergänge und Grenzen ins Bundesgebiet. Die ersten Besucher sind schon da!

MOSAIK, ab 14,–/qm!

ATALA BAD & WOHNEN

VILLEROY & BOCH

ICH WAR DABEI AM 9.11.

»Ende des Kalten Krieges«. Demontage des Checkpoint Charlie: Feierstunde der Außenminister von BRD, DDR und den vier Siegermächten des Zweiten Weltkriegs in der Friedrichstraße. Nach deren Ansprachen wird die Kontrollbaracke mit einem Kran von der Straßenmitte entfernt. 22. Juni 1990

"End of the Cold War". Dismantling Checkpoint Charlie: The hour of celebration at Friedrichstraße for the Foreign Ministers of West Germany, East Germany and the four victorious forces of World War II. After their speeches the control barracks were removed from the middle of the street with a crane. June 22nd, 1990.

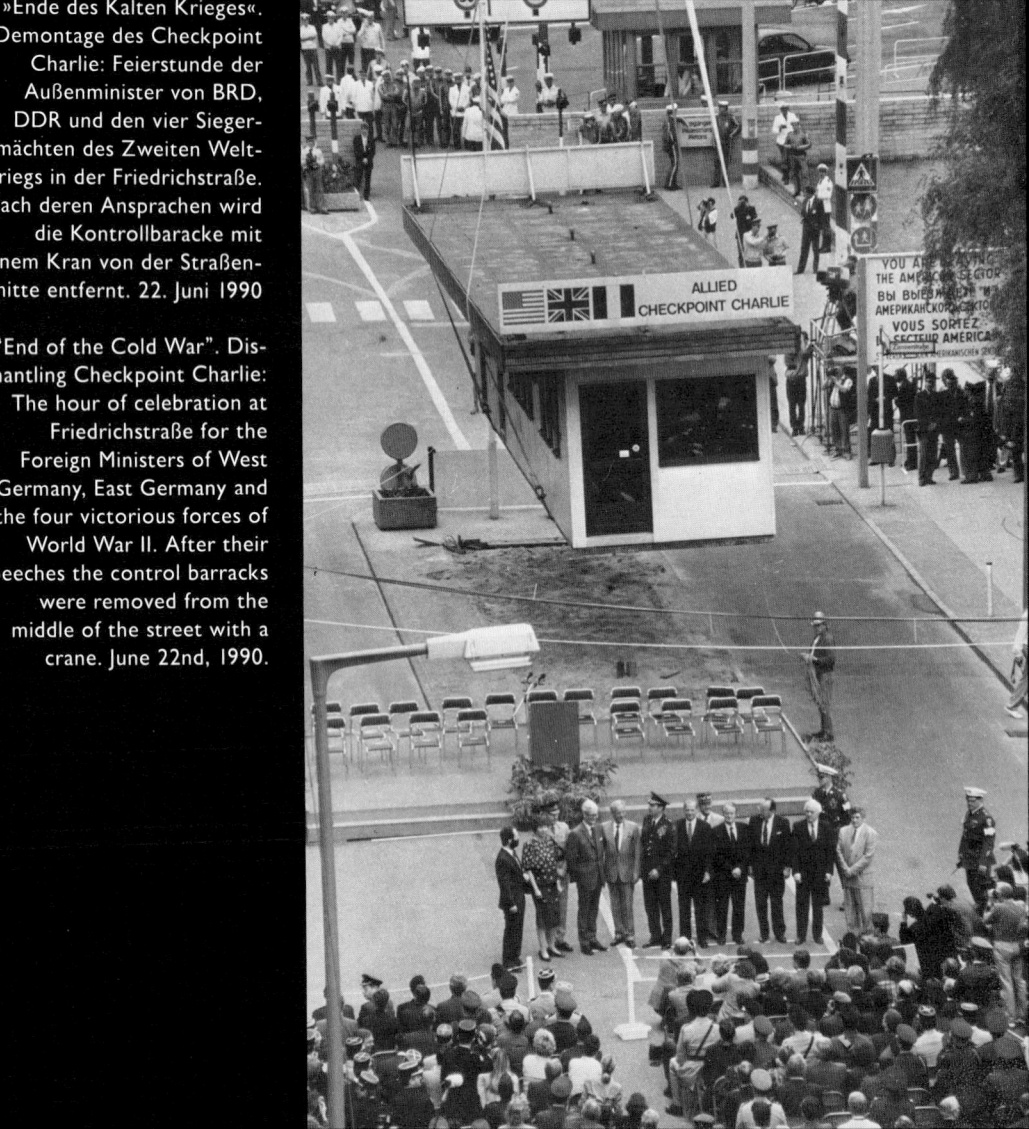

CHARLIE'S RETIRED 10. NOV. 1989

Hans-Jürgen Dyck, Haus am Checkpoint Charlie, Berlin
**Chronologie der Berliner Mauer
im Rahmen des Weltgeschehens, 1961–1990**

Berliner Mauer

1961

15. Juni
Der DDR-Staatsratsvorsitzende Walter Ulbricht verlangt auf der Grundlage des sowjetischen Deutschland-Memorandums vom 4. Juni (Ankündigung eines separaten Friedensvertrages zwischen der UdSSR und der DDR und damit volle Souveränitätsrechte der DDR über die Zufahrtswege nach West-Berlin) eine Neutralisierung West-Berlins und erklärt:
»Niemand hat die Absicht, eine Mauer zu errichten.«

13. August
Beginn des Mauerbaus; bewaffnete Verbände der DDR riegeln Ost-Berlin mit Stacheldraht und Straßensperren ab. Seit Jahresbeginn sind 155.402 Personen aus Ost-Berlin und der DDR geflüchtet.

15. August
Der erste Volksarmist springt in der Bernauer Straße im Bezirk Wedding über den Stacheldraht in den Westen. Sein Photo geht um die Welt.

19.–21. August
Der amerikanische Vizepräsident Lyndon B. Johnson besucht Bonn und West-Berlin. Johnson bekräftigt die Entschlossenheit der USA, die Freiheit West-Berlins zu verteidigen.

23. August
Die DDR verbietet Westberlinern das Betreten von Ost-Berlin.

24. August
Erstmals wird ein Flüchtling bei dem Versuch, durch den Humboldthafen nach West-Berlin zu schwimmen, von Volkspolizisten erschossen.

23. Oktober
Das Innenministerium der DDR verfügt, daß Mitglieder der amerikanischen Militärmission in Zivil sich gegenüber der Volkspolizei auszuweisen haben. Daraufhin lassen die Amerikaner am 25. Oktober Panzer auffahren und erzwingen den unkontrollierten Zugang.

Weltgeschehen

1961

3./4. Juni
Treffen zwischen US-Präsident John F. Kennedy und dem sowjetischen Ministerpräsidenten Nikita Chruschtschow in Wien.

15. Dezember
Der SS-Obersturmbannführer Adolf Eichmann wird in Jerusalem wegen Verbrechen gegen die Menschlichkeit zum Tode verurteilt und am 31. Mai 1962 hingerichtet.

1962

16./17. Juni
In dem »Nationalen Dokument« der Nationalen Front in der DDR wird der Grundsatz der Zweistaatlichkeit bekräftigt.

19. Juni
In Ost-Berlin wird mit dem Bau einer zweiten Sperrmauer hinter der bisherigen Mauer begonnen, wodurch auch in Berlin ein sogenannter »Todesstreifen« entsteht.

17. August
Der Ostberliner Bauarbeiter Peter Fechter wird bei dem Versuch, über die Mauer zu flüchten, von Grenzsoldaten der DDR angeschossen und verblutet, ohne daß ihm Hilfe geleistet wird.

1963

Juni
Schikanen durch DDR-Behörden im Straßenverkehr nach West-Berlin.

21. Juni
Maßnahmen der DDR-Regierung zur Errichtung eines »Grenzgebiets« zwischen DDR und West-Berlin.

26. Juni
US-Präsident John F. Kennedy besucht West-Berlin und wird von der Bevölkerung begeistert gefeiert.

28. Juni — 4. Juli
Der sowjetische Parteichef Nikita Chruschtschow besucht die DDR aus Anlaß des 70. Geburtstags von Walter Ulbricht.

15. Juli
Der SPD-Politiker Egon Bahr formuliert in Tutzing (Bayern) seine Thesen vom »Wandel durch Annäherung« für die Beziehungen zwischen der Bundesrepublik Deutschland und der DDR.

Juli bis September
Erneut Schikanen durch DDR-Behörden auf den Interzonen-Autobahnen nach West-Berlin.

1962

18. März
Waffenstillstand in Algerien; am 3. Juli proklamiert Frankreich die Unabhängigkeit des Landes.

22. Oktober
Beginn der Kuba-Krise; US-Präsident John F. Kennedy protestiert gegen die Errichtung sowjetischer Raketenbasen auf Kuba, am 24. Oktober verhängen die Amerikaner eine Seeblockade und erreichen am 28. Oktober ein Einlenken des sowjetischen Ministerpräsidenten Nikita Chruschtschow. Die Welt stand am Rande eines atomaren Krieges.

26. Oktober
Die »*Spiegel*-Affäre« (Verdacht des Geheimnisverrats) erregt die bundesdeutsche Öffentlichkeit, der *Spiegel*-Verleger Rudolf Augstein und weitere Mitarbeiter werden festgenommen.

1963

22. Januar
Deutsch-französischer Freundschaftsvertrag wird von Bundeskanzler Konrad Adenauer und dem französischen Staatspräsidenten Charles de Gaulle unterzeichnet.

19. Juni
US-Präsident John F. Kennedy stellt sein Programm zur Lösung der Rassenprobleme vor.

5. August
Das von den USA, Großbritannien und der Sowjetunion unterzeichnete Atomteststoppabkommen verbietet Atomversuche in der Atmosphäre, im Weltraum und unter Wasser.

16. Oktober
Der Deutsche Bundestag wählt Ludwig Erhard als Nachfolger von Konrad Adenauer zum neuen Bundeskanzler.

18./19. Oktober
Sir Alec Douglas-Home wird nach dem Rücktritt von Harold Macmillan neuer britischer Premierminister.

22. November
US-Präsident John F. Kennedy wird in Dallas/Texas ermordet; sein Nachfolger wird der bisherige Vizepräsident Lyndon B. Johnson.

17. Dezember
Erstes Passierscheinabkommen zwischen dem Westberliner Senat und der DDR.

1964

2. Januar
In der DDR werden neue Personalausweise mit dem Vermerk »Bürger der Deutschen Demokratischen Republik« ausgegeben.

13. März
Auf Anweisung des Staatssekretärs für Hoch- und Fachschulwesen wird der Regimekritiker Prof. Robert Havemann von seinen »Verpflichtungen entbunden« (=Verlust seines Lehrstuhles für Physikalische Chemie an der Ostberliner Humboldt-Universität).

12. Juni
Die Sowjetunion und die DDR unterzeichnen einen Vertrag über Freundschaft, gegenseitigen Beistand und Zusammenarbeit. Darin wird West-Berlin als »selbständige politische Einheit« bezeichnet.

24. September
Zweites Passierscheinabkommen unterzeichnet: Nach dieser Vereinbarung können Westberliner in der Zeit vom 30. Oktober bis 12. November 1964 einmal, vom 19. Dezember 1964 bis 3. Januar 1965 zweimal und zu Ostern und Pfingsten 1965 je einmal Verwandte in Ost-Berlin besuchen.

4./5. Oktober
Die größte Massenflucht: 57 Personen gelingt es, durch einen Tunnel in den Westteil der Stadt zu flüchten (Bernauer Straße, Bezirk Wedding).

2. November
DDR-Rentner dürfen erstmals wieder ihre Verwandten im Westen besuchen.

25. November
Die DDR-Regierung beschließt mit Wirkung vom 1. Dezember den Zwangsumtausch von DM-Beträgen in DDR-Mark für westliche Besucher.

1964

16. Februar
Willy Brandt wird auf einem außerordentlichen Parteitag der SPD zum neuen Vorsitzenden gewählt.

2. August
Im Golf von Tonking kommt es zu einem Feuergefecht zwischen nordvietnamesischen und US-Schiffen, wenige Tage später bombardieren amerikanische Kampfflugzeuge nordvietnamesische Flottenstützpunkte (Beginn des direkten militärischen Eingreifens der USA in Vietnam).

14. Oktober
Sturz von Nikita Chruschtschow; Leonid Breschnew wird neuer Parteichef.

15. Oktober
Die britischen Konservativen verlieren die Wahlen, Harold Wilson (Labour Party) wird neuer Premierminister.

1965

April
Wegen einer Sitzung des Deutschen Bundestages in West-Berlin werden die Straßen und Schienenwege nach West-Berlin teilweise gesperrt. Sowjetische und DDR-Düsenjäger veranstalten Störflüge über dem Westteil der Stadt.

5. Mai
Walter Ulbricht gibt eine Erklärung ab, in der es heißt, daß ein wiedervereinigtes Deutschland nur noch als ein sozialistisches Deutschland möglich ist.

8. Oktober
Das Internationale Olympische Komitee beschließt, zu den Olympischen Spielen 1968 erstmals zwei deutsche Mannschaften zuzulassen.

25. November
Das dritte Passierscheinabkommen über Verwandtenbesuche zum Jahreswechsel 1965/66 wird unterzeichnet.

1966

Erste Jahreshälfte
Briefwechsel und Gespräche zwischen der SPD und der SED über einen Redneraustausch. Am 29. Juni wird der Redneraustausch von der SED abgesagt.

7. März
Viertes Passierscheinabkommen für Ostern und Pfingsten.

1. April
Die Deutsche Akademie der Wissenschaften in Ost-Berlin gibt den Ausschluß von Professor Robert Havemann bekannt.

13. August
Fünfter Jahrestag des Mauerbaus, Militärparade der DDR-Grenztruppen und der SED-Kampfgruppen in Ost-Berlin.

1965

24. Januar
Tod von Sir Winston Churchill.

Februar
Der Vietnamkrieg nimmt an Intensität zu, Beginn des systematischen Luftkrieges durch die USA.

31. Juli
Die USA entsenden weitere 75.000 Soldaten nach Vietnam.

11. November
Die britische Kolonie Südrhodesien erklärt unter dem Ministerpräsidenten Ian Smith einseitig ihre Unabhängigkeit und weigert sich, Garantien für eine künftige Mehrheitsregierung aus Afrikanern abzugeben; Großbritannien verhängt wirtschaftliche Sanktionen.

1966

Januar
Nach kriegerischen Auseinandersetzungen beschließen Indien und Pakistan auf einer Friedenskonferenz, den Streit um Kaschmir friedlich zu regeln. Indira Gandhi wird indische Premierministerin.

29. März
Frankreich übergibt den Vertretern der NATO-Staaten ein Memorandum über den Beschluß, sich aus der NATO zurückzuziehen.

Mai
Ideologischer Beginn der »Großen Proletarischen Kulturrevolution« unter Mao Tse-tung in der Volksrepublik China, in deren Verlauf es zu schweren innenpolitischen Auseinandersetzungen kommt.

1. Dezember
Große Koalition zwischen CDU und SPD; Kurt Georg Kiesinger wird Bundeskanzler, Willy Brandt Vizekanzler und Außenminister.

6. Oktober
Unterzeichnung eines Übereinkommens über die Arbeit einer Passierscheinstelle für Härtefälle (dringende Familienangelegenheiten).

Weihnachten
Erstmals keine allgemeine Passierscheinregelung mehr zu den Feiertagen.

1967

20. Februar
Die Volkskammer beschließt ein »Gesetz über die Staatsbürgerschaft der DDR«. Mit diesem Gesetz wird eine eigene Staatsbürgerschaft der DDR eingeführt.

1. Dezember
Unter Vorsitz von Walter Ulbricht bildet die Volkskammer einen Ausschuß zur Ausarbeitung einer neuen sozialistischen Verfassung.

1967

19. April
Tod von Altbundeskanzler Konrad Adenauer.

21. April
Militärputsch in Griechenland; Georgios Papadopoulos wird während der darauffolgenden Militärdiktatur Ministerpräsident.

9. Mai
Die Außenminister der NATO-Staaten (ohne Frankreich) beschließen die Doktrin der »flexible response«.

30. Mai
Die Unabhängigkeitserklärung der Provinz Biafra führt zum Bürgerkrieg in Nigeria, der am 15. Januar 1970 mit der bedingungslosen Kapitulation Biafras endet.

2. Juni
Studentendemonstrationen bei dem Besuch des Schahs von Persien in West-Berlin; Benno Ohnesorg wird dabei von der Polizei erschossen.

5.–10. Juni
»Sechstagekrieg« im Nahen Osten; Israel besetzt West-Jordanien sowie Ost-Jerusalem, die Sinai-Halbinsel, den Gaza-Streifen und die Golan-Höhen.

Juli
Blutige Rassenkrawalle in mehreren Städten der USA.

9. Oktober
Ernesto (Che) Guevara wird in Bolivien erschossen.

1968

6. Januar
Die Sowjetunion protestiert gegen die Bundespräsenz in West-Berlin (Sitzungen der Bundestagsausschüsse und der Fraktionen sowie des Kabinetts in West-Berlin etc.).

6. April
In einem Volksentscheid stimmen 94,49 % der Wahlberechtigten für eine neue DDR-Verfassung, in der die »führende Rolle« der kommunistischen Partei festgeschrieben wird.

10./11. Juni
Einführung des Paß- und Visumzwanges für Transitreisende zwischen der Bundesrepublik und West-Berlin.

1968

Januar/Februar
Im Rahmen der Tet-Offensive des Vietkong wird auch die Kaiserstadt Hue besetzt; die Amerikaner verstärken ihre in Vietnam stehenden Truppen auf über 500.000 Mann. Im März stellen die USA die Bombenangriffe auf Nordvietnam vorläufig ein, im Laufe des Jahres verstärkt sich in den USA und weltweit der Protest gegen den Vietnamkrieg.

4. April
Der schwarze amerikanische Bürgerrechtler Martin Luther King, der 1964 für seinen gewaltlosen Kampf gegen die Rassentrennung in den USA den Friedensnobelpreis erhalten hatte, wird in Memphis ermordet.

Mai
Studentenunruhen und ein Generalstreik führen in Frankreich zu einer Staatskrise.

30. Mai
Der Deutsche Bundestag verabschiedet die Notstandsgesetze. Dies und der Krieg der USA in Vietnam sind die Hauptursachen für die das ganze Jahr anhaltenden Studentenunruhen.

6. Juni
Der amerikanische Senator Robert F. Kennedy wird in Los Angeles ermordet.

1. Juli
Der Atomwaffensperrvertrag (Vertrag über die Nichtverbreitung von Kernwaffen) wird von den USA, Großbritannien und der Sowjetunion unterzeichnet; zahlreiche weitere Staaten schließen sich diesem Vertrag später an.

20./21. August
Militärverbände aus fünf Staaten des Warschauer Paktes marschieren unter Führung der Sowjetunion in die ČSSR ein und beenden gewaltsam den Reformkommunismus der KPČ (»Prager Frühling«) unter Alexander Dubček.

1969

21. Februar
Brief von Walter Ulbricht an Außenminister Willy Brandt, in dem bei Verzicht auf die Abhaltung der Bundesversammlung in West-Berlin Besuchsmöglichkeiten in Ost-Berlin in Aussicht gestellt werden. Dieses Ansinnen wird zurückgewiesen.

22. Oktober
Der Deutsche Bundestag wählt Willy Brandt zum Bundeskanzler. In seiner Regierungserklärung (28. Oktober) erklärt Brandt die Bereitschaft zu gleichberechtigten Verhandlungen mit der DDR.

1969

20. Januar
Richard M. Nixon übernimmt das Präsidentenamt in den USA.

5. März
Die Bundesversammlung wählt in West-Berlin Gustav Heinemann (SPD) zum neuen Bundespräsidenten.

27. April
Charles de Gaulle tritt nach einem für seine Politik negativ ausgegangenen Plebiszit als französischer Staatspräsident zurück; Nachfolger wird Georges Pompidou.

20. Juli
Als erste Menschen betreten die amerikanischen Astronauten Neil Armstrong und Edwin Aldrin den Mond.

3. September
Ho Chi Minh, weltweit Symbolfigur des vietnamesischen Kampfes gegen die USA, stirbt in Hanoi.

September
Militärputsch in Libyen gegen die Monarchie unter Führung von Muammar Gaddafi.

1. Oktober
Olof Palme wird zum Vorsitzenden der schwedischen Sozialdemokraten gewählt; er wird am 14. Oktober als Nachfolger von Tage Erlander Ministerpräsident.

1970

19. März
Treffen zwischen Bundeskanzler Willy Brandt und Ministerpräsident Willi Stoph in Erfurt.

26. März
Beginn der Verhandlungen der vier Mächte über Berlin.

21. Mai
Treffen zwischen Bundeskanzler Willy Brandt und Ministerpräsident Willi Stoph in Kassel.

1970

16. April
Die USA und die Sowjetunion beginnen in Wien mit Verhandlungen über die Begrenzung der strategischen Rüstung (SALT).

30. April
Auf Anordnung von US-Präsident Richard M. Nixon greifen amerikanische Truppen auch in Kambodscha ein.

14. Mai
In Berlin-Dahlem wird der wegen Kaufhausbrandstiftung inhaftierte Andreas Baader von Mitgliedern der Baader-Meinhof-Gruppe gewaltsam befreit.

27. November
Beginn der Verhandlungen zwischen Michael Kohl, Staatssekretär beim Ministerrat der DDR, und Egon Bahr, Staatssekretär im Bundeskanzleramt.

Jahresende
Beginn der Installierung von Selbstschußanlagen an der innerdeutschen Grenze, nicht jedoch um West-Berlin.

18. Juni
Überraschender Wahlsieg der Konservativen in Großbritannien, Edward Heath wird neuer Premierminister.

12. August
Bundeskanzler Willy Brandt und der sowjetische Ministerpräsident Alexej Kossygin unterzeichnen mit den jeweiligen Außenministern den »Moskauer Vertrag« (Normalisierung der Beziehungen zwischen den beiden Staaten, Gewaltverzicht).

8. Oktober
Der Literaturnobelpreis wird dem sowjetischen Schriftsteller Aleksandr Solschenizyn zuerkannt, der 1974 wegen seines Buches »Der Archipel GULAG« die sowjetische Staatsbürgerschaft verliert und ausgewiesen wird.

7. Dezember
Bundeskanzler Willy Brandt und der polnische Ministerpräsident Jósef Cyrankiewicz unterzeichnen mit den jeweiligen Außenministern den »Warschauer Vertrag« (Normalisierung der Beziehungen zwischen den beiden Staaten, Gewaltverzicht, Unverletzlichkeit der bestehenden Grenzen, insbesondere der Oder-Neiße-Linie als Westgrenze Polens). Brandts Kniefall am Mahnmal des Warschauer Ghettos erregt weltweites Aufsehen.

14. Dezember
Norm- und Preiserhöhungen führen zu einem Streik der Danziger Werftarbeiter, der Aufstand greift auf weitere polnische Städte über. Nach blutigen Zusammenstößen zwischen Arbeitern und der Polizei tritt Parteichef Wladyslaw Gomulka am 20. Dezember zurück und wird durch Edward Gierek ersetzt.

1971

31. Januar
Nach 19jähriger Unterbrechung wird der Telefonverkehr zwischen Ost- und West-Berlin in begrenztem Rahmen wiederaufgenommen.

3. Mai
Erich Honecker wird als Nachfolger von Walter Ulbricht, der sein Amt aus »Altersgründen« aufgibt, zum Ersten Sekretär des ZK der SED gewählt.

13. August
Zehnter Jahrestag des Mauerbaus.

1971

März
Westpakistanische Truppen marschieren in Ost-Pakistan ein, um Separationsbestrebungen (Unabhängigkeitserklärung am 26. März) zu unterdrücken.

14. April
»Pingpong-Diplomatie« zwischen den USA und der Volksrepublik China: Der chinesische Ministerpräsident Tschou En-lai empfängt eine amerikanische Tischtennismannschaft.

3. September
Unterzeichnung des Viermächte-Abkommens über Berlin durch die drei Westmächte und die Sowjetunion.

17. Dezember
Unterzeichnung des Transit-Abkommens zwischen der Bundesrepublik und der DDR.

20. Dezember
Unterzeichnung der Vereinbarung zwischen dem Senat von West-Berlin und der Regierung der DDR über Erleichterungen und Verbesserungen des Reise- und Besucherverkehrs sowie über den Gebietsaustausch zur Regelung der Frage von Enklaven.

1972

6. Januar
Die Bundesrepublik wird von Erich Honecker erstmals als »Ausland« bezeichnet.

15. Januar
Einführung des paß- und visafreien Reiseverkehrs zwischen der DDR und der ČSSR.

Ostern
Die DDR ermöglicht im Vorgriff auf das Berlin-Abkommen Reisen von Westberlinern nach Ost-Berlin und in die DDR (erste Besuchsmöglichkeit seit sechs Jahren). Diese Regelung gilt auch an Pfingsten. Mehr als eine Million Westberliner machen davon Gebrauch.

26. Mai
Unterzeichnung des Verkehrsvertrages zwischen der Bundesrepublik und der DDR.

3. Juni
Inkrafttreten des Viermächte-Abkommens und damit auch des Transit-Abkommens sowie der Regelung über den Reise- und Besucherverkehr und des Gebietsaustauschs.

24. Juli
Aufnahme des Selbstwählfernsprechdiensts zwischen West-Berlin und zunächst 32 Ortsnetzen in der DDR.

20. Oktober
Willy Brandt erhält für seine Ostpolitik den Friedensnobelpreis zugesprochen.

25. Oktober
Die Volksrepublik China wird in die UNO aufgenommen, gleichzeitig wird Taiwan ausgeschlossen.

1972

28. Januar
Der Bundeskanzler und die Ministerpräsidenten der Länder verkünden den sogenannten »Radikalenerlaß«: Bewerber für den und Angehörige des öffentlichen Dienstes haben jederzeit für die freiheitlich-demokratische Grundordnung einzutreten. In der Folgezeit werden deshalb Tausende auf ihre Verfassungstreue hin überprüft.

Februar
US-Präsident Richard M. Nixon zu Besuch in der Volksrepublik China.

März/April
Nach einer nordvietnamesischen Offensive erlebt Vietnam die heftigsten Kämpfe seit der Tet-Offensive von 1968; in der Folgezeit erneut schwere Bombenangriffe der USA auf Nordvietnam.

17. Mai
Nach äußerst kontroversen innenpolitischen Auseinandersetzungen werden die Ostverträge vom Deutschen Bundestag ratifiziert.

26. Mai
Die USA und die Sowjetunion unterzeichnen das SALT-Abkommen.

Juni
Die führenden Köpfe der »Rote Armee Fraktion« (RAF) werden von der Polizei gefaßt: Andreas Baader, Holger Meins, Jan-Carl Raspe, Gudrun Ensslin und Ulrike Meinhof.

3. Oktober
Die DDR-Behörden geben an Personen mit ständigem Wohnsitz in West-Berlin Mehrfachberechtigungsscheine aus, die ein Vierteljahr gültig sind und bis zu acht Besuche in der DDR und Ost-Berlin ermöglichen.

17. Oktober
Erstmals können DDR-Bürger auch vor Erreichen des Rentenalters in dringenden Familienangelegenheiten in die Bundesrepublik reisen.

21. Dezember
Unterzeichnung des Grundlagenvertrags zwischen der Bundesrepublik und der DDR.

1973

26. Januar
Kurt Hager, Mitglied des Politbüros und Sekretär des ZK der SED, wendet sich gegen die These vom Fortbestand einer einheitlichen deutschen Kulturnation. Er unterstreicht die These von der Herausbildung der sozialistischen Kultur in der DDR.

9. Februar
Großbritannien und Frankreich erkennen die DDR völkerrechtlich an und nehmen als 70. bzw. 71. Staat diplomatische Beziehungen zur DDR auf.

März
Akkreditierung von westdeutschen Korrespondenten in der DDR.

1. August
Tod von Walter Ulbricht.

18. September
Die DDR wird als 133., die Bundesrepublik als 134. Staat in die UNO aufgenommen.

5. September
Acht arabische Terroristen des »Schwarzen September« überfallen während der Olympischen Spiele in München die Unterkunft der israelischen Mannschaft. Ein Befreiungsversuch mißlingt, alle elf israelischen Geiseln, ein Polizeibeamter und fünf Terroristen kommen ums Leben, drei werden verhaftet.

1973

1. Januar
Dänemark, Irland und — nach heftigen innenpolitischen Auseinandersetzungen — Großbritannien werden Mitglied in der EWG.

27. Januar
Das in Paris unterzeichnete Waffenstillstandsabkommen beendet die Verwicklung der USA in den Vietnamkrieg, die USA beginnen mit dem Abzug ihrer Truppen.

17. Mai
Ein Ausschuß des US-Senats beginnt mit der Untersuchung des Watergate-Skandals; Präsident Richard M. Nixon tritt deshalb im August 1974 zurück.

11. September
Militärputsch in Chile; der sozialistische Präsident Salvador Allende wird gestürzt und ermordet, sein Nachfolger wird General Augusto Pinochet. In der Folgezeit kommt es in Chile zu zahlreichen Menschenrechtsverletzungen.

Oktober
»Jom-Kippur-Krieg«, Ägypten und Syrien überfallen Israel. Nach anfänglichen Erfolgen der Aggressoren gelingt es Israel, den Angriff abzuwehren und seinerseits vorzudringen.

7. November
Die Bundesregierung beschließt wegen des arabischen Ölboykotts ein Energiesicherungsgesetz (Sonntagsfahrverbote, Geschwindigkeitsbegrenzungen).

1974

14. März
Unterzeichnung des Protokolls zwischen den Regierungen der Bundesrepublik und der DDR über die Errichtung »Ständiger Vertretungen« (anstelle von Botschaften). Ihre offizielle Tätigkeit nehmen sie am 2. Mai auf.

6. Mai
Rücktritt von Willy Brandt im Zusammenhang mit der Spionageaffäre Guillaume.

4. September
Die USA und die DDR nehmen diplomatische Beziehungen auf.

14. September
Die Staatsbank der DDR ersetzt auf den neuen Banknoten den Begriff »Mark der Deutschen Notenbank« durch »Mark der DDR«.

27. September
Die Volkskammer der DDR beschließt eine neue Verfassung: Der Begriff »deutsche Nation« entfällt.

7. Oktober
25. Jahrestag der Gründung der DDR.

10. Dezember
Auf Anordnung des Finanzministeriums der DDR werden Rentner und Jugendliche unter 16 Jahren beim Besuch der DDR oder von Ost-Berlin vom Mindestumtausch befreit (Inkrafttreten am 20. Dezember).

1975

7. Oktober
Der Gründungstag der DDR wird erstmals als Nationalfeiertag begangen.

25. November
Der griechische Präsident Georgios Papadopoulos wird durch einen Militärputsch gestürzt, das Land kehrt im darauffolgenden Jahr zur Demokratie zurück.

1974

28. März
In Rumänien wird Nicolae Ceaușescu (Parteichef seit 1965, Staatsratvorsitzender seit 1967) nach einer Verfassungsänderung zum ersten Staatspräsidenten der »Sozialistischen Republik Rumänien« gewählt.

25. April
Der portugiesische Generalstabschef António Spínola stürzt die Regierung; in der Folgezeit Übergang des Landes zur Demokratie, die portugiesischen Kolonien werden unabhängig.

19. Mai
Valéry Giscard d'Estaing wird zum neuen französischen Staatspräsidenten gewählt.

26. Oktober
Die arabische Gipfelkonferenz in Rabat erkennt die PLO mit ihrem Chef Jassir Arafat als einzige legitime Vertretung des palästinensischen Volkes an.

1975

5. April
Tod des taiwanesischen Staatschefs Tschiang Kai-schek.

13. April
Beginn des Bürgerkrieges im Libanon nach blutigen Zusammenstößen zwischen Palästinensern und christlichen Falangisten.

29. Oktober
Übereinkunft zwischen dem Außenministerium der DDR und dem Innensenator von West-Berlin über Rettungsmaßnahmen bei Unglücksfällen an der Sektorengrenze.

19. Dezember
Die DDR und die Bundesrepublik vereinbaren die Erneuerung der Transitautobahn Marienborn-Berlin. Die Transitpauschale für den Verkehr zwischen der Bundesrepublik und West-Berlin wird für 1976 bis 1979 auf 400 Millionen DM pro Jahr festgelegt (1980 bis 1989: 525 Millionen DM, 1990 bis 1999: 860 Millionen DM pro Jahr).

1976

13. August
15. Jahrestag des Mauerbaus. 13 von 20 Omnibussen, in denen Mitglieder der Jungen Union an einer Sternfahrt nach West-Berlin teilnehmen wollen, werden von den DDR-Grenzbehörden wegen Verdachts des Mißbrauchs der Transitwege zurückgewiesen.

16. November
Der regimekritische Liedermacher Wolf Biermann wird während einer Tournee durch die Bundesrepublik von den DDR-Behörden ausgebürgert.

26. November
Hausarrest für Professor Robert Havemann (bis 9. Mai 1979).

17. April
Ende des kambodschanischen Bürgerkrieges mit der Eroberung Phnom Penhs durch die Roten Khmer, deren Terrorherrschaft in den folgenden Jahren etwa eine Million Menschen zum Opfer fallen.

1. August
In Helsinki wird die Schlußakte der Konferenz über Sicherheit und Zusammenheit in Europa (KSZE) unterzeichnet. Auch wenn in der Folgezeit u. a. die in der Akte festgeschriebene Achtung der Menschenrechte von den osteuropäischen Staaten immer wieder verletzt wird, so bildet das Vertragswerk doch eine wichtige Grundlage, auf die sich Bürgerrechtler in den osteuropäischen Staaten bei ihren Forderungen nach Einhaltung der Grund- und Menschenrechte immer wieder berufen.

9. September
Der Friedensnobelpreis wird dem sowjetischen Bürgerrechtler Andrej Sacharow zuerkannt, was zu Protesten der Sowjetunion führt; Sacharow wird später die Ausreise zur Annahme des Preises verweigert.

11. November
Die portugiesische Kolonie Angola wird unabhängig. Es folgt ein jahrelanger Bürgerkrieg, in den auch Kuba auf seiten der Kommunisten eingreift.

20. November
Tod des spanischen Caudillo Francisco Franco; unter König Juan Carlos kehrt das Land zur Demokratie zurück.

1976

24. März
Militärputsch in Argentinien gegen Isabel Perón, General Jorge Videla übernimmt die Macht.

5. April
James Callaghan wird zum neuen britischen Premierminister gewählt.

9. Mai
Selbstmord von Ulrike Meinhof im Gefängnis Stuttgart-Stammheim.

16. Juni
Blutige Unruhen in Soweto, der überwiegend von Schwarzen bewohnten Vorstadt von Johannesburg.

25. Juni
Streiks in den polnischen Städten Radom und Ursus wegen chronischer Versorgungsmängel; Bildung des »Komitees zur Verteidigung der Arbeiter«, die eigentliche Keimzelle der späteren polnischen Gewerkschaft »Solidarität«.

9. September
Tod von Mao Tse-tung.

2. November
Jimmy Carter wird zum neuen US-Präsidenten gewählt.

27. November
Die »Sozialistische Internationale« wählt Willy Brandt zum Vorsitzenden.

18. Dezember
Chile entläßt den KP-Chef Luis Corvalán aus der Haft in die Sowjetunion, die dafür den sowjetischen Regimekritiker Wladimir Bukowski in die Schweiz ausreisen läßt.

1977

1. März
Die DDR-Behörden erheben nun auch für von West- nach Ost-Berlin einfahrende Pkws eine Straßenbenutzungsgebühr in Höhe von 10 DM (für Reisen in das Gebiet der DDR bestand diese Regelung bereits seit 1951). Die Straßenbenutzungsgebühr im Verkehr von und nach West-Berlin (Transitverkehr) wurde seit dem 1. Januar 1972 nicht mehr individuell erhoben, sondern von der Bundesregierung durch die Transitpauschale abgegolten.

23. August
Festnahme von Rudolf Bahro. Wegen der in der Bundesrepublik erfolgten Veröffentlichung seines regimekritischen Buches »Die Alternative« wird er am 30. Juni 1978 zu acht Jahren Haft verurteilt, jedoch am 11. Oktober 1979 vorzeitig in die Bundesrepublik entlassen.

1977

Januar
Zahlreiche tschechoslowakische Intellektuelle veröffentlichen die Charta 77, in der mehr demokratische Grundrechte gefordert werden; die Regierung verstärkt den Druck auf Oppositionelle.

7. April
In Karlsruhe wird Generalbundesanwalt Siegfried Buback von der RAF ermordet.

22. Juli
Der frühere stellvertretende chinesische Regierungschef Teng Hsiao-ping wird rehabilitiert. Unter seiner Führung öffnet sich China in der Folgezeit gegenüber dem Westen.

30. Juli
In Oberursel wird der Vorstandsvorsitzende der Dresdner Bank, Jürgen Ponto, von der RAF ermordet.

7. Oktober
Festveranstaltung anläßlich des Nationalfeiertages der DDR; abends kommt es bei einem Konzert zu Tumulten auf dem Ostberliner Alexanderplatz (drei Todesopfer, darunter zwei Volkspolizisten).

5. September
Der Präsident der Arbeitgeberverbände, Hanns-Martin Schleyer, wird von der RAF entführt. Am 13. Oktober erfolgt durch arabische Terroristen die Entführung einer Lufthansa-Maschine nach Mogadischu, am 18. Oktober stürmt eine Sondereinheit des Bundesgrenzschutzes die Maschine und befreit die Geiseln. In derselben Nacht begehen Andreas Baader, Jan-Carl Raspe und Gudrun Ensslin im Gefängnis Stuttgart-Stammheim Selbstmord. Einen Tag später wird Schleyer ermordet aufgefunden.

19. November
Der Besuch des ägyptischen Staatspräsidenten Anwar As Sadat in Israel macht den Weg zur Aussöhnung zwischen den beiden Ländern frei.

10. Dezember
Der Friedensnobelpreis geht an die Gefangenenhilfsorganisation Amnesty International. Der Friedensnobelpreis für 1976 wird nachträglich den Begründerinnen der nordirischen Friedensbewegung, Betty Williams und Mairead Corrigan, für ihr Engagement zur friedlichen Beilegung des Nordirland-Konflikts verliehen.

1978

10. Januar
Schließung des *Spiegel*-Büros in Ost-Berlin durch das Außenministerium der DDR wegen der Veröffentlichung eines Manifests von einem angeblich in der DDR ansässigen »Bund Demokratischer Kommunisten Deutschlands«.

15. Januar
Der CDU-Vorsitzende Helmut Kohl und der Parlamentarische Geschäftsführer der CDU/CSU-Bundestagsfraktion, Philipp Jenninger, werden am Grenzübergang Bahnhof Friedrichstraße von DDR-Behörden zurückgewiesen.

21. Juni
Beginn der Verhandlungen zwischen den Regierungen der DDR und der Bundesrepublik über den Bau einer Autobahn Berlin-Hamburg (Unterzeichnung der Vereinbarung am 16. November).

September
Beginn des Wehrkundeunterrichts in der DDR für die Klassen 9 und 10.

1978

16. März
Aldo Moro, Präsident der italienischen Christdemokraten, wird von den »Roten Brigaden« entführt und am 9. Mai ermordet aufgefunden.

17. September
Der israelische Ministerpräsident Menachem Begin und der ägyptische Staatspräsident Anwar As Sadat unterzeichnen in Camp David ein Rahmenabkommen für eine Friedenslösung im Nahen Osten. Sie erhalten dafür den Friedensnobelpreis 1978.

16. Oktober
Der polnische Kardinal Karol Wojtyla wird als Nachfolger von Johannes Paul I. zum Papst gewählt.

15. Dezember
Die USA kündigen die Aufnahme voller diplomatischer Beziehungen zur Volksrepublik China ab 1. Januar 1979 bei gleichzeitigem Abbruch der Beziehungen zu Taiwan an.

14. November
Der Bundesminister für innerdeutsche Beziehungen, Egon Franke, warnt vor dem Mißbrauch der Transitwege nach West-Berlin durch kommerzielle Fluchthelfer.

29. November
Unterzeichnung des Protokolls zwischen den Regierungen der DDR und der Bundesrepublik über die Überprüfung, Erneuerung und Ergänzung der Markierung der bestehenden, rund 1393 km langen innerdeutschen Grenze.

1979

14. April
Eine Verordnung schränkt die Arbeitsmöglichkeiten für westdeutsche Korrespondenten in der DDR erheblich ein: Interviews und Befragungen werden genehmigungspflichtig, Reisen außerhalb von Ost-Berlin sind meldepflichtig.

7. Juni
Ausschluß von Stefan Heym und acht weiteren Mitgliedern des Bezirksverbandes Ost-Berlin aus dem Schriftstellerverband der DDR.

28. Juni
Die Volkskammer der DDR beschließt das 3. Strafrechtsänderungsgesetz, das erhebliche Verschärfungen des politischen Strafrechts mit sich bringt.

14. Dezember
Abschluß der Amnestie anläßlich des 30. Jahrestages der Gründung der DDR.

1979

16. Januar
Nach ständig anwachsendem innenpolitischem Druck verläßt der Schah von Persien, Resa Pahlevi, das Land.

30. Januar
In einem Referendum stimmt die weiße Bevölkerung Rhodesiens einer neuen Verfassung und damit der Machtübergabe an die schwarze Bevölkerungsmehrheit zu.

1. Februar
Ajatollah Ruhollah Khomeini kehrt in den Iran zurück und übernimmt die Macht.

5. März
Ende des Grenzkriegs zwischen Vietnam und der Volksrepublik China.

3. Mai
Die Konservativen gewinnen die britischen Unterhauswahlen, Margaret Thatcher wird Premierministerin.

Juni
In den neun Mitgliedsstaaten der EG finden erstmals Direktwahlen zum Europäischen Parlament statt.

18. Juni
Die USA und die Sowjetunion unterzeichnen das SALT-II-Abkommen; wegen des Einmarsches der Sowjetunion in Afghanistan wird das Abkommen von den USA nicht ratifiziert.

17. Oktober
Der Friedensnobelpreis geht an Mutter Theresa für ihr Wirken in den Elendsvierteln Kalkuttas.

1980

1. Januar
Wegfall der Straßenbenutzungsgebühr bei Fahrten nach Ost-Berlin und in die DDR. Die Bundesregierung zahlt dafür von 1980 bis 1989 eine jährliche Pauschale von 50 Millionen DM.

13. Oktober
Inkrafttreten der Erhöhung des Zwangsumtausches für Besuche in Ost-Berlin und der DDR auf 25 DM pro Tag. Die Regelung gilt auch für Rentner. Die Besuche gehen drastisch zurück.

4. November
Iraner besetzen die amerikanische Botschaft in Teheran und nehmen fast 70 amerikanische Geiseln. Am 25. April 1980 scheitert ein amerikanischer Befreiungsversuch.

12. Dezember
NATO-Doppelbeschluß: Stationierung neuer atomarer Mittelstreckenraketen in Europa und Angebot an die Sowjetunion zu Verhandlungen über Mittelstreckenraketen.

27. Dezember
Sowjetische Truppen marschieren in Afghanistan ein.

1980

22. Januar
Der sowjetische Bürgerrechtler Andrej Sacharow wird in Moskau festgenommen und ohne Richterspruch nach Gorki verbannt.

18. April
Rhodesien wird unter dem neuen Namen Zimbabwe von Großbritannien in die Unabhängigkeit entlassen.

4. Mai
Tod des jugoslawischen Staats- und Parteichefs Josip Broz Tito.

2. August
Auf dem Bahnhof von Bologna fordert ein Attentat italienischer Neofaschisten mindestens 83 Todesopfer.

August
Streiks in zahlreichen polnischen Städten; Verhandlungen zwischen der Regierung und einem überbetrieblichen Streikkomitee führen am 31. August zur Gründung der ersten unabhängigen polnischen Gewerkschaft »Solidarität« unter dem Vorsitz von Lech Walesa. Am 6. September tritt Edward Gierek als Parteichef zurück, Nachfolger wird Stanislaw Kania.

12. September
Militärputsch in der Türkei, General Kenan Evren wird neuer Staatspräsident.

23. September
Beginn des iranisch-irakischen Kriegs.

4. November
Ronald Reagan gewinnt die amerikanischen Präsidentschaftswahlen gegen Jimmy Carter.

1981

13. August
20. Jahrestag des Mauerbaus; »Kampfdemonstration« bewaffneter Verbände in Ost-Berlin.

20. November
Gemäß den Vereinbarungen zwischen der Bundesrepublik und der DDR wird der Teltow-Kanal in Berlin (zum ersten Mal seit Ende des Zweiten Weltkrieges) für den zivilen Güterschiffsverkehr von und nach West-Berlin geöffnet.

1982

15. Februar
Das Innenministerium der DDR erweitert den Katalog der »dringenden Familienangelegenheiten«, bei denen DDR-Bürgern Reisen in den Westen genehmigt werden können. Der Kreis der Personen im berufstätigen Alter wird dadurch erweitert.

9. April
Tod des DDR-Regimekritikers Robert Havemann im Alter von 72 Jahren.

1981

1. Januar
Griechenland wird zehntes Mitglied der EG.

23. Februar
In Spanien scheitert der Putschversuch einiger Offiziere.

28. Februar
Zwischen 50.000 und 100.000 Personen demonstrieren in Brokdorf gegen Atomkraftwerke; am Rande kommt es auch zu Ausschreitungen.

10. Mai
Der Sozialist François Mitterrand wird zum französischen Staatspräsidenten gewählt.

Juli
Straßenschlachten mit rassistischem Hintergrund in verschiedenen Städten Großbritanniens.

6. Oktober
Der ägyptische Staatspräsident Anwar As Sadat wird in Kairo ermordet.

10. Oktober
In Bonn demonstrieren etwa 300.000 Anhänger der Friedensbewegung.

13. Dezember
In Polen wird das Kriegsrecht verhängt und die Gewerkschaft »Solidarität« verboten. Tausende von Mitgliedern sowie die gesamte Führungsspitze der Gewerkschaft werden interniert.

1982

2. April
Argentinien besetzt die Falklandinseln (britische Kronkolonie), im Anschluß kommt es zu schweren Kämpfen zwischen argentinischen und britischen Streitkräften, die die Insel zurückerobern. Am 15. Juni kapitulieren die argentinischen Truppen.

16. September
Falange-Truppen verüben in libanesischen Palästinenserlagern in Beirut Massaker mit Duldung durch israelischen Einheiten.

20. November
Die letzten Teilstücke der Autobahn Berlin-Hamburg werden freigegeben.

1983

10. April
Der Tod des Transitreisenden Rudolf Burkert während einer Vernehmung im DDR-Kontrollpunkt Drewitz (Herzanfall) führt zu Protesten der Bundesregierung und zu einer Verschlechterung des innerdeutschen Klimas.

8. Juni
Roland Jahn, in der Jenaer Friedensbewegung aktiv, wird gegen seinen Willen aus der DDR in die Bundesrepublik abgeschoben.

27. September
Kinder, die das 14. Lebensjahr noch nicht vollendet haben, werden vom Mindestumtausch befreit.

30. Dezember
Vereinbarung, daß die in West-Berlin liegenden Anlagen der S-Bahn von der Deutschen Reichsbahn der DDR an die Westberliner Verkehrsbetriebe übergeben werden (zum 9. Januar 1984).

1. Oktober
Bundeskanzler Helmut Schmidt wird durch ein konstruktives Mißtrauensvotum gestürzt, Helmut Kohl wird mit den Stimmen von CDU/CSU und FDP zum neuen Bundeskanzler gewählt.

7. November
Die vom türkischen Militärregime erarbeitete neue Verfassung (parlamentarisches Regierungssystem mit starker Stellung der Militärs) wird in einem Referendum gebilligt. Im November 1983 finden Parlamentswahlen statt, die vor dem Militärputsch existierenden Parteien sind jedoch nicht zugelassen.

10. November
Tod des sowjetischen Staats- und Parteichefs Leonid Breschnew.

1983

23. März
Der amerikanische Präsident Ronald Reagan kündigt ein Forschungsprogramm für die Stationierung von Defensivwaffen im Weltraum an (SDI).

24. Mai
In Österreich kommt es zu einer Koalition zwischen SPÖ und FPÖ; Nachfolger des zurückgetretenen Bundeskanzlers Bruno Kreisky wird Fred Sinowatz.

25. Mai
Die irakische Regierung erlaubt türkischen Truppen das Betreten irakischen Gebiets zur Verfolgung kurdischer Freiheitskämpfer.

14. Juni
Zweiter »Tag des Nationalen Protests« in Chile gegen das Militärregime unter General Augusto Pinochet, es kommt zu Massenverhaftungen; weitere Protesttage folgen.

22. Juli
Aufhebung des Kriegsrechts in Polen und Amnestie für ca. 800 Gefangene; einige führende Angehörige der Gewerkschaft »Solidarität« bleiben aber weiterhin inhaftiert.

5. Oktober
Der Friedensnobelpreis wird dem polnischen Arbeiterführer Lech Walesa zugesprochen und am 10. Dezember von seiner Frau Danuta in Oslo entgegengenommen.

1984

Januar
Mehrere DDR-Bürger erzwingen über die US-Botschaft sowie über die Ständige Vertretung der Bundesrepublik in Ost-Berlin ihre Ausreise in den Westen.

Frühjahr
In einer einmaligen Aktion dürfen ca. 25.000 Personen legal aus der DDR in die Bundesrepublik übersiedeln.

6. April
35 DDR-Bürger, die über die Prager Botschaft der Bundesrepublik ihre Ausreise durchsetzen wollen, kehren freiwillig in die DDR zurück, nachdem ihnen eine baldige Übersiedlung zugesagt wurde.

27. Juni
Vorübergehende Schließung der Ständigen Vertretung der Bundesrepublik in Ost-Berlin wegen der Besetzung durch 55 DDR-Bürger, die so ihre Übersiedlung in den Westen erzwingen wollen.

1. August
Der Mindestumtausch für Rentner wird auf 15 DM gesenkt.

2. Oktober
DDR-Bürger versuchen, über die Besetzung der Prager Botschaft der Bundesrepublik ihre Ausreise in den Westen zu erzwingen; die Botschaft wird vorübergehend geschlossen.

Ende November
Der Abbau der Selbstschußanlagen an der innerdeutschen Grenze wird abgeschlossen. (Die maximale Dichte wurde am 31. August 1983 auf einer Länge von 439,5 km der 1393 km langen innerdeutschen Grenze registriert)

15.–22. Oktober
Im Rahmen einer »Friedenswoche« beteiligen sich über eine Million Menschen in der Bundesrepublik an Demonstrationen; zwischen Stuttgart und Neu-Ulm wird eine 108 km lange Menschenkette gebildet.

30. Oktober
Erste demokratische Wahlen in Argentinien seit nahezu zehn Jahren.

1984

9. Februar
Tod des sowjetischen Staats- und Parteichefs Juri Andropow.

28. August
Leichte Lockerung der Apartheid-Politik in Südafrika: Erstmals dürfen Inder und Mischlinge eigene Parlamentsabgeordnete wählen.

25. September
Jordanien nimmt seine 1979 abgebrochenen Beziehungen zu Ägypten wieder auf.

26. September
Großbritannien und die Volksrepublik China paraphieren eine Vereinbarung über die Zukunft der britischen Kronkolonie Hongkong nach dem Auslaufen des bis 1997 gültigen Pachtvertrages.

Oktober
Der Nobelpreis für Literatur geht an den tschechischen Schriftsteller Jaroslav Seifert, den Friedensnobelpreis erhält der südafrikanische Bischof Desmond Tutu für sein Engagement zur Abschaffung der Apartheid.

19. Oktober
Der polnische Priester Jerzy Popieluszko, der der Gewerkschaft »Solidarität« nahesteht, wird in der Nähe von Thorn von drei Sicherheitsbeamten entführt und später ermordet.

31. Oktober
Die indische Premierministerin Indira Gandhi wird von zwei Angehörigen ihrer Leibwache ermordet, Nachfolger wird ihr Sohn Rajiv Gandhi.

1985

Ende Oktober
Der Abbau der Minenfelder an der innerdeutschen Grenze wird abgeschlossen.

31. Dezember
Aus der DDR konnten im zurückliegenden Jahr ca. 1,6 Millionen Rentner sowie rund 66.000 Personen in dringenden Familienangelegenheiten in den Westen reisen.

3. Dezember
Giftgaskatastrophe in Bhopal (Indien); mehr als 3.000 Menschen sterben, über 200.000 werden verletzt, Hunderttausende flüchten aus der Stadt.

1985

1. Februar
Der Vorstandsvorsitzende der Motoren- und Turbinen-Union, Ernst Zimmermann, wird von Terroristen der RAF in der Nähe von München erschossen.

5. März
Nach fast einem Jahr wird der Streik der britischen Bergarbeiter offiziell beendet.

10. März
Tod des sowjetischen Staats- und Parteichefs Konstantin Tschernenko.

11. März
Das ZK der KPdSU wählt Michail Gorbatschow zum neuen Generalsekretär (»Glasnost« = Transparenz und »Perestrojka« = Umbau werden im Laufe seiner Amtszeit zu den bestimmenden Schlagworten der sowjetischen Politik).

8. Mai
40. Jahrestag des Endes des Zweiten Weltkriegs. Der deutsche Bundespräsident Richard von Weizsäcker hält eine Rede, die auch international breite Anerkennung und Zustimmung findet.

12. Juni
Portugal und Spanien unterzeichnen die EG-Mitgliedsverträge; ihre Mitgliedschaft beginnt am 1. Januar 1986.

2. Juli
Andrej Gromyko, seit 1957 Außenminister der Sowjetunion, wird vom Obersten Sowjet zum Staatsoberhaupt gewählt.

29. Juli
Der sowjetische Parteichef Michail Gorbatschow kündigt ein einseitiges sowjetisches Atomtestmoratorium an, das bis Ende des Jahres gelten soll und verlängert werden würde, sofern die USA ebenfalls ihre Atomtests einstellen würden.

September
Schwere Rassenunruhen in Birmingham und im Londoner Stadtteil Brixton.

1986

11. Februar
Agentenaustausch auf der Glienicker Brücke zwischen West-Berlin und der DDR; unter den von der östlichen Seite Freigelassenen ist auch der sowjetische Regimekritiker Anatoli Schtscharanskij.

28. Februar
Der schwedische Ministerpräsident Olof Palme wird in Stockholm von unbekannten Attentätern erschossen.

25. April
Der bisher größte Reaktorunfall in der Geschichte der friedlichen Nutzung der Kernenergie ereignet sich in der ukrainischen Stadt Tschernobyl. Große Teile der Bevölkerung der umliegenden Gegenden werden evakuiert, in ganz Europa kommt es zu radioaktivem Niederschlag.

9. Juli
In der Nähe von München fällt der Siemens-Manager Karl Heinz Beckurts einem Bombenanschlag der RAF zum Opfer.

10. Oktober
In Bonn erschießen Terroristen der RAF den Leiter der Politischen Abteilung des Auswärtigen Amtes, Gerold von Braunmühl.

12. Oktober
Das Gipfeltreffen zwischen US-Präsident Ronald Reagan und dem sowjetischen Parteichef Michail Gorbatschow in der isländischen Hauptstadt Reykjavik scheitert am Problem SDI.

19. Dezember
Die Verbannung des sowjetischen Bürgerrechtlers Andrej Sacharow und seiner Frau Jelena Bonner nach Gorki wird aufgehoben.

1986

25. April
Die Oberbürgermeister von Saarlouis und Eisenhüttenstadt unterzeichnen die erste deutsch-deutsche Vereinbarung über eine Städtepartnerschaft.

6. Mai
Unterzeichnung des Kulturabkommens zwischen der Bundesrepublik und der DDR.

13. August
25. Jahrestag des Mauerbaus.

1987

8. Juni
Während eines Rockkonzertes vor dem direkt an der Mauer gelegenen Reichstag in West-Berlin kommt es in Ost-Berlin zu schweren Zusammenstößen zwischen Jugendlichen und der Polizei; u. a. werden Rufe laut wie: »Die Mauer muß weg!« und »Gorbatschow!«

17. Juli
Der Staatsrat der DDR beschließt eine Amnestie zum 38. Jahrestag der Gründung der DDR; mehr als 20.000 Gefangene werden entlassen.

1987

Juni
Regierungsfeindliche Demonstrationen und Straßenschlachten in Südkorea; Staatspräsident Chun Doo Hwan sieht sich gezwungen, mit der Opposition zu verhandeln, ein innenpolitisches Reformprogramm wird verabschiedet.

30. Juni
Der Oberste Sowjet beschließt umfassende politische und wirtschaftliche Reformgesetze.

22. Juli
Der sowjetische Parteichef Michail Gorbatschow schlägt eine doppelte Nullösung für nukleare Kurz- und Mittelstreckenraketen vor.

23. August
Protestdemonstrationen in den Hauptstädten Estlands, Lettlands und Litauens anläßlich des Jahrestages der Unterzeichnung des Hitler-Stalin-Paktes (1939), in dessen Folge die drei Länder von der Sowjetunion annektiert wurden.

15. November
Demonstrationen in Rumänien gegen die schlechte Versorgungslage.

8. Dezember
US-Präsident Ronald Reagan und der sowjetische Parteichef Michail Gorbatschow unterzeichnen in Washington ein Abkommen über die globale Abschaffung aller landgestützten nuklearen Mittelstreckenraketen.

9. Dezember
Beginn des Palästinenseraufstandes (»Intifada«) in den von Israel besetzten Gebieten.

17. Dezember
Milos Jakeš wird als Nachfolger von Gustav Husák neuer Parteichef der Kommunistischen Partei der Tschechoslowakei.

1988

17. Januar
An der offiziellen »Kampfdemonstration« zum Gedenken der Ermordung von Karl Liebknecht und Rosa Luxemburg nehmen auch zahlreiche Demonstranten unabhängiger Gruppen teil. Über 100 Personen aus oppositionellen Kreisen werden an diesem und den folgenden Tagen vom Staatssicherheitsdienst der DDR festgenommen; zahlreiche Demonstranten dürfen ausreisen, andere, darunter die Bürgerrechtler Freya Klier, Stephan Krawczyk und Ralf Hirsch, werden später gegen ihren Willen in den Westen abgeschoben, nachdem man sie vor die »Alternative« Aussiedlung oder hohe Haftstrafe gestellt hatte.

1. Juli
Inkrafttreten des Gebietsaustausches in Berlin; die Gesamtlänge der Mauer um West-Berlin beträgt jetzt 155 km, davon zwischen West- und Ost-Berlin 43,1 km und zwischen West-Berlin und der DDR 111,9 km.

31. Dezember
Seit dem 13. August 1961 haben insgesamt 616.751 Personen die DDR legal oder illegal verlassen; 383.181 Personen konnten legal aussiedeln, 178.182 Personen flohen »ohne besonderes Risiko« (zumeist über Drittländer), 40.101 Personen wurden als sogenannte »Sperrbrecher« registriert (»Flucht unter Gefahr für Leib und Leben« über das Grenzsicherungssystem an der innerdeutschen Grenze bzw. die Berliner Mauer) und (seit dem 1. Januar 1979) 15.287 politische Häftlinge wurden von der Bundesregierung freigekauft. (In den Jahren 1963 bis 1978 wurden mehr als 10.000 politische Häftlinge freigekauft, jedoch statistisch nicht gesondert erfaßt.)

1988

Februar
Mehrwöchige Unruhen in den Sowjetrepubliken Armenien und Aserbaidschan um die autonome Region Berg Karabach, die zu Aserbaidschan gehört, aber zu 80 % von Armeniern bewohnt wird, die den Anschluß an Armenien fordern. Am 18. Juli beschließt das Präsidium des Obersten Sowjet den Verbleib von Berg Karabach bei der Republik Aserbaidschan, der Konflikt schwelt jedoch weiter.

8. Februar
Eine internationale Historikerkommission, von der österreichischen Regierung eingesetzt, kritisiert das Verhalten des amtierenden österreichischen Bundespräsidenten Kurt Waldheim als früherer Offizier der deutschen Wehrmacht, spricht ihn jedoch vom Vorwurf, Kriegsverbrechen begangen zu haben, frei.

22. Mai
Der langjährige Generalsekretär der ungarischen KP, János Kádár, wird von Károly Grosz abgelöst, der parteilose Biochemiker Bruno Straub vom Parlament zum neuen Staatspräsidenten gewählt (29. Juni).

8. August
Nach mehrtägigen Verhandlungen verkündet UN-Generalsekretär Perez de Cuellar einen Waffenstillstand zwischen Iran und Irak.

23. August
Anläßlich des Jahrestages der Unterzeichnung des Hitler-Stalin-Paktes demonstrieren Hunderttausende in den baltischen Republiken der Sowjetunion für nationale Unabhängigkeit.

1. Oktober
Der sowjetische Parteichef Michail Gorbatschow wird zum neuen Staatsoberhaupt gewählt.

3. Oktober
Tod von Franz Josef Strauß.

5. Oktober
Volksbefragung in Chile: Die Mehrheit entscheidet sich für ein Ende der Militärdiktatur und für den Übergang zur Demokratie.

8. November
George Bush, bisher Vizepräsident der USA, wird zum Präsidenten gewählt.

16. November
Die Volkspartei unter Benazir Bhutto gewinnt die Parlamentswahlen in Pakistan.

24. November
Der Reformpolitiker Miklos Németh wird zum neuen ungarischen Ministerpräsidenten gewählt.

13. Dezember
PLO-Chef Jassir Arafat verurteilt vor der Vollversammlung der UNO den Terrorismus und bietet Israel Friedensgespräche an.

1989

19. Januar
Honecker erklärt, daß die Mauer noch in 50 und 100 Jahren bestehen werde, wenn die Gründe, die zu ihrer Errichtung führten, nicht beseitigt seien.

5./6. Februar
Bei einem Fluchtversuch nach West-Berlin wird der 20jährige Chris Gueffroy von DDR-Grenzsoldaten erschossen.

8. März
Bei dem Versuch, mit einem selbstgebauten Gasballon nach West-Berlin zu flüchten, stürzt der DDR-Bürger Winfried Freudenberg (32) nach Überqueren der Grenze ab und verunglückt tödlich.

2. Mai
Ungarn beginnt mit dem Abbau des »Eisernen Vorhangs«, in der Folgezeit kommt es zu einer Massenflucht von DDR-Bürgern. Im September erlaubt Ungarn DDR-Bürgern auch offiziell die Ausreise. Insgesamt setzen sich bis Ende Oktober mehr als 50.000 DDR-Bürger über Ungarn in die Bundesrepublik Deutschland ab.

8. August
Die Ständige Vertretung der Bundesrepublik in Ost-Berlin wird geschlossen, nachdem über 100 ausreisewillige DDR-Bürger dort Zuflucht gesucht haben.

1989

7. Januar
Tod des japanischen Kaisers Hirohito.

15. Januar
Das von den 35 Teilnehmerstaaten verabschiedete Schlußdokument der Wiener KSZE-Nachfolgekonferenz ebnet den Weg zu neuen Verhandlungen über konventionelle Abrüstung in Europa.

29. Januar
Wahlen zum Westberliner Abgeordnetenhaus, Mehrheit für eine SPD/AL-Koalition; zum ersten Mal ziehen die rechtsextremen Republikaner in ein Landesparlament ein.

15. Februar
Die letzten sowjetischen Truppenverbände verlassen Afghanistan.

26. März
In der Sowjetunion finden Wahlen zum ersten Kongreß der Volksdeputierten statt, der künftig als höchstes Staatsorgan fungiert. In den meisten Wahlbezirken stehen erstmals mehrere Kandidaten zur Auswahl.

13. August
Seit dem 13. August 1961 wurden seitens der bundesdeutschen und Westberliner Behörden insgesamt 191 Todesfälle bei Fluchtversuchen aus der DDR und Ost-Berlin registriert, davon 111 an der innerdeutschen Grenze und 80 an der Grenze zu West-Berlin.

23. August
Die Botschaft der Bundesrepublik in Prag wird wegen Zuflucht von über 100 DDR-Bürgern, die so ihre Ausreise durchsetzen wollen, geschlossen.

8. September
Die DDR-Bürger, die in der Ständigen Vertretung Zuflucht gesucht haben, verlassen diese freiwillig. Ihnen wird Straffreiheit sowie juristischer Beistand zugesichert, jedoch keine Ausreisegarantie.

19. September
Die Botschaft der Bundesrepublik in Warschau wird wegen Überfüllung mit DDR-Flüchtlingen geschlossen.

25. September
Die Montagsdemonstrationen in Leipzig nehmen von Woche zu Woche zu; am 25. September demonstrieren ca. 8.000, am 9. Oktober ca. 70.000, am 23. Oktober ca. 300.000 Personen für Reisefreiheit und demokratische Reformen in der DDR.

30. September/1. Oktober
Über 6.000 ausreisewillige DDR-Bürger in den bundesdeutschen Botschaften in Prag und Warschau werden mit Sonderzügen durch die DDR ins Bundesgebiet gebracht.

3. Oktober
Die DDR setzt den visafreien Besucherverkehr mit der ČSSR aus (die ČSSR war bis dato das einzige Land, das DDR-Bürger nur mit Personalausweis besuchen konnten).

4. Oktober
Erneut können mehr als 6.000 ausreisewillige DDR-Bürger die Prager Botschaft der Bundesrepublik verlassen; sie werden mit Zügen ins Bundesgebiet gebracht.

April bis Juni
Nach dem Tod des früheren chinesischen Parteichefs Hu Yaobang kommt es zu Studentendemonstrationen. Am 13. Mai beginnen mehrere tausend Studenten auf dem Pekinger »Platz des Himmlischen Friedens« einen Hungerstreik, am 4. Juni antwortet die chinesische Führung mit dem Militär: Die Demonstranten auf dem »Platz des Himmlischen Friedens« werden von der chinesischen Armee zusammengeschossen und von Panzern niedergewalzt.

2. April
PLO-Chef Jassir Arafat wird in Tunis zum Präsidenten des im November 1988 ausgerufenen unabhängigen Staates Palästina gewählt.

17. April
Die seit Ausrufung des Kriegsrechts im Dezember 1981 verbotene unabhängige polnische Gewerkschaft »Solidarität« wird erneut offiziell zugelassen.

25. Mai
Der neue Kongreß der Volksdeputierten wählt auf seiner konstituierenden Sitzung nach kontroverser Debatte Michail Gorbatschow zum Staatspräsidenten.

4. Juni
Parlamentswahlen in der Volksrepublik Polen. Der Sejm wählt zum ersten Mal in der polnischen Nachkriegsgeschichte einen nichtkommunistischen Politiker, Tadeusz Mazowiecki, zum Regierungschef. Am 29. Dezember wird die Volksrepublik Polen umbenannt in »Republik Polen«.

16. Juni
Imre Nagy, Ministerpräsident in Ungarn zur Zeit des Volksaufstandes von 1956 und am 16. Juni 1958 als »Hochverräter« hingerichtet, wird im Zuge der politischen und wirtschaftlichen Reformen rehabilitiert und unter großer Anteilnahme der Bevölkerung feierlich bestattet. Anläßlich des 33. Jahrestages des Volksaufstandes von 1956 proklamiert der ungarische Parlamentspräsident am 23. Oktober die »Republik Ungarn«. Am 21. Dezember beschließt das ungarische Parlament seine Selbstauflösung.

Juli
Massenstreiks sowjetischer Bergleute in Sibirien und in der Ukraine. Die Arbeiter fordern wirtschaftliche Unabhängigkeit der Gruben und bessere Lebensbedingungen.

7./8. Oktober
Festveranstaltungen zum 40. Jahrestag der DDR-Gründung in Ost-Berlin. Sowohl in Ost-Berlin als auch in anderen Städten kommt es zu Gegendemonstrationen, über 1.000 Personen werden festgenommen, die Sicherheitskräfte gehen teilweise mit äußerster Härte vor. Auch in den folgenden Tagen reißen die Proteste gegen die SED nicht mehr ab.

18. Oktober
Unter dem Druck der Fluchtwelle und der Demonstrationen wird Erich Honecker von allen Staats- und Parteiämtern entbunden, sein Nachfolger wird Egon Krenz.

27. Oktober
Der Staatsrat der DDR verkündet eine Amnestie für alle wegen »Republikflucht« verurteilten Personen sowie für diejenigen, die in Zusammenhang mit Demonstrationen festgenommen wurden, sofern sie keine Gewalttaten begangen haben.
Erneut können über tausend ausreisewillige DDR-Bürger aus der Warschauer und Prager Botschaft der Bundesrepublik ins Bundesgebiet ausreisen.

1. November
Nach der Wiedereinführung des visafreien Verkehrs zwischen der DDR und der ČSSR setzen sich bis Mitte des Monats über 60.000 DDR-Bürger via ČSSR ins Bundesgebiet ab, nachdem nun die ČSSR DDR-Bürger in Übereinstimmung mit der Regierung der DDR offiziell ausreisen läßt.

4. November
Die größte Demonstration in der Geschichte der DDR: In Ost-Berlin gehen etwa eine Million Menschen für demokratische Reformen auf die Straße.

7. November
Der gesamte Ministerrat der DDR tritt zurück.

8. November
Das gesamte Politbüro der SED tritt zurück, Egon Krenz wird jedoch als Generalsekretär bestätigt.

30. November
In Bad Homburg fällt der Vorstandssprecher der Deutschen Bank AG, Alfred Herrhausen, einem Bombenanschlag der RAF zum Opfer.

November/Dezember
Am 17. November lösen Sicherheitskräfte in Prag eine Protestdemonstration von ca. 30.000 Teilnehmern mit brutaler Härte auf. Einen Tag später wird das »Bürgerforum« gegründet. Am 24. November wird Alexander Dubček auf dem Prager Wenzelsplatz von den Massen begeistert gefeiert, die gesamte KP-Führung tritt zurück. Am 27. November werden alle politischen Gefangenen freigelassen. Zwei Tage später wird das Machtmonopol der KPČ aus der Verfassung gestrichen. Am 10. Dezember tritt Gustav Husák unter dem Druck der Massendemonstrationen als Staatspräsident zurück. Alexander Dubček wird am 28. Dezember zum Parlamentspräsidenten gewählt, am 29. Dezember erfolgt die Wahl Václav Havels zum Staatspräsidenten.

9. November
In den Abendstunden öffnet die DDR völlig überraschend die Mauer nach West-Berlin sowie die Grenzen zur Bundesrepublik, es kommt zu unbeschreiblichen Jubelszenen. Ab sofort gilt Reise- und Ausreisefreiheit für alle DDR-Bürger. In den Folgetagen besuchen Millionen DDR-Bürger die Bundesrepublik und West-Berlin; zahlreiche weitere Grenzübergänge werden eingerichtet.

13. November
Hans Modrow, bisher Dresdner Bezirkschef der SED, wird von der Volkskammer zum neuen Ministerpräsidenten der DDR gewählt.

3. Dezember
Unter dem Druck der Massendemonstrationen tritt das Politbüro der SED einschließlich des Generalsekretärs Egon Krenz zurück.

6. Dezember
Egon Krenz legt auch sein Amt als Vorsitzender des Staatsrates der DDR nieder, Nachfolger wird Manfred Gerlach, Vorsitzender der Liberal demokratische Partei Deutschlands (LDPD). Der Staatsrat beschließt eine weitere Amnestie.

7. Dezember
In der DDR beginnen die Gespräche am »Runden Tisch« zwischen Regierungsparteien und Vertretern der verschiedenen oppositionellen Gruppen.

9. Dezember
Der Ostberliner Anwalt Gregor Gysi wird auf einem Sonderparteitag der SED zum neuen Vorsitzenden gewählt.

11. Dezember
Neue Massendemonstrationen in der DDR, insbesondere in Leipzig. Der Ruf: »Deutschland, einig Vaterland!« tritt immer mehr in den Vordergrund.

22. Dezember
Öffnung eines Grenzüberganges für Fußgänger am Brandenburger Tor.

24. Dezember
Aufhebung des Visumzwangs sowie des Mindestumtausches bei Reisen in die DDR und nach Ost-Berlin.

14. Dezember
In Moskau stirbt der Atomphysiker und Friedensnobelpreisträger Andrej Sacharow.

Dezember
Am 17. Dezember gehen Sicherheitskräfte in der rumänischen Stadt Temesvar mit brutaler Härte gegen Demonstranten vor. Drei Tage später steht Rumänien am Rande des Bürgerkrieges. Am 22. Dezember flüchtet Staats- und Parteichef Nicolae Ceaușescu aus Bukarest, am 25. Dezember werden er und seine Frau von einem Militärgericht zum Tode verurteilt und erschossen. Der Umsturz und der blutige Terror der Geheimpolizei fordern mehrere tausend Todesopfer.

22. Dezember
Der sowjetische Parteichef Michail Gorbatschow beruft wegen des Austritts der litauischen KP aus der KPdSU ein ZK-Plenum ein.

31. Dezember
Im Jahr 1989 haben insgesamt 343.854 Personen die DDR legal oder illegal verlassen.

31. Dezember 1989/1. Januar 1990
Jahreswechsel — Hunderttausende feiern Silvester am Brandenburger Tor; die Bilanz dieser »Silvesterfeier des Jahrhunderts« stimmt jedoch traurig:
271 Verletzte und Schäden an der Quadriga auf dem Tor, wo sich zeitweise mehr als 500 Personen aufhielten.

1990

3. Januar
Einem Aufruf der SED-PDS folgend, demonstrieren 250.000 Menschen in Treptow (Ost-Berlin) gegen Neonazismus. Bauarbeiter der DDR beginnen im Bezirk Schwerin mit dem Abbau der Grenzsicherungsanlagen.

12. Januar
Eine Regierungskrise in der DDR kann beigelegt werden, nachdem Ministerpräsident Hans Modrow darauf verzichtet, eine Behörde für Verfassungsschutz (anstelle des aufgelösten Staatssicherheitsdiensts und dessen Nachfolgeorganisation »Amt für Nationale Sicherheit«) einzurichten.

15. Januar
Mehrere tausend Demonstranten stürmen in Ost-Berlin die Zentrale des ehemaligen Staatssicherheitsdienstes. In Leipzig demonstrieren über 100.000 Menschen für die deutsche Einheit.

23. Januar
DDR-Grenztruppen beginnen, die Mauer durch einen Zaun zu ersetzen. Insgesamt sollen am Leuschnerdamm 320 Meter Mauer fallen, »offenbar wegen der besonders farbenprächtigen Graffiti, die die DDR-Außenhandelsfirma Limex nun an zahlungskräftige Interessenten verkauft« (so der Westberliner *Tagesspiegel* am 24. Januar).

28. Januar
Die am Runden Tisch vertretenen Gruppierungen beschließen, die Volkskammerwahlen auf den 18. März vorzuverlegen.

1990

Anfang Januar
Schwere Unruhen an der iranisch-sowjetischen Grenze auf Grund der Forderung der in beiden Staaten lebenden Aserbaidschaner nach Vereinigung.

11. Januar
Der sowjetische Staats- und Parteichef Michail Gorbatschow trifft in Litauen ein und fordert das Land zum Verbleib in der Sowjetunion auf. Hunderttausende begrüßen ihn freundlich, demonstrieren aber gleichzeitig für die Unabhängigkeit des Landes.

Mitte Januar
Schwere Unruhen in der Sowjetunion; in Georgien kommt es zu Demonstrationen für die Unabhängigkeit der Republik, zwischen Aserbaidschan und Armenien herrscht Bürgerkrieg. Die sowjetische Führung verhängt den Ausnahmezustand und entsendet Truppen in das Krisengebiet. Erst gegen Ende des Monats normalisiert sich die Situation wieder ein wenig.

15. Januar
Das bulgarische Parlament streicht einstimmig die führende Rolle der Kommunistischen Partei aus der Verfassung des Landes.

19. Januar
Der langjährige Vorsitzende der SPD-Bundestagsfraktion, Herbert Wehner, stirbt im Alter von 83 Jahren in Bad Godesberg.

21. Januar
Rund 100.000 Menschen demonstrieren mit einer 500 km langen Menschenkette zwischen Lwow und Kiew für die Unabhängigkeit der Ukraine.

29. Januar
Der ehemalige Staats- und Parteichef Erich Honecker wird aus dem Krankenhaus in die Untersuchungshaftanstalt Rummelsburg (Ost-Berlin) eingewiesen. Einen Tag später wird er wegen Haftunfähigkeit aus gesundheitlichen Gründen wieder auf freien Fuß gesetzt und nach Lobetal (Kreis Bernau) in das dortige kirchliche Pflegeheim gebracht.

1. Februar
DDR-Ministerpräsident Hans Modrow legt unter dem Motto »Für Deutschland, einig Vaterland« einen Stufenplan für ein geeintes Deutschland vor.

4. Februar
Nach einem Beschluß des Parteivorstandes heißt die ehemalige SED (zwischenzeitlich SED-PDS) nur noch PDS (Partei des Demokratischen Sozialismus).

6. Februar
Bundeskanzler Helmut Kohl kündigt in Bonn an, der DDR sofortige Verhandlungen über eine Wirtschafts- und Währungsunion anzubieten.

10. Februar
Nach Gesprächen mit dem sowjetischen Staats- und Parteichef Michail Gorbatschow in Moskau erklärt Bundeskanzler Helmut Kohl, daß die UdSSR die deutsche Wiedervereinigung als eine Angelegenheit betrachte, die allein von den Deutschen entschieden werden kann.

13. Februar
Bundeskanzler Helmut Kohl und DDR-Ministerpräsident Hans Modrow verständigen sich in Bonn auf erste Schritte zu einer Vereinigung der beiden deutschen Staaten.

19. Februar
Zwischen Reichstag und Brandenburger Tor beginnen Grenztruppen der DDR mit dem Abbau der Mauer. Auf dem Stück bis zum Checkpoint Charlie soll ein 1,50 Meter hoher Drahtzaun an Stelle der Mauer errichtet werden.

14. März
Beginn der »Vier plus Zwei«-Verhandlungen (die vier Siegermächte des Zweiten Weltkriegs sowie die beiden deutschen Staaten) auf Beamtenebene in Bonn über die äußeren Aspekte der deutschen Einheit.

22. Januar
Die jugoslawische KP verzichtet auf einem Sonderparteitag auf ihr in der Verfassung garantiertes Machtmonopol.

4. Februar
Einen Tag vor dem Beginn einer Plenarsitzung des ZK der KPdSU demonstrieren rund 300.000 Menschen in Moskau gegen das Machtmonopol der Partei.

11. Februar
In Südafrika wird nach fast 28jähriger Haft der schwarze Nationalistenführer Nelson Mandela freigelassen. Zwei Tage später ruft er in Soweto im Fußballstadion Soccer City vor etwa 120.000 Menschen — die ihm einen triumphalen Empfang bereiten — erneut zum Kampf gegen die Apartheid auf.

24. Februar
Erste freie Parlamentswahl in der Sowjetrepublik Litauen.

25. Februar
Hunderttausende demonstrieren in Moskau und anderen Städten der Sowjetunion für mehr Demokratie.

10. März
Die UdSSR und Ungarn unterzeichnen ein Abkommen über den Abzug der sowjetischen Truppen aus Ungarn bis zum Juni 1991.

11. März
Das litauische Parlament erklärt die Unabhängigkeit der Republik Litauen; die Sowjetunion verhängt in der Folgezeit eine Wirtschaftsblockade.

16. März
Der Übersiedlerstrom aus der DDR hält unvermindert an. Seit Jahresbeginn haben sich insgesamt 141.772 Übersiedler gemeldet.

18. März
Die »Allianz für Deutschland« gewinnt die ersten freien Wahlen in der DDR (48,15 %: CDU 40,91 %; DSU 6,32 %; DA 0,92 %), die SPD erhält 21,84 %, die PDS 16,33 %. Auf die im »Bündnis 90« zusammengeschlossenen Bürgerbewegungen entfallen lediglich 2,9 %.

3. April
Erich Honecker wird vom Pfarrhaus Lobetal in ein sowjetisches Militärhospital nach Beelitz (Bezirk Potsdam) verlegt.

7. April
Eröffnung des Grenzüberganges Brunnenstraße Ecke Bernauer Straße.

10. April
Nach heftigen Auseinandersetzungen einigen sich SPD und AL im Westberliner Senat über die Zukunft des Potsdamer Platzes. Gemeinsam mit dem Ostberliner Magistrat soll ein Wettbewerb ausgelobt werden, der den Wunsch von Daimler-Benz, dort ein Dienstleistungszentrum zu errichten (was von der AL bisher strikt abgelehnt worden ist), berücksichtigt.

12. April
Erstmals seit 1946 fahren wieder Linienbusse über die innerstädtische Grenze. Ostern (15./16. April) gibt es 43 Möglichkeiten, den Westteil der Stadt zu verlassen.
In der DDR bilden die »Allianz für Deutschland«, SPD und Liberale eine Große Koalition. Der CDU-Vorsitzende Lothar de Maizière wird von der Volkskammer zum Ministerpräsidenten gewählt.

28. April
Mit Hilfe von Westberliner Firmen beginnen Bautrupps der Volksarmee mit dem Abriß der Mauer vor dem Brandenburger Tor.

5. Mai
Beginn der Außenministerkonferenz der vier Siegermächte des Zweiten Weltkrieges sowie der Bundesrepublik und der DDR über die äußeren Bedingungen der deutschen Einigung in Bonn (»Vier plus Zwei«-Gespräche; erste Deutschland-Konferenz seit 1959). Hauptthemen: Militärischer Status des vereinten Deutschlands, polnische Westgrenze, Ablösung der alliierten Rechte in Deutschland.

13. März
Der sowjetische Kongreß der Volksdeputierten billigt die Einführung eines Präsidialsystems in der UdSSR, das Machtmonopol der KPdSU wird aus der Verfassung gestrichen. Zwei Tage später wird Michail Gorbatschow zum ersten Staatspräsidenten der UdSSR gewählt. In seiner Antrittsrede bekräftigt er das Recht der Deutschen auf staatliche Einheit.

21. März
Mit Namibia wird die letzte Kolonie in Afrika unabhängig.

25. März/8. April
Erste freie Wahlen in Ungarn. Das konservative »Ungarische Demokratische Forum« erhält 164 von 386 Sitzen, die Liberalen gewinnen 92 Mandate, die »Ungarische Sozialistische Partei« (die aus der früheren KP hervorgegangen ist) wird mit 33 Sitzen lediglich viertstärkste Partei.

30. März
Das Parlament von Estland beschließt mit großer Mehrheit den Beginn einer Übergangsperiode, die schließlich zur vollen staatlichen Souveränität führen soll.

13. April
Die Sowjetunion gesteht erstmals offiziell ihre Schuld an dem Massenmord von etwa 15.000 polnischen Offizieren während des Zweiten Weltkriegs ein, der bisher (von sowjetischer Seite) der deutschen Wehrmacht angelastet worden war.

4. Mai
Unabhängigkeitserklärung der Republik Lettland von der Sowjetunion.

20. Mai
Bei den ersten freien Wahlen in Rumänien gewinnt die »Front zur Nationalen Rettung« die absolute Mehrheit, ihr Kandidat Ion Iliescu wird mit über 80 % der Stimmen zum Präsidenten gewählt.

Juni
In der Monatshälfte werden acht von 30 steckbrieflich gesuchten mutmaßlichen RAF-Terroristen in der DDR festgenommen.

6. Mai
Die Kommunalwahlen in der DDR bestätigen das Kräfteverhältnis der Volkskammerwahl vom 18. März. In Ost-Berlin wird die SPD stärkste Partei und stellt künftig den Oberbürgermeister.

18. Mai
Unterzeichnung des Staatsvertrages zur Währungs-, Wirtschafts- und Sozialunion zwischen den beiden deutschen Staaten in Bonn.

9. Juni
Die Vorbehalte der Westalliierten vom 12. Mai 1949 gegenüber dem vollen Stimmrecht der Westberliner Vertreter in Bundestag und Bundesrat werden zurückgezogen.

12. Juni
Knapp 42 Jahre nach der Spaltung der Stadtverwaltung treffen der Ostberliner Magistrat und der Senat von Berlin (West) im Roten Rathaus in Ost-Berlin zu einer ersten gemeinsamen Sitzung zusammen und beschließen — neben einer Erklärung zur Wiederherstellung der Einheit der Stadt —, zunächst 86 durch die Mauer unterbrochene Straßenverbindungen wiederherzustellen.

13. Juni
An der Bernauer Straße beginnt der endgültige Abriß der Mauer.

21. Juni
Bundestag und Volkskammer stimmen dem deutsch-deutschen Staatsvertrag zur Währungs-, Wirtschafts- und Sozialunion zu.

22. Juni
Der Bundesrat stimmt — bis auf das Saarland und Niedersachsen — dem deutsch-deutschen Staatsvertrag zu.
Der westalliierte Übergang Checkpoint Charlie — ein Symbol der Ost-West-Konfrontation — wird in einer feierlichen Zeremonie im Beisein der Außenminister der vier Siegermächte des Zweiten Weltkriegs sowie der beiden deutschen Staaten, der drei westalliierten Stadtkommandanten und der Bürgermeisterin Ingrid Stahmer sowie des Ostberliner Oberbürgermeisters Tino Schwierzina abgebaut.

27. Juni
Regierungsvereinbarung zwischen der Bundesrepublik und der DDR über den Wegfall der Personenkontrollen an der innerdeutschen Grenze und in Berlin ab 1. Juli 1990.

7. Juni
Die Staaten des Warschauer Paktes kündigen in Moskau an, ihr militärisches Bündnis Schritt für Schritt in eine politische Vertragsgemeinschaft umzuwandeln.

9. Juni
Erste freie Wahlen in der Tschechoslowakei; die führenden Kräfte der demokratischen Wende, das tschechische »Bürgerforum« und dessen slowakische Schwesterorganisation »Öffentlichkeit gegen die Gewalt« (OF/VNP) erringen die absolute Mehrheit der Sitze, die tschechoslowakische KP erhält 13,6 % der Stimmen.

10./17. Juni
Die aus der ehemaligen KP hervorgegangene Bulgarische Sozialistische Partei gewinnt bei den Parlamentswahlen die absolute Mehrheit.

12. Juni
Das russische Parlament beschließt die Souveränität der russischen Föderation, ohne jedoch aus der Sowjetunion auszuscheiden.

Mitte Juni
Schwere Unruhen in Bukarest nach der gewaltsamen Räumung des von Studenten besetzten und zur »kommunistenfreien Zone« erklärten Universitätsplatzes. Zehntausende von Iliescu-treuen Bergarbeitern und Polizisten machen Jagd auf Oppositionelle.

21. Juni
Bundestag und Volkskammer erklären, daß ein vereintes Deutschland die Oder-Neiße-Linie als endgültige polnische Westgrenze anerkennen wird. Bundeskanzler Helmut Kohl spricht von einer »bitteren, aber notwendigen« Entscheidung.

22. Juni
Demontage des Checkpoint Charly an der Friedrichstraße »Symbolisches Ende des Kalten Kriegs«.
Dismantling of Checkpoint-Charly at Friedrichstraße. Symbolic end of cold war.

29. Juni
Bundespräsident Richard von Weizsäcker wird erster Gesamtberliner Ehrenbürger seit der Spaltung der Stadtverwaltung Ende 1948.

30. Juni
Mit Ablauf des Tages entfallen die Grenzkontrollen an der innerdeutschen Grenze und zu West-Berlin, die Währungs-, Wirtschafts- und Sozialunion tritt in Kraft, sieben noch geschlossene U-Bahnhöfe in Ost-Berlin werden wieder geöffnet und das Berliner Nahverkehrssystem wächst weiter zusammen. Außerdem wird das Notaufnahmeverfahren für DDR-Bürger, die in die Bundesrepublik übersiedeln, abgeschafft.

Hans-Jürgen Dyck, Haus am Checkpoint Charlie, Berlin
**Chronology of the Berlin Wall
within the context of world history, 1961—1990**

Berlin Wall	**World History**
1961	**1961**

Berlin Wall

1961

15 June
Walter Ulbricht, President of the State Council of the German Democratic Republic (GDR) demands the neutralisation of West Berlin on the basis of the Soviet Memorandum on Germany dated 4 June and announcing a separate peace treaty between the USSR and the GDR ensuring that country full rights of sovereignty over the access routes to West Berlin. Ulbricht declares: "No one has the intention of building a wall."

13 August
Building of the Wall begins; armed units of the GDR throw a cordon of barbed wire around East Berlin and set up road blocks. Since the beginning of this year, 155,402 people had fled from East Berlin and the GDR.

15 August
The first soldier of the People's Army jumps the wire to the West at Bernauer Strasse in Wedding. A photo that went round the world.

19—21 August
The American Vice President Lyndon B. Johnson visits Bonn and West Berlin. Johnson confirms the determination of the USA to defend the freedom of West Berlin.

23 August
The GDR forbids West Berliners to enter East Berlin.

24 August
For the first time a refugee is shot by People's Police while attempting to swim across the Humboldt Basin to West Berlin.

23 October
The GDR Ministry of the Interior decrees that members of US military missions in civilian clothing must show means of identification to members of the People's Police. In response, the Americans call up tanks and forcibly obtain access without inspection.

World History

1961

3—4 June
Meeting between US President John F. Kennedy and Soviet Prime Minister Nikita Khrushchev in Vienna.

15 December
Ex-SS-Obersturmbannführer Adolf Eichmann is condemned to death in Jerusalem for crimes against humanity. He is executed on 31 May 1962.

1962

16—17 June
The "National Document" of the National Front in the GDR confirms the principle of dual statehood.

19 June
Work begins in East Berlin with the construction of a second wall behind the previous one, thus creating a so-called "death strip" in Berlin, too.

17 August
East Berlin building worker Peter Fechter is shot while attempting to escape over the wall and, not receiving medical aid, bleeds to death.

1963

June
GDR authorities harass transit travellers to West Berlin.

21 June
The GDR government takes measures to set up a "frontier area" between the GDR and West Berlin.

26 June
US President John F. Kennedy visits West Berlin and is greeted enthusiastically by the population.

28 June — 4 July
Soviet Party Leader Nikita Khrushchev visits the GDR on the occasion of Walter Ulbricht's 70th birthday.

15 July
At Tutzing in Bavaria, the SPD politician Egon Bahr formulates his plan for "Change through Rapprochement" for the relationship between the Federal Republic of Germany and the GDR.

July to September
Renewed harassment by GDR authorities on interzonal motorways to West Berlin.

17 December
First agreement on visitors' permits between the West Berlin Senate and the GDR.

1962

18 March
Truce in Algeria; on 3 July France declares the country's independence.

22 October
Beginning of the Cuba crisis; US President John F. Kennedy protests against the setting up of Soviet rocket bases on Cuba. On 24 October the Americans impose a maritime blockade forcing the Soviet Prime Minister Nikita Khrushchev to intervene. The world is on the brink of an atomic war.

26 October
The *Spiegel* Affair (suspicion of betrayal of secrets) causes public excitement in West Germany, and the editor of *Der Spiegel*, Rudolf Augstein is arrested along with other staff members.

1963

22 January
Franco-German Treaty of Friendship is signed by the Federal German Chancellor Konrad Adenauer and the French President Charles de Gaulle.

19 June
US President John F. Kennedy presents his programme for solving the racial problems of the USA.

5 August
The Atomic Test Ban Agreement signed by the USA, Great Britain and the Soviet Union bans atomic experiments in the atmosphere, in space and under water.

16 October
The West German Bundestag (Lower Chamber of Parliament) elects Ludwig Erhard to succeed Konrad Adenauer as Chancellor.

18—19 October
After the resignation of Harold Macmillan, Sir Alec Douglas-Home becomes the new British Prime Minister.

22 November
US President John F. Kennedy is assassinated in Dallas, Texas; his successor is the previous Vice President Lyndon B. Johnson.

1964

2 January
New identity cards stating nationality as "Citizen of the GDR" are issued in the GDR.

13 March
At the instigation of the State Secretary for Higher Education, the regime critic Professor Robert Havemann is "relieved of his commitments" (i.e. removed from the Chair of Physical Chemistry at East Berlin's Humboldt University).

12 June
The Soviet Union and the GDR sign a Treaty of Friendship, Mutual Aid and Co-operation. Here West Berlin is described as "an independent political entity".

24 September
Second agreement on visitors' permits signed. This agreement allows West Berliners to visit relatives in East Berlin once between 30 October and 12 November 1964, twice between 19 December 1964 and 3 January 1965 and once at both Easter and Whitsun.

4—5 October
The biggest mass escape: 57 people manage to escape through a tunnel to the western part of the city (Bernauer Strasse, Wedding).

2 November
GDR old-age pensioners are allowed to visit relatives in the West for the first time again.

25 November
The GDR government decides to introduce a compulsory exchange amount of D-Marks into GDR Marks for Western visitors as from 1 December.

1964

16 February
At a special party conference of Germany's Social Democratic Party (SPD), Willy Brandt is elected new Chairman.

2 August
There is an exchange of fire between North Vietnamese and US warships in the Gulf of Tonking. Several days later, American planes bomb North Vietnam naval bases (beginning of direct US military intervention in Vietnam).

14 October
Nikita Khrushchev deposed; Leonid Brezhnev becomes new party leader.

15 October
The British Conservative Party loses the General Election. Harold Wilson (Labour Party) becomes the new Prime Minister.

1965

April
Because of a session of the West German Federal Parliament (Bundestag) in West Berlin, roads and railways to Berlin are partially blocked. Soviet and GDR jet fighters buzz the western part of Berlin.

1965

24 January
Death of Sir Winston Churchill.

February
The Vietnam War increases in intensity. Commencement of systematic aerial warfare by the USA.

5 May
Walter Ulbricht publishes a statement declaring that a reunification of Germany is only possible for a Socialist Germay.

8 October
The International Olympic Committee decides to allow two German teams to participate for the first time in the 1968 Olympic Games.

25 November
The third agreement on visitors' permits to visit relatives at Christmas and New Year 1965-66 is signed.

1966

First half of the year
Correspondence and discussions between the SPD and the SED concerning an exchange of speakers. On 29 June the SED cancels the exchange of speakers.

7 March
Fourth agreement on visitors' permits for Easter and Whitsun.

1 April
The German Academy of Sciences in East Berlin announces the expulsion of Professor Robert Havemann.

13 August
Fifth anniversary of the construction of the Wall, military parade of GDR border troops and SED combat groups in East Berlin.

6 October
Signature of agreement governing the work of a Permit Office for Cases of Hardship (urgent family matters).

Christmas
For the first time, no general agreement on visitors' permits for the Christmas-New Year holidays.

31 July
The USA sends 75,000 more soldiers to Vietnam.

11 November
The British colony of Southern Rhodesia declares its unilateral independence under Prime Minister Ian Smith, and refuses to give guarantees for future majority rule by black Africans; Great Britain imposes economic sanctions.

1966

January
After a military confrontation, India and Pakistan agree to a peaceful settlement of the Kashmir question at a peace conference. Indira Gandhi becomes Prime Minister of India.

29 March
France hands the NATO Member States a memorandum on its decision to withdraw from NATO.

May
Ideological beginnings of the "Great Proletarian Cultural Revolution" under Mao Tse-tung in the People's Republic of China in the course of which serious internal unrest breaks out.

1 December
Great Coalition between German Christian Democrats (CDU) and Social Democrats (SPD); Kurt Georg Kiesinger becomes Federal Chancellor, Willy Brandt Vice Chancellor and Foreign Minister.

1967

20 February
The East German Volkskammer (lower house of parliament) passes the "GDR Citizenship Act". This law introduces a separate GDR citizenship.

1 December
Chaired by Walter Ulbricht, the East German parliament forms a committee to draft a new Socialist Constitution.

1968

6 January
The Soviet Union protests against the presence of the Federal Republic in West Berlin (sessions of committees of the West German Bundestag, parliamentary and cabinet meetings in West Berlin).

6 April
In a referendum 94,4 % of the people entitled to vote decide for a new constitution of the GDR, in which the leading part of the communist party is stipulated.

1967

19 April
Death of former Federal Chancellor Konrad Adenauer.

21 April
Military coup in Greece; Georgios Papadopoulos becomes Prime Minister during the subsequent military dictatorship.

9 May
The Foreign Ministers of the NATO Member States (excluding France) adopt the doctrine of "flexible response".

30 May
The Declaration of Independence by Biafra leads to civil war in Nigeria, ending on 15 January 1970 with the unconditional surrender of Biafra.

2 June
Student demonstrations during the Shah of Persia's visit to West Berlin in the course of which Benno Ohnesorg is shot and killed by police.

5—10 June
"Six-day War" in the Near East; Israel occupies West Jordan and East Jerusalem, the Sinai Peninsula, the Gaza Strip and the Golan Heights.

July
Bloody race riots in several US cities.

9 October
Ernesto (Che) Guevara is shot and killed in Bolivia.

1968

January—February
As part of the Tet Offensive of the Viet Cong the imperial city of Hue is occupied; the Americans increase their troop strength in Vietnam to over 500,000 men. In March the USA temporarily stops its bombings of North Vietnam. During the year there are growing protests in the USA and worldwide against the Vietnam War.

10–11 June
Introduction of passport and visa obligations for transit travellers between the Federal Republic and West Berlin.

1969

21 February
Letter from Walter Ulbricht to Foreign Minister Willy Brandt hinting at a relaxation of the regulations for visits to East Berlin if meetings of the Federal Parliament in West Berlin are abandoned. This proposal is rejected.

22 October
The West German Federal Parliament elects Willy Brandt as Chancellor. In his government address (28. October) Brandt states his readiness to enter into negotiations with the GDR on equal terms.

4 April
The black American civil rights leader Martin Luther King, who had won the 1964 Nobel Peace Prize for his non-violent resistance to racial segregation in the USA, is assassinated in Memphis.

May
Student unrest and a general strike lead to a national crisis in France.

30 May
The German Bundestag passes the Emergency Legislation. This and the US war in Vietnam are the main causes of the student unrest lasting throughout the year.

6 June
The American Senator Robert F. Kennedy is assassinated in Los Angeles.

1 July
The Atomic Weapons Non-proliferation Treaty is signed by the USA, Great Britain and the Soviet Union; numerous other states later append their signatures to this treaty.

20–21 August
Troops of five Warsaw Pact countries, led by the Soviet Union, march into Czechoslovakia and put a forcible end to the "Communism with a Human Face" of the Czech Communist Party ("Prague Spring") under Alexander Dubček.

1969

20 January
Richard M. Nixon becomes President of the USA.

5 March
The German Federal Assembly, meeting in West Berlin, elects Gustav Heinemann (SPD) as the new Federal President.

27 April
After a plebiscite rejecting his policies, Charles de Gaulle resigns as President of France and is succeeded by Georges Pompidou.

20 July
The American astronauts Neil Armstrong and Edwin Aldrin are the first men on the moon.

1970

19 March
Meeting between Federal Chancellor Willy Brandt and East German Prime Minister Willi Stoph in Erfurt.

26 March
Start of Four Power negotiations on Berlin.

21 May
Meeting between Federal Chancellor Willy Brandt and East German Prime Minister Willi Stoph in Kassel.

27 November
Start of negotiations between Michael Kohl, State Secretary of the East German Council of Ministers, and Egon Bahr, State Secretary of the Federal Chancellory.

End of the year
Commencement of installation of trip-gun systems along the border between the two Germanies, though not around West Berlin.

3 September
Ho Chi Minh, worldwide symbol of Vietnam's fight against the USA, dies in Hanoi.

September
Military coup against the monarchy in Libya led by Muammar Gaddafi.

1 October
Olof Palme is elected Chairman of the Swedish Social Democrats, succeeding Tage Erlander as Prime Minister on 14 October.

1970

16 April
In Vienna, negotiations begin between the USA and the Soviet Union on Strategic Arms Limitations (SALT).

30 April
US President Richard M. Nixon gives the order for US troops to intervene in Cambodia, too.

14 May
In Berlin-Dahlem, Andreas Baader, sentenced for setting fire to a department store, is forcibly liberated by members of the terrorist Baader-Meinhof Group.

18 June
Surprising election victory for the Conservatives in Great Britain. Edward Heath becomes the new Prime Minister.

12 August
Federal Chancellor Willy Brandt, Soviet Prime Minister Alexei Kosygin and the Foreign Ministers of both countries sign the "Moscow Agreement" (normalisation of relationships between the two countries, renunciation of force).

8 October
The Nobel Prize for Literature is awarded to the Soviet author Alexander Solzhenitsyn, who loses his Soviet citizenship and is expelled from the country in 1974 because of his book "The GULAG Archipelago".

7 December
Federal Chancellor Willy Brandt and the Polish Prime Minister Józef Cyrankiewicz and their respective Foreign Ministers sign the "Warsaw Agreement" (normalisation of relationships between the two countries, renunciation of force, inviolability of existing frontiers, particularly the Oder-Neisse line as Poland's western border). Brandt goes down on his knees in front of the monument to victims of the Uprising in the Warsaw Ghetto, a gesture which moves the world.

14 December
Increased work norms and prices lead to a strike at a Danzig shipyard. This rebellion spreads to other Polish towns. After bloody clashes between workers and the police, Party Leader Wladyslaw Gomulka resigns on 20 December and is replaced by Edward Gierek.

1971

31 January
After an interruption of 19 years telephonic communication between East and West Berlin is reinstated to a limited extent.

3 May
Erich Honecker becomes First Secretary of the Central Committee of the SED in succession to Walter Ulbricht, who resigns "for reasons of age".

13 August
10th Anniversary of the erection of the Wall.

3 September
Signature of the Four-Power Agreement on Berlin by the three Western Allies and the Soviet Union.

17 December
Signature of the Transit Agreement between the Federal Republic and the GDR.

20 December
Signature of the Agreement between the Senate of West Berlin and the Government of the GDR on relaxations and improvements in regulations for travel and visiting, on exchanges of territory and the regulation of the question of enclaves.

1971

March
Troops from West Pakistan march into East Pakistan in order to suppress the separatist movement (independence declared on 26 March).

14 April
"Ping-pong Diplomacy" between the USA and the People's Republic of China: Prime Minister Chou En-lai gives a reception for a table-tennis team from the USA.

20 October
Willy Brandt is awarded the Nobel Peace Prize for his policies towards Eastern Europe.

25 October
The People's Republic of China is admitted to the UNO. Simultaneously Taiwan is excluded.

1972

6 January
Erich Honecker refers to the Federal Republic as a "foreign country" for the first time.

15 January
Introduction of passport- and visa-free travel between the GDR and Czechoslovakia.

Easter
In advance of the Berlin Agreement, the GDR enables West Berliners to visit East Berlin and the GDR (first opportunity for six years). This arrangement also applies to Whitsun. More than one million West Berliners take advantage of it.

26 May
Signature of the Traffic Agreement between the Federal Republic and the GDR.

3 June
Four-Power Agreement comes into force, as do the Agreements for Transit Travellers, the Regulation of Travel and Visits, and the Exchange of Territory.

24 July
Subscriber telephone dialling becomes possible between West Berlin and, at the outset, 32 exchanges in the GDR.

3 October
The GDR authorities issue to residents of West Berlin multiple permits valid for three months and allowing up to eight visits to the GDR and East Berlin.

17 October
For the first time, GDR citizens who have not reached the age of retirement can also travel to the Federal Republic in the case of urgent family matters.

21 December
Signature of the Foundation Treaty between the Federal Republic and the GDR.

1972

28 January
The Federal Chancellor and the Prime Ministers of the Federal German "Länder" announce the so-called "Radicals Decree": holders of and applicants for civil service posts must at all times give their support to the country's free and democratic constitutional structure. Consequently the loyalty to the constitution of thousands of individuals is examined.

February
US President Richard M. Nixon visits the People's Republic of China.

March-April
Following a North Vietnamese offensive, Vietnam experiences the worst fighting since the Tet Offensive of 1968; USA bombing raids on North Vietnam increase in force.

17 May
After extremely controversial discussions the two Eastern European Treaties are ratified by the West German Bundestag.

26 May
The USA and the Soviet Union sign the SALT Agreement.

June
The leading individuals in the "Rote Armee Fraktion" ("Red Army Party") are arrested by the police: Andreas Baader, Holger Meins, Jan-Carl Raspe, Gudrun Ensslin and Ulrike Meinhof.

5 September
Eight Arab terrorists of "Black September" attack the quarters of the Israeli team during the Olympic Games in Munich. A rescue attempt fails, all the Israeli hostages, one policeman and five terrorists die, three terrorists are arrested.

1973

26 January
Kurt Hagen, member of the Politbureau and secretary of the Central Committee of the East German Socialist Unity Party (SED) turns against the theory of the continuation of a united German nation as a cultural unit. He underlines the theory of the creation of a Socialist culture in the GDR.

9 February
Great Britain and France recognise the GDR as a separate state and become the 70th and 71st countries respectively to establish diplomatic relations with the GDR.

March
Accreditation of West German correspondents in the GDR.

1 August
Death of Walter Ulbricht.

18 September
The GDR becomes the 133rd, the Federal Republic the 134th member of the United Nations.

1973

1 January
Denmark, Ireland and — after violent internal debate — Great Britain join the European Economic Community.

27 January
A truce signed in Paris ends US involvement in the Vietnam War. The USA begins to withdraw its troops.

17 May
A US Senate Commission begins to investigate the Watergate Affair; President Richard M. Nixon resigns as a result in August 1974.

11 September
Military coup in Chile; the Socialist President Salvador Allende is deposed and murdered. His successor is General Augusto Pinochet. Numerous violations of human rights follow in Chile.

October
"Yom Kippur War"; Egypt and Syria attack Israel. After initial successes, the aggressors are beaten back by the Israelis and forced to retreat.

7 November
The Federal German government passes the Energy Saving Act as a result of the Arab oil boycott (no Sunday driving, speed restrictions).

25 November
The Greek President Georgios Papadopoulos is deposed in a military coup. The following year, democracy is re-introduced to the country.

1974

14 March
Signature of the Protocol between the governments of the Federal Republic and the GDR on the setting up of "permanent diplomatic representations" (in place of embassies). These begin official operations on 2 May.

6 May
Willy Brandt resigns in connection with the Guillaume espionage affair.

4 September
The USA and the GDR establish diplomatic relations.

14 September
On the new banknotes the State Bank of the GDR replaces the term "Marks of the German Currency Bank" with "GDR Marks".

27 September
The Volkskammer of the GDR adopts a new constitution omitting the concept of the "German nation".

7 October
25th Anniversary of the foundation of the GDR.

10 December
At the instigation of the GDR Ministry of Finances, old-age pensioners and young people below the age of 16 from the Federal Republic and West Berlin are not required to exchange the minimum amount of foreign currency when visiting the GDR (as from 20 December).

1975

7 October
The date the GDR was founded is celebrated for the first time as the National Holiday.

29 October
Agreement is reached between the GDR Foreign Ministry and West Berlin's Senator for the Interior on how to deal with accidents occurring at the sector border.

1974

28 March
After a change in the Romanian constitution, Nicolae Ceauşescu (party leader since 1965, State Council Chairman since 1967) is elected as the first State President of the "Socialist Republic of Romania".

25 April
The Chief of the Portuguese General Staff António Spínola deposes the government. The country moves towards democracy. Portugal's colonies achieve independence.

19 May
Valéry Giscard d'Estaing becomes the new President of France.

26 October
Arab summit conference in Rabat recognises the PLO and its leader Yassir Arafat as the sole legitimate representatives of the Palestinian people.

1975

5 April
Death of the Taiwanese leader Chiang Kai-shek.

13 April
Civil war in the Lebanon begins after bloody clashes between Palestinians and Christian Falangists.

17 April
End of Cambodian civil war with the conquest of Phnom Penh by the Red Khmer, whose reign of terror claims about a million lives over the following years.

19 December
The GDR and the Federal Republic agree to resurface the transit motorway from Marienborn to Berlin. The transit lump-sum paid by the West German government for traffic between the Federal Republic and West Berlin is set at 400 million DM per year for the period from 1976 to 1979 (1980 to 1989: 525 million DM; 1990 to 1999: 860 million DM per year).

1976

13 August
15th Anniversary of the erection of the Wall. 13 out of 20 coaches in which members of the Young CDU were travelling to Berlin from all over West Germany are turned back by GDR border authorities under suspicion of abuse of the transit facilities.

16 November
The regime critic and chansonnier Wolf Biermann is deprived of his GDR citizenship while on a tour to the Federal Republic.

26 November
Professor Robert Havemann placed under house arrest (until 9 May 1979).

1 August
The concluding document of the Conference for Security and Co-operation in Europe (CSCE) is signed in Helsinki. Even though the respect for human rights guaranteed in the document is frequently flouted by Eastern European countries, the treaty represents an important foundation-stone on which civil-rights movements in Eastern Europe can repeatedly base their demands for the observance of fundamental human rights.

9 September
The Nobel Peace Prize is awarded to the Soviet civil-rights leader Andrei Sakharov, which leads to protests in the Soviet Union; Sakharov is later refused an exit permit to accept the prize.

11 November
The Portuguese colony of Angola gains its independence. Years of civil war follow, in which Cuba intervenes on the Communist side.

20 November
Death of the Spanish Caudillo Francisco Franco; Spain returns to democracy under King Juan Carlos.

1976

24 March
Military coup in Argentina against Isabel Perón. General Jorge Videla assumes power.

5 April
James Callaghan becomes the new British Prime Minister.

9 May
The terrorist Ulrike Meinhof commits suicide in prison in Stuttgart-Stammheim.

16 June
Bloody fighting in the Johannesburg township of Soweto, mainly inhabited by blacks.

25 June
Strikes in the Polish towns of Radom and Ursus as a result of chronic food shortages; formation of the "Committee for Workers' Defence", the real nucleus of the Polish trade-union "Solidarity".

9 September
Death of Mao Tse-tung.

2 November
Jimmy Carter is elected the new President of the USA.

27 November
The "Socialist International" elects Willy Brandt as Chairman.

18 December
Chile releases the leader of the Chilean Communist Party, Luis Corvalán, to the Soviet Union in return for the release to Switzerland of the Soviet regime critic Vladimir Bukovsky.

1977

1 March
The GDR authorities now also charge a road-use fee of 10 DM (payable since 1951 by visitors to the GDR) for cars driving into East Berlin from West Berlin. The road-use fee for transit traffic to and from West Berlin had not been charged individually since 1 January 1972, but paid by the Federal Government as a lump-sum.

23 August
Rudolf Bahro arrested. For criticising the regime in his book "The Alternative", published in the Federal Republic, he is sentenced on 30 June 1978 to eight years imprisonment, but is released to the Federal Republic on 11 October 1979.

7 October
Celebrations to mark the GDR National Holiday; during a concert on East Berlin's Alexander Square violence erupts (three dead, two of them People's Police men).

1977

January
Numerous Czech intellectuals publish the Charta 77 in which they demand more fundamental democratic rights; the government increases its pressure on the forces of opposition.

7 April
In Karlsruhe, Federal Attorney General Siegfried Buback is murdered by the RAF (Red Army Party).

22 July
Former deputy leader of the Chinese government, Teng Hsiao-ping, is rehabilitated. Under his leadership China begins to open up to the West.

30 July
The Chairman of the Board of Directors of the Dresdner Bank, Jürgen Ponto, is murdered by the RAF in Oberursel.

5 September
The President of the Employers' Associations, Hanns-Martin Schleyer, is abducted by the RAF. On 13 October, Arab terrorists hijack a Lufthansa plane to Mogadishu. On 18 October a special unit of Federal Border Protection Troops storms the plane and frees the hostages. That same night Andreas Baader, Jan-Carl Raspe and Gudrun Ensslin commit suicide in prison in Stuttgart-Stammheim. One day later Schleyer's dead body is found.

19 November
The visit of Egypt's President Anwar As Sadat to Israel opens the way to reconciliation between the two countries.

10 December
The Nobel Peace Prize is awarded to the prisoners' aid association Amnesty International. The Nobel Peace Prize for 1976 is belatedly awarded to the founders of the Northern Irish peace movement, Betty Williams and Malread Corrigan, for their commitment to a peaceful solution of the conflict in Northern Ireland.

1978

10 January
Closure of the office of *Spiegel* magazine in East Berlin by the GDR Foreign Ministry for publication of a Manifesto issued by a "Federation of Democratic Communists" apparently resident in the GDR.

15 January
Helmut Kohl, Chairman of the West German Christian Democratic Union (CDU) and Philipp Jenninger, Parliamentary Head of the CDU/CSU coalition party are sent back by the GDR authorities at the checkpoint of Friedrichstraße Railway Station.

21 June
Start of negotiations between the governments of the GDR and the Federal Republic of Germany on the building of a Berlin-Hamburg motorway (agreement signed on 16 November).

September
GDR schools begin to teach Military Knowledge as a school subject to Grades 9 and 10.

14 November
Federal Minister for Inner German Relations, Egon Franke, warns against misuse of transit routes to West Berlin by commercial escape dealers.

29 November
Signature of the Protocol between the governments of the GDR and the Federal Republic of Germany on the Examination, Renewal and Supplementation of Markings of the existing, 1393-kilometre-long inner-German border.

1978

16 March
Aldo Moro, President of the Italian Christian Democrats, is kidnapped by the "Red Brigades", and his dead body is found on 9 May.

17 September
At Camp David, Israel's Prime Minister Menachem Begin and the Egyptian President Anwar As Sadat sign a general agreement on a peaceful solution to the Near East conflict. For this they are jointly awarded the 1978 Nobel Peace Prize.

16 October
The Polish Cardinal Karol Wojtyla is elected Pope to succeed John Paul I.

15 December
The USA announce the establishment of full diplomatic relations with the People's Republic of China as from 1 January 1979. Relations with Taiwan are to be broken off on the same date.

1979

14 April
A decree considerably restricts working conditions for West German correspondents in the GDR; interviews and street reporting require permits. Travel outside East Berlin has to be reported.

7 June
Stefan Heym and eight other members of the East Berlin Section are expelled from the Writers' Association of the GDR.

28 June
The Volkskammer (GDR Parliament) passes the 3rd Criminal Law Amendment Act containing considerably stricter treatment for political offenders.

14 December
Amnesty to mark the 30th Anniversary of the GDR.

1979

16 January
As a result of constantly growing internal pressure, the Shah of Persia, Resa Pahlevi, leaves the country.

30 January
In a referendum, the white population of Rhodesia approves a new constitution and, with it, the transference of power to the black majority.

1 February
Ayatollah Ruhollah Khomeini returns to Iran and assumes power.

5 March
End of the frontier conflict between Vietnam and the People's Republic of China.

3 May
The Conservatives win the British General Election. Margaret Thatcher becomes Prime Minister.

June
The first direct elections to the European Parliament take place in the nine Member States of the Common Market.

18 June
The USA and the Soviet Union sign the SALT II agreement; because of the intervention of Soviet troops in Afghanistan, the agreement is not ratified by the USA.

17 October
The Nobel Peace Prize is awarded to Mother Theresa for her work in the slums of Calcutta.

4 November
Iranians occupy the American Embassy in Teheran and take almost seventy Americans hostage. An American liberation attempt on 25 April 1980 is unsuccessful.

12 December
The NATO Double Agreement: stationing of new medium-range missiles in Europe and offer to negotiate with the Soviet Union on medium-range missiles.

27 December
Soviet troops occupy Afghanistan.

1980

1 January
Road-use charge abolished for journeys to East Berlin and the GDR. In its place the Federal government pays from 1980 to 1989 an annual lump-sum of 50 million DM.

13 October
Increase of compulsory minimum exchange amount for visits to East Berlin and the GDR to 25 DM per day. These regulations also apply to old-age pensioners. Drastic reduction in the number of visitors.

1980

22 January
The Soviet civil-rights activist Andrei Sakharov is arrested in Moscow and banished to Gorki without trial.

18 April
Under the new name Zimbabwe, Rhodesia is declared independent of Great Britain.

4 May
Death of Yugoslavia's Head of State and Party Leader Josip Broz Tito.

2 August
A bomb outrage committed by Italian neo-Fascists at Bologna Station claims at least 83 lives.

August
Strikes in numerous Polish cities and towns; negotiations between the government and a strike committee made up of representatives from several places lead, on 31 August, to the foundation of the first independent Polish trade union "Solidarity" under the chairmanship of Lech Walesa. On 6 September Edward Gierek resigns as leader of the party. He is succeeded by Stanislaw Kania.

12 September
Military coup in Turkey. General Kenan Evren becomes the new President.

23 September
War between Iran and Iraq begins.

4 November
Ronald Reagan wins the American presidential elections against Jimmy Carter.

1981

13 August
20th Anniversary of the erection of the Wall. "Action Demonstration" of armed units in East Berlin.

20 November
In accordance with the agreements between the Federal Republic and the GDR, the Teltow Canal in Berlin is opened for civilian freight traffic to and from West Berlin (for the first time since the end of the Second World War).

1981

1 January
Greece becomes the tenth member of the European Community.

23 February
An attempted coup by several Spanish officers fails.

28 February
Between 50,000 and 100,000 people demonstrate in Brokdorf against atomic power stations; the demonstration is accompanied by some excesses.

10 May
The Socialist François Mitterrand is elected President of France.

July
Street fighting with racial background in several British cities.

6 October
The Egyptian President Anwar As Sadat is assassinated in Cairo.

10 October
Some 300,000 supporters of the peace movement demonstrate in Bonn.

13 December
In Poland martial law is declared and the trade union "Solidarity" is banned. Thousands of members and the entire top leadership of the union are interned.

1982

15 February
The GDR Ministry of the Interior expands the catalogue of "urgent family events" for which GDR citizens can obtain permission to travel to the West. The number of non-pensioners who can travel is thus greatly extended.

9 April
Death of GDR regime critic Robert Havemann at the age of 72.

20 November
The final sections of the motorway from Berlin to Hamburg are opened.

1982

2 April
Argentina occupies the Falkland Islands (a British Crown Colony). Bitter fighting between Argentinian and British troops follows. The latter recapture the islands, while the former capitulate on 15 June.

16 September
Falangist troops massacre occupants of Palestinian camps in Beirut, the Lebanon, with tacit assent of Israeli units.

1983

10 April
The death of the transit traveller Rudolf Burkert of a heart attack during interrogation at the GDR Drewitz control point leads to protests from the Federal government and to a worsening of the inner-German political climate.

8 June
Roland Jahn, active in the Jena Peace Movement, is expelled from the GDR to the Federal Republic against his will.

27 September
Children under the age of 14 are freed from the obligation to exchange the fixed minimum amount of 25 DM per day.

30 December
The GDR Reichsbahn agrees to transfer to the West Berlin Transport Authority the West Berlin sections of the Berlin S-Bahn (suburban electric railway) on 9 January 1984.

1 October
As the result of a constructive vote of no confidence, Federal Chancellor Helmut Schmidt is toppled from power. Helmut Kohl is elected the new Federal Chancellor by the votes of the CDU/CSU and the FDP (Liberals).

7 November
The new constitution worked out by the Turkish military regime (parliamentary system of government with strong military backing) is passed in a referendum. In November 1983, elections to parliament are to take place, but the parties which existed before the military coup are forbidden to participate.

10 November
Death of the Soviet Head of State and Party Leader Leonid Brezhnev.

1983

23 March
The American President Ronald Reagan announces a research programme for the stationing of defensive weapons in space (SDI).

24 May
In Austria a coalition is formed between Socialists (SPÖ) and Freedom Party (FPÖ); Chancellor Bruno Kreisky resigns and is replaced by Fred Sinowatz.

25 May
The Iraqi government allows Turkish troops to enter Iraqi territory to persecute Kurdish freedom fighters.

14 June
The second "Day of National Protest" in Chile against the military junta of General Augusto Pinochet results in mass arrests; further days of protest follow.

22 July
Martial law in Poland ends with an amnesty for around 800 prisoners; some leading members of "Solidarity" remain under arrest.

1984

January
Several citizens of the GDR use the US Embassy and the Permanent Representation of the Federal Republic in East Berlin to force their government to allow them to leave for the West.

Spring
A unique gesture allows some 25,000 people to move legally from the GDR to the Federal Republic of Germany.

6 April
35 GDR citizens who had wanted to obtain permission to leave via the Federal German Embassy in Prague return to the GDR of their own accord, having been assured that emigration visas will soon be granted.

27 June
Temporary closure of the Permanent Representation of the Federal Republic in East Berlin after its occupation by 55 GDR citizens who had tried to obtain permission to leave for the West in this way.

1 August
The minimum exchange amount for visits to the GDR by old-age pensioners is reduced to 15 DM per day.

2 October
GDR citizens attempt to obtain permission to emigrate to the West by occupying the Federal German Embassy in Prague; the Embassy is temporarily closed.

5 October
The Nobel Peace Prize is awarded to the Polish workers' leader Lech Walesa and accepted on his behalf by his wife Danuta on 10 December in Oslo.

15–22 October
Within the framework of a "Peace Week", over one million people in the Federal Republic participate in demonstrations; between Stuttgart and New-Ulm a 108-kilometre-long human chain is formed.

30 October
First democratic elections in Argentina for over ten years.

1984

9 February
Death of the Soviet Head of State and Party Leader Yuri Andropov.

28 August
Slight relaxation of apartheid policies in South Africa: for the first time Indians and Coloureds are permitted to elect their own Members of Parliament.

25 September
Jordan re-establishes diplomatic relations with Egypt for the first time since 1979.

26 September
Great Britain and the People's Republic of China initial an agreement on the future of the British Crown Colony of Hong Kong when the lease expires in 1997.

October
The Nobel Prize for Literature is awarded to the Czech writer Jaroslav Seifert, the Peace Prize goes to the South African Bishop Desmond Tutu for his work towards the abolition of apartheid.

19 October
The Polish priest Jerzy Popieluszko, an adherent of the "Solidarity" movement, is abducted near Torún by three security policemen and later murdered.

Late November
Removal of the last trip-gun installations along the inner-German border (maximum number registered on 31 August 1983 along 439.5 km of the 1393-kilometre-long inner-German border).

1985

Late October
Removal of the last minefields along the inner-German border.

Year ending 31 December
Some 1.6 million old-age pensioners and 66,000 others were able to visit the West on urgent family business.

31 October
The Indian Prime Minister Indira Gandhi is murdered by two members of her bodyguard. She is succeeded by her son Rajiv Gandhi.

3 December
Poison-gas catastrophe in Bhopal, India; over 3,000 people die and more than 200,000 are injured. Hundreds of thousands flee the city.

1985

1 February
The chairman of the board of the Motor and Turbine Union, Ernst Zimmermann, is shot dead by RAF terrorists near Munich.

5 March
After almost a year the British miners' strike is officially ended.

10 March
Death of the Soviet Head of State and Party Leader Konstantin Tchernenko.

11 March
The Central Committee of the Soviet Communist Party elects Mikhail Gorbachev as its new General Secretary ("glasnost" = transparence and "perestroika" = re-formation become the watchwords of Soviet politics during his term of office).

8 May
40th Anniversary of the end of the Second World War. The West German President Richard von Weizsäcker holds a speech which is also well received on a broad international basis.

12 June
Portugal and Spain sign the EC Membership Treaty; they will become Members of the European Community on 1 January 1986.

2 July
Andrei Gromyko, Foreign Minister of the USSR since 1957, is elected Head of State by the Supreme Soviet.

29 July
Soviet Party Leader Mikhail Gorbachev announces a unilateral Soviet atomic test moratorium to last until the end of the year and which will be extended if the USA also stops its atomic tests.

September
Serious race riots in Birmingham and the London suburb of Brixton.

1986

11 February
Exchange of agents on Glienicke Bridge between West Berlin and the GDR; those freed by the East include the Soviet regime critic Anatoli Shcharanski.

28 February
The Swedish Prime Minister Olof Palme is shot and killed in Stockholm by unknown assassins.

25 April
The biggest accident with a nuclear reactor in the history of the peaceful utilisation of atomic energy occurs in the Ukrainian town of Chernobyl. Large population groups living in the surrounding area are evacuated, there is radioactive fall-out all over Europe.

9 July
Near Munich the Siemens manager Karl Heinz Beckurts is killed in a bomb attack perpetrated by RAF terrorists.

10 October
In Bonn RAF terrorists shoot the head of the political department of the West German Foreign Office, Gerold von Braunmühl.

12 October
The summit conference between US President Ronald Reagan and the Soviet Party Leader Mikhail Gorbachev in the Icelandic capital Reykjavik come to grief on the question of SDI.

19 December
The banishment of the Soviet regime critic and civil-rights activist Andrei Sakharov and his wife Yelena Bonner to Gorki is ended.

1986

25 April
The Lord Mayors of Saarlouis and Eisenhüttenstadt sign the first inner-German twin-town agreement.

6 May
Signature of cultural agreement between the Federal Republic of Germany and the GDR.

13 August
25th Anniversary of the erection of the Wall.

1987

8 June
During a rock concert in front of the Deutsche Reichstag in West Berlin, which stands right alongside the Wall, there are serious clashes in East Berlin between young people and the police, including cries such as: "The Wall must go!" and "Gorbachev!"

17 July
On the occasion of the 38th Anniversary of the foundation of the GDR, the GDR State Council issues an amnesty leading to the release of over 20,000 prisoners.

1987

June
Anti-government demonstrations and street fighting in South Korea; President Chun Doo Hwan is forced to negotiate with the opposition. A programme of internal reforms is passed.

30 June
The Supreme Soviet passes comprehensive political and economic reform bills.

22 July
Soviet Party Leader Mikhail Gorbachev suggests the Double Zero Solution for nuclear short- and medium-range missiles.

23 August
Protest demonstrations in the capitals of Estonia, Latvia and Lithuania on the occasion of the anniversary of the signature of the Hitler-Stalin Pact (1939) as a result of which the three countries were annexed by the Soviet Union.

15 November
Demonstrations in Romania against the bad supply situation.

8 December
US President Ronald Reagan and the Soviet Party Leader Mikhail Gorbachev sign an agreement on the global scrapping of all land-based medium-range nuclear missiles.

9 December
Start of Palestinian uprising ("Intifada") in the Israeli-controlled areas.

17 December
Miklos Jakeš succeeds Gustav Husák as leader of the Czechoslovak Communist Party.

1988

17 January
Numerous demonstrators from independent groups also participate in the official "action demonstration" in memory of the murder of Karl Liebknecht and Rosa Luxemburg. Over 100 people from the ranks of the opposition are arrested on this and the following day by the GDR Staatssicherheitsdienst (Secret Police); many demonstrators are allowed to leave the country, others, including Freya Klier, Stephan Krawczyk and Ralf Hirsch, members of the civil rights movement, are later expelled to the West against their will, having been given the "alternative" of emigration or long prison sentences.

1 July
The agreement on the exchange of territory in Berlin comes into force; the total length of the Wall around West Berlin now amounts to 155 km, of which 43.1 km separate West and East Berlin, and 111.9 km West Berlin from the GDR.

31 December
Since 13 August 1961 a total of 616,751 persons have left the GDR legally or illegally: 383,181 were given permission to leave, 178,182 people fled "without particular risk" (mainly via third countries), 40,101 persons are registered as so-called "border-breakers" ("escape at risk of life and limb" across the border security system along the inner- German border or the Berlin Wall) and 15,287 political prisoners have been ransomed by the Federal Government. (From 1963 to 1978 over 10,000 political prisoners were ransomed but not statistically recorded separately).

1988

February
Several weeks of unrest in the Soviet Republics of Armenia and Azerbaijan in connection with the autonomous region of Nagorno-Karabakh, belonging to Azerbaijan but with an 80 % Armenian population who demand integration with Armenia. On 18 July the Presidium of the Supreme Soviet decrees that Nagorno-Karabakh should remain part of Azerbaijan, but the conflict festers on.

8 February
An international commission of historians set up by the Austrian government criticises the behaviour of the Austrian Federal President Kurt Waldheim as a former officer of the German Army but acquits him of the charge of having committed atrocities during the war.

22 May
The long-serving General Secretary of the Hungarian Communist Party, János Kádár, is succeeded by Károly Grosz. The biochemist Bruno Straub, with no party affiliations, is elected new State President by the Hungarian parliament (29 June).

8 August
After several days of negotiations, UN General Secretary Perez de Cuellar announces a truce between Iran and Iraq.

23 August
On the occasion of the anniversary of the signature of the Hitler-Stalin Pact, hundreds of thousands demonstrate in the Baltic Republics of the Soviet Union for national independence.

1 October
The Soviet Party Leader Mikhail Gorbachev is elected new Head of State.

3 October
Death of Franz-Josef Strauß.

5 October
Plebiscite in Chile: the majority of people vote to end the military dictatorship and to return to democracy.

8 November
George Bush, former Vice President of the USA, is elected President.

16 November
The People's Party, led by Benazir Bhutto, wins the parliamentary elections in Pakistan.

24 November
The reformist politician Miklos Németh is elected new Prime Minister of Hungary.

13 December
PLO leader Yassir Arafat denounces terrorism before the UN General Assembly and offers Israel peace talks.

1989

19 January
Honecker states that the Wall will still be standing in 50 or even 100 years' time unless the reasons which led to its erection are not eliminated.

5–6 February
During an attempted escape to West Berlin, 20-year-old Chris Gueffroy is shot by GDR border soldiers.

8 March
During an attempt to flee to West Berlin in a home-made gas balloon, GDR citizen Winfried Freudenberg (32) crashes and is killed after having crossed the border.

2 May
Hungary begins to dismantle the "Iron Curtain", and this results in a mass exodus of GDR citizens. In September Hungary also permits GDR citizens to leave officially. By the end of October more than 50,000 GDR citizens have travelled via Hungary to the Federal Republic.

8 August
The Permanent Representation of the Federal Republic in East Berlin is closed after over 100 GDR citizens wishing to leave the country had sought refuge there.

13 August
Since 13 August 1961, Federal German and West Berlin authorities have registered a total of 191 deaths during escape attempts from the GDR and East Berlin, of which 111 occurred along the inner-German border and 80 along the border to West Berlin.

1989

7 January
Death of the Japanese Emperor Hirohito.

15 January
The concluding document of the Second CSCE conference, held in Vienna, is signed by 35 participating countries and smoothes the way to new negotiations on conventional disarmament in Europe.

29 January
Elections to the West Berlin city parliament. Majority for a coalition between SPD and the "green" Alternative Liste (AL); for the first time members of the extreme right-wing Republican Party are elected to a State Parliament.

15 February
The last Soviet troops leave Afghanistan.

26 March
In the Soviet Union elections to the first Congress of Peoples' Deputies take place. This is to function as the highest organ of the state. In most constituencies several candidates can be chosen from for the first time.

April to June
Student demonstrations follow the death of the former Chinese Communist Party Leader Hu Yaobang. On 15 May several thousand students begin a hunger strike on Tiananmen Square in Peking. On 4 June the Chinese government replies by sending in the army: the demonstrators on Tiananmen Square are shot down by troops and mown down by tanks.

23 August
The Embassy of the Federal Republic in Prague is closed because it by now housed over 100 GDR citizens who wished to obtain permission to leave their country.

8 September
The GDR citizens who had sought refuge in the Permanent Representation leave voluntarily. They are promised freedom from prosecution and legal aid, but not given guarantees that they will be allowed to leave.

19 September
The Embassy of the Federal Republic in Warsaw is closed due to occupation by GDR citizens.

25 September
The Monday demonstrations in Leipzig get larger by the week; on 25 September some 8,000 people, on 9 October about 70,000 and on 23 October some 300,000 demonstrate for freedom to travel and democratic reforms in the GDR.

30 September—1 October
Over 6,000 GDR citizens who occupied the Federal German Embassies in Prague and Warsaw are conveyed by special trains through the GDR to the Federal Republic.

3 October
The GDR stops visa-free travel to Czechoslovakia (the only country which GDR citizens had been able to visit with their identity cards only).

4 October
Once again over 6,000 GDR citizens can leave the Federal German Embassy in Prague; they are conveyed by train to the Federal Republic.

7—8 October
Celebrations to mark the 40th Anniversary of the founding of the GDR in East Berlin. Both in East Berlin and in other cities there are counter-demonstrations, over a thousand people are arrested, and security forces react in some cases with extreme brutality. Protests against the East German SED continue during the days that follow.

2 April
In Tunis, PLO leader Yassir Arafat is elected President of the independent State of Palestine proclaimed in November 1988.

17 April
The independent Polish trade union "Solidarity", forbidden since the proclamation of martial law in December 1981, is once more officially tolerated.

25 May
After a controversial debate during its constituent assembly, the new Congress of Peoples' Deputies elects Mikhail Gorbachev State President.

4 June
General elections in the People's Republic of Poland. For the first time in the post-war history of Poland, the Sejm elects a non-Communist politician, Tadeusz Mazowiecki head of government. On 29 December the People's Republic of Poland is renamed Republic of Poland.

16 June
Imre Nagy, Prime Minister of Hungary at the time of the 1956 uprising and executed for "high treason" on 16 June 1958 is rehabilitated in the wake of the political and economic reforms, and his remains solemnly re-interred amid moving scenes of national mourning. To mark the 33rd Anniversary of the popular uprising of 1956, the President of the Hungarian Parliament proclaims the "Republic of Hungary" on 23 October. On 21 December the Hungarian Parliament dissolves itself.

July
Mass strikes of Soviet miners in Siberia and the Ukraine. The miners demand economic independence for the mines and better living conditions.

30 November
In Bad Homburg the spokesman of the Board of Directors of the Deutsche Bank AG, Alfred Herrhausen is killed in a bomb attack by RAF terrorists.

18 October
Under the pressure of the wave of refugees and demonstrations, Erich Honecker is relieved of all government and party offices, his successor is Egon Krenz.

27 October
The GDR State Council announces an amnesty for all individuals sentenced for attempted flight from the Republic and for those arrested in connection with demonstrations, provided they have not committed violence.
Once again, over a thousand GDR citizens are permitted to leave via the Embassies of the Federal Republic in Warsaw and Prague.

1 November
After the re-introduction of visa-free travel between the GDR and Czechoslovakia, over 60,000 GDR citizens reach the Federal Republic now that the government of Czechoslovakia is officially permitting GDR citizens to leave, in agreement with the GDR government.

4 November
The largest demonstration in the history of the GDR: some one million people throng the streets, calling for democratic reforms.

7 November
The GDR Council of Ministers resigns en bloc.

8 November
The Politbureau of the SED resigns en bloc, Egon Krenz is confirmed in office as General Secretary of the party.

9 November
This evening the GDR, to everyone's complete surprise, opens up the Wall to West Berlin and the border to the Federal Republic. There are indescribable scenes of jubilation. As from today, GDR citizens are free to travel or leave the country completely. In the days that follow, millions of GDR citizens visit the Federal Republic and West Berlin; many more border crossing points are opened.

13 November
Hans Modrow, former head of the Dresden section of the SED, is elected new Prime Minister of the GDR by the Volkskammer.

3 December
Under the pressure of mass demonstrations, the Politbureau of the SED, including General Secretary Egon Krenz, resigns.

November—December
On 17 November security troops in Prague break up a protest demonstration staged by some 30,000 people with considerable brutality. One day later the "Citizens' Forum" is founded. On 24 November Alexander Dubček is enthusiastically received by the masses on Wenceslas Square in Prague. The entire leadership of the Czech Communist Party resigns. On 27 November all political prisoners are released. Two days later the Communist Party's power monopoly is deleted from the constitution. On 12 December President Gustav Husák resigns in response to the pressure of mass demonstrations. Alexander Dubček is elected President of the Czech parliament on 28 December, and on 29 December Václav Havel is elected State President.

6 December
Egon Krenz also resigns as Chairman of the GDR State Council. His successor is Manfred Gerlach, Chairman of the Liberal Democratic Party (LDPD). The State Council passes another amnesty.

7 December
Talks at the "Round Table" begin in Berlin between parties of the ruling coalition and representatives of the various opposition groups.

9 December
The East Berlin attorney Gregor Gysi is elected new Chairman of the SED at a special party conference.

11 December
New mass demonstrations in the GDR, particularly in Leipzig. The call: "Germany, one united Fatherland!" is heard more and more frequently.

22 December
A border crossing point for pedestrians is opened at the Brandenburg Gate.

24 December
Visas and the minimum exchange regulations are abolished for visits to the GDR and East Berlin.

31 December
In 1989 a total of 343,854 people left the GDR legally or illegally.

31 December 1989 — 1 January 1990
The beginning of the New Year is celebrated by hundreds of thousands at the Brandenburg Gate; the balance-sheet of this "New Year of the Century" is an unhappy one, however: 271 people are injured and on top of the gate, where at times over 500 people had been standing, the Quadriga is damaged.

14 December
Death occurs in Moscow of the atomic physicist and Nobel Peace Prizewinner Andrei Sakharov.

December
On 17 December security police brutally break up a demonstration in the Romanian city of Temesvar. Three days later Romania is on the edge of civil war. On 22 December Head of State and Party Leader Nicolae Ceauşescu flees Bucarest. On 25 December he and his wife are condemned to death by a military tribunal and shot. The revolution and the security police's bloody reign of terror costs several thousand lives.

22 December
Soviet Party Leader Mikhail Gorbachev summons a plenary meeting of the Central Committee to deal with the withdrawal of the Lithuanian Communists from the USSR Communist Party.

1990

3 January
Following a call from the newly-constituted SED-PDS party, 250,000 people demonstrate in Treptow (East Berlin) against neo-Nazism.
GDR building workers in Schwerin District (northern East Germany) begin to dismantle the border security installations.

1990

Early January
Serious disturbances on the border between Iran and the Soviet Union as a result of demands for union made by Azerbaijanis on both sides of the frontier.

12 January
A government crisis in the GDR is avoided when Prime Minister Hans Modrow dispenses with the setting up of an Office for the Protection of the Constitution (to replace the now-abolished State-Security Office and its successor, the "Office for National Security").

15 January
Several thousand demonstrators storm the headquarters of the former State Security Service in East Berlin. In Leipzig, over 100,000 people demonstrate for German unity.

23 January
GDR border troops begin to replace the Wall with a fence. A total of 320 metres of wall are to be demolished along the Leuschnerdamm, "apparently because of the particularly colourful graffiti, which the GDR foreign-trade company Limex now intends to sell to wealthy interested parties" (according to *Der Tagesspiegel* on 24 January).

28 January
The groups represented at the "Round Table" decide to bring the elections to the Volkskammer forward to 18 March.

29 January
The former Head of both State and Party, Erich Honecker is removed from hospital and placed in Rummelsburg Remand Centre (East Berlin). One day later he is released as being too ill to undergo arrest and removed to a church nursing home in Lobetal (Bernau District).

1 February
Under the motto "For a united German Fatherland", GDR Prime Minister Hans Modrow presents a step-by-step plan for a unified Germany.

4 February
In accordance with a resolution of the party leadership, the former SED (with the interim name SED-PDS) is now to be simple called PDS (Party of Democratic Socialism).

6 February
The Federal German Chancellor Helmut Kohl announces his offer of immediate negotiations with the GDR on economic and monetary union.

11 January
The Soviet Party Leader and Head of State, Mikhail Gorbachev, travels to Lithuania and calls on the country to remain in the Soviet Union. Hundreds of thousands welcome him but simultaneously demonstrate for the independence of their country.

Mid January
Serious disturbances in the Soviet Union. In Georgia there are demonstrations for independence, while civil war rages between Azerbaijan and Armenia. The Soviet leadership declares a state of emergency and sends troops to the critical area. Only at the end of the month does the situation relax somewhat.

15 January
The Bulgarian parliament unanimously deletes the reference to the leading role of the Communist Party from the country's constitution.

19 January
Herbert Wehner, for many years Chairman of the parliamentary SPD party in West Germany, dies in Bad Godesberg at the age of 83.

21 January
Some 100,000 people demonstrate for Ukrainian independence by forming a 500-kilometre-long human chain from Lvov to Kiev.

22 January
At a special party conference the Yugoslav Communist Party also renounces the monopoly of power guaranteed to it by the constitution.

4 February
One day before the start of a plenary session of the USSR Communist Party, around 300,000 people demonstrate in Moscow against the party's monopoly of power.

11 February
After almost 28 years in prison, the black nationalist leader Nelson Mandela is released in South Africa. Two days later, in the presence of some 120,000 people who have prepared a triumphant reception for him at the football stadium Soccer City, he renews his call to fight apartheid.

24 February
First free parliamentary elections in the Soviet republic of Lithuania.

10 February
After talks with the Soviet Head of State and Party Leader Mikhail Gorbachev in Moscow, Chancellor Helmut Kohl reports that the USSR considers the reunification of Germany to be a matter which can be settled by the Germans alone.

13 February
Federal Chancellor Helmut Kohl and GDR Prime Minister Hans Modrow agree in Bonn on the first steps towards a unification of the two German states.

19 February
GDR border troops begin to demolish the Wall between the Reichstag and the Brandenburg Gate. From here to Checkpoint Charlie a 1.5-metre-high wire fence is to replace the Wall.

14 March
Beginning of the "Four plus Two" negotiations (between representatives of the four victorious Allies of the Second World War and the two German states) at civil-service level in Bonn. External aspects of German unity are discussed.

16 March
The flood of emigrants from the GDR continues unchecked. Since the beginning of the year a total of 141,772 have registered as immigrants.

18 March
The "Alliance for Germany" wins the first free elections in the GDR (48.15 %: CDU 40.91 %; DSU 6.32 %; DA 0.92 %), the SPD wins 21.84 %, the PDS 16.33 %. The citizens' action groups under the collective label "Federation 90" only poll 2.9 %.

3 April
Erich Honecker is moved from Lobetal vicarage to a Soviet military hospital in Beelitz (Potsdam District).

7 April
Opening of a border crossing point on Brunnenstrasse (corner of Bernauer Strasse).

25 February
Hundreds of thousands demonstrate for more democracy in Moscow and other cities of the Soviet Union.

10 March
The USSR and Hungary sign an agreement on the withdrawal of Soviet troops from Hungary by June 1991.

11 March
The Lithuanian parliament declares the independent Republic of Lithuania; the Soviet Union then imposes an economic embargo.

13 March
The Soviet Congress of Peoples' Deputies agrees to the introduction of a presidential system in the USSR. The Communist Party's monopoly of power is deleted from the constitution. Two days later Mikhail Gorbachev is elected as first State President of the USSR. In his inaugural address he confirms the right of the German people to national union.

21 March
The last colony in Africa, Namibia, gains its independence.

25 March—8 April
First free elections in Hungary. The conservative "Hungarian Democratic Forum" obtains 164 out of 386 seats, the Liberals 92. The "Hungarian Socialist Party" (successor to the former Communist Party) becomes the fourth- largest party with 33 seats.

30 March
The parliament of Estonia votes by a large majority for a transition period leading to full national sovereignty.

13 April
For the first time the Soviet Union admits its guilt in the mass execution of some 15,000 Polish officers during the Second World War. Up to now the Soviet Union had blamed the German Wehrmacht for this atrocity.

4 May
The republic of Latvia declares itself independent of the Soviet Union.

10 April
Following lively discussions the SPD and the Alternative List in the West Berlin Senate agree on the future of Potsdam Square. In conjunction with the East Berlin Magistrate a competition is to be organised taking into account the wishes of the Daimler-Benz company concerning the setting up of a service centre there (a suggestion previously strictly rejected by the "green" AL).

12 April
For the first time since 1946 regular bus services cross the border between the two halves of the city. Easter (15—16 April) sees 43 crossing points between East and West.
In the GDR the "Alliance for Germany", the SPD and the Liberals form a Large Coalition. The CDU chairman Lothar de Maizière is elected Prime Minister by the Volkskammer.

28 April
With the aid of West Berlin companies, sappers of the People's Army begin to demolish the Wall in front of the Brandenburg Gate.

5 May
The foreign ministers of the four victorious Allies of the Second World War plus those of the Federal Republic and the GDR meet in Bonn to confer on the external conditions for the unification of Germany ("Four plus Two"); first conference on the future of Germany since 1959. Main topics: military status of the united Germany, Poland's Western border, dissolution of the rights of the Allies in Germany.

6 May
Local-government elections in the GDR confirm the distribution of power that resulted from the elections to the Volkskammer on 18 March. In East Berlin the SPD becomes the strongest party and will nominate the future Lord Mayor.

18 May
Signature of the agreement on monetary, economic and social union between the two German states in Bonn.

9 June
The reservations of the Western Allies, dating from 12 May 1949, towards the full voting entitlement of the West Berlin deputies in the Federal German Bundestag (lower chamber) and Bundesrat (upper chamber) are withdrawn.

20 May
During the first free elections in Romania the "National Salvation Front" obtains an absolute majority. Their candidate Ion Iliescu is elected President by over 80 % of the votes.

June
In the first half of this month eight out of thirty presumed RAF terrorists for whom warrants had been issued are arrested in the GDR.

7 June
In Moscow the Member States of the Warsaw Pact announce their decision to transform their military alliance step by step into a political community.

9 June
First free elections in Czechoslovakia; the leading forces for democratic change, the Czech "Citizens' Forum" and its Slovak sister organization "The Public against Force" (OF/VNP) obtain an absolute majority of seats, while the Czech Communist Party only polls 13.6 % of the votes.

10—17 June
The Bulgarian Socialist Party, which had grown out of the former Communist Party, wins an absolute majority in the parliamentary elections.

12 June
The Russian parliament declares the sovereignty of the Russian Federation without however leaving the Soviet Union.

Mid June
Serious riots in Bucharest after clearance of the University Square of students who had declared it a "Communist-free Zone". Tens of thousands of miners and policemen supporting Iliescu begin to persecute the opposition.

21 June
The West German Bundestag and the GDR Volkskammer declare the intent of a unified Germany to recognise the Oder-Neisse Line as the definitive Western frontier of Poland. Federal Chancellor Helmut Kohl talks of a "bitter but necessary" decision.

12 June
Just 42 years after the split between the two halves of the City Council the Magistrate of East Berlin and the Senate of West Berlin meet in the "Red-brick Town Hall" of East Berlin for a preliminary joint session, pass a declaration on the re-establishment of the unity of the city and decide to re-connect 86 streets which had been divided by the Wall.

13 June
The final demolition of the Wall begins along Bernauer Strasse.

21 June
The Bundestag and the Volkskammer accept the agreement on monetary, economic and social union between the two German states.

22 June
With the exception of the Saar and Lower Saxony, the Bundesrat (Upper Chamber of the West German parliament) accepts the German-German Agreement.
The Allied Crossing Point "Checkpoint Charlie" — a symbol of East-West confrontation — is dismantled in a solemn ceremony attended by the foreign ministers of the four victorious Allies of the Second World War, of the two German states, of the three City Commandants of West Berlin and Mayor Ingrid Stahmer together with East Berlin's Lord Mayor Tino Schwierzina.

27 June
Government agreement between the Federal Republic and the GDR on the abolition of identity inspections along the inner-German border and in Berlin as from 1 July 1990.

29 June
Federal President Richard von Weizsäcker becomes the first Honorary Citizen of a United Berlin since the division of the city administration in 1948.

1 July
As of today border identity inspections along the inner-German border and in Berlin cease, the Agreement on Monetary, Economic and Social Union comes into force, seven Underground Railway stations in East Berlin, previously still closed are opened once more, and Berlin's local public-transport network is reunited. Additionally, the emergency integration procedure for GDR citizens moving to the Federal Republic is discontinued.

Wolfgang G. Fischer, 1933 in Wien geboren, Kunsthistoriker, Schriftsteller und Kunsthändler (Fischer Fine Art in London). Das leidenschaftliche Interesse für Zeitgeschichte ist bereits wichtiger Bestandteil seiner Romane *Wohnungen* (1969) und *Möblierte Zimmer* (1972) und verstärkt sich neben seiner Beschäftigung mit der Kunst unseres Jahrhunderts (siehe z. B. *Gustav Klimt und Emilie Flöge,* Wien 1987) bis zum Mauerbuch. Fischer ist Mitglied des österreichischen und Internationalen P.E.N. Clubs und sieht seine Rolle sowohl als Kunstvermittler (deutsche und österreichische Kunst nach England und in die westliche Hemisphäre, englische Kunst nach Kontinentaleuropa) als auch als »Wortmeister und unabhängiger Chronist«. Sein Hauptwohnsitz ist seit 1963 London, seine Nebenwohnsitze Wien und Grundlsee (Steiermark).

Fritz von der Schulenburg wurde 1938 in Berlin geboren. Er ist einer der führenden Photographen im Bereich der Innenarchitektur und arbeitet regelmäßig für Zeitschriften wie *The World of Interiors, House & Garden, Connoisseur, Ambiente* und *Architektur & Wohnen*. Seit 1985 sind mehrere Bücher mit seinen Photographien erschienen: *The English Garden Room* (deutsch: *Wohngärten*), *Living in Scotland, The Curtain Book* und *Neo-Classicism in the North*.

Wolfgang G. Fischer, born in Vienna in 1933, art historian, writer and art dealer (Fischer Fine Art, London). His passionate interest in contemporary history has already found expression in his novels *Wohnungen* (Interiors, 1969) and *Möblierte Zimmer* (Lodgings in Exile, 1972), and now in this book on the Wall of Berlin. Apart from that he closely follows developments in 20th century art (for example in his book *Gustav Klimt and Emilie Flöge,* Vienna, 1987). Fischer is a member of the Austrian and of the International P.E.N. Club. He sees his task partly in mediating German and Austrian Art to Britain and the Western hemisphere, British art to Continental Europe, and also in playing the part of an independent chronicler. Since 1963 he has mainly lived in London, but also in Vienna and Grundlsee (Steiermark).

Fritz von der Schulenburg was born in Berlin in 1938. He is one of the leading photographers in the field of interior decoration and design and regularly works for journals like *The World of Interiors, House & Garden, Connoisseur, Ambiente* and *Architektur & Wohnen*. Since 1985, several books with his photographs have appeared: *The English Garden Room, Living in Scotland, The Curtain Book* and *Neo-Classicism in the North*.